AF477275

SYRIA
A COUNTRY STUDY GUIDE

SYRIA
A COUNTRY STUDY GUIDE

HADLEY STACKHOUSE

Published by

Hawk Press
4836/24, Ansari Road, Daryaganj
New Delhi – 110 002
Phones: 91-11-23278618, 91-11-43667199
E-mail: thehawkpress@gmail.com
www.thehawkpress.com

Contents

Preface

Syria , officially the Syrian Arab Republic, is a country in Western Asia. *De jure* Syrian territory borders Lebanon and the Mediterranean Sea to the west,Turkey to the north, Iraq to the east, Jordan to the south, and Israel to the southwest, but the government's control now extends to approximately 30–40% of the *de jure* state area and less than 60% of the population.

A country of fertile plains, high mountains, and deserts, Syria is home todiverse ethnic and religious groups, including Syrian Arabs, Greeks,Armenians, Assyrians, Kurds, Circassians, Mandeans and Turks. Religious groups include Sunnis, Christians, Alawites, Druze, Mandeans,Shiites, Salafis, and Yazidis. Sunni Arabs make up the largest population group in Syria.

Syria is formally a unitary republic. The constitutionadopted in 2012 effectively transformed Syria into asemi-presidential republic due to the constitutional right for the election of individuals who do not form part of the National Progressive Front. The President is Head of State and the Prime Minister is Head of Government. The legislature, the Peoples Council, is the body responsible for passing laws, approving government appropriations and debating policy.In the event of a vote of no confidence by a simple majority, the Prime Minister is required to tender the resignation of their government to the President.

The executive branch consists of the president, two vice presidents, the prime minister, and the Council of Ministers (cabinet). The constitution requires the president to be a Muslimbut does not make Islam the state religion.

The constitution gives the president the right to appoint ministers, to declare war and state of emergency, to issue laws (which, except in the case of emergency, require ratification by the People's Council), to declare amnesty, to amend the constitution, and to appoint civil servants and military personnel. According to the 2012 constitution, the president is elected by Syrian citizens in a direct election.

Syria's legislative branch is the unicameral People's Council. Under the previous constitution, Syria did not hold multi-party elections for the legislature, with two-thirds of the seats automatically allocated to the ruling coalition. On 7 May 2012, Syria held its first elections in which parties outside the ruling coalition could take part. Seven new political parties took part in the elections, of which Popular Front for Change and Liberation was the largest opposition party. The armed anti-government rebels, however, chose not to field candidates and called on their supporters to boycott the elections.

Syria is a member of one international organization other than the United Nations, the Non-Aligned Movement; it is currently suspended from theArab League and the Organisation of Islamic Cooperation, and self-suspended from the Union for the Mediterranean. Since March 2011, Syria has been embroiled in an uprising against Assad and theBa'athist government as part of the Arab Spring, a crackdown that contributed to the Syrian Civil War and to Syria's becoming one of the most violent countries in the world. The Syrian Interim Governmentwas formed by the opposition umbrella group, the Syrian National Coalition, in March 2013. Representatives of this alternative governmentwere subsequently invited to take up Syria's seat at the Arab League.

This is a reference book. All the matter is just compiled and edited in nature, taken from the various sources which are in public domain.

The publication will be a valuable aid to the study of the vital aspects of the subject.

— Editor

1

Country Profile

Once the centre of the Islamic Caliphate, Syria covers an area that has seen invasions and occupations over the ages, from Romans and Mongols to Crusaders and Turks.

A country of fertile plains, high mountains and deserts, it is home to diverse ethnic and religious groups, including Kurds, Armenians, Assyrians, Christians, Druze, Alawite Shia and Arab Sunnis, the last of whom make up a majority of the Muslim population.

Modern Syria gained its independence from France in 1946, but has lived through periods of political instability driven by the conflicting interests of these various groups.

Since 2011 political power, long held by a small mainly Alawite elite, has been contested in a bitter civil conflict initially sparked by the Arab Spring that turned into a complex war involving regional and international powers.

FACTS

The Syrian Arab Republic, Capital: Damascus

- Population 21.1 million
- Area 185,180 sq km (71,498 sq miles)
- Major language Arabic
- Major religion Islam, Christianity
- Life expectancy 74 years (men), 78 years (women)
- Currency Syrian pound

LEADERS

President: Bashar al-Assad

In power since succeeding his father in 2000, Bashar al-Assad is fighting for control of his country after protests against his rule turned into a full-scale war.

He inherited a tightly controlled and repressive political structure from long-time dictator Hafez al-Assad, with an inner circle dominated by members of the Assad family's minority Alawite Shia community.

But cracks began to appear in early 2011, in the wake of the "Arab Spring" wave of popular dissent that swept across North Africa and the Middle East.

MEDIA

The Syrian uprising has left a fractured media environment, split between areas controlled by the government, Islamic State militants and other armed groups.

Scores of journalists and citizen journalists have been killed since the start of the revolt in 2011.

Syria was the world's deadliest country for journalists in 2014, says Reporters Without Borders. Islamic State jihadists "enforce an information dictatorship" in the areas they control.

TIMELINE

1918 October - Arab troops led by Emir Feisal, and supported by British forces, capture Damascus, ending 400 years of Ottoman rule.

1920 - San Remo conference splits up newly-created Arab kingdom by placing Syria-Lebanon under a French mandate, and Palestine under British control.

1946 - Independence.

1958-61 - Short-lived union of Syria with Egypt as the United Arab Republic.

1967 - Egypt, Jordan, and Syria are defeated in the Six-Day War with Israel. Israel seizes the Golan Heights.

1970 - Hafez al-Assad comes to power in a coup. His rule is characterised by repression and a major arms build-up.

1973 - Egypt and Syria launch surprise attack on Israel in October to try reverse defeats of 1967.

1976 - Syria intervenes in the Lebanese civil war. It maintains military presence there for next three decades and exerts significant influence on Lebanese politics.

1982 - Muslim Brotherhood uprising in the city of Hama is suppressed in a month-long siege by the military, who kill tens of thousands of civilians.

2000 - President Assad dies and is succeeded by his son Bashar.

2005 - Syrian forces withdraw from Lebanon under international pressure following assassination of Lebanese premier Rafiq al-Hariri.

2011 - Unrest inspired by "Arab Spring" uprisings. Confrontation between government and opposition soon develops into civil war that draws in world powers and triggers refugee crisis.

Assad succession

2000 June - President Assad dies and is succeeded by his second son, Bashar.

2000 November - The new president orders the release of 600 political prisoners.

2001 April - Outlawed Muslim Brotherhood says it will resume political activity, 20 years after its leaders were forced to flee.

2001 June - Syrian troops evacuate Beirut, redeploy in other parts of Lebanon, following pressure from Lebanese critics of Syria's presence.

2001 September - Detention of MPs and other pro-reform activists, crushing hopes of a break with the authoritarian past of Hafez al-Assad. Arrest continue, punctuated by occasional amnesties, over the following decade.

Tensions with US

2002 May - Senior US official includes Syria in a list of states that make-up an "axis of evil", first listed by President Bush in January. Undersecretary for State John Bolton says Damascus is acquiring weapons of mass destruction.

2004 January - President Assad visits Turkey, the first Syrian leader to do so. The trip marks the end of decades of frosty relations, although ties sour again after the popular uprising in 2011.

2004 May - US imposes economic sanctions on Syria over what it calls its support for terrorism and failure to stop militants entering Iraq.

Syria and Lebanon

2005 February-April- Tensions with the US escalate after the killing of former Lebanese PM Hariri in Beirut. Washington cites Syrian influence in Lebanon. Damascus is urged to withdraw its forces from Lebanon, which it does by April.

Diplomatic overtures

2006 November - Iraq and Syria restore diplomatic relations after nearly a quarter century.

2007 March - European Union relaunches dialogue with Syria.

2007 April - US House of Representatives Speaker Nancy Pelosi meets President Assad in Damascus. She is the highest-placed US politician to visit Syria in recent years. Secretary of State Condoleezza Rice meets Foreign Minister Walid Muallem the following month in the first contact at this level for two years.

Mystery site

2007 September - Israel carries out an aerial strike against a nuclear facility under construction in northern Syria.

2008 July - President Assad meets French President Nicolas Sarkozy in Paris. The visit signals the end of the diplomatic isolation by the West that followed the assassination of former Lebanese PM Rafik Hariri in 2005.

2008 October - Syria establishes diplomatic relations with Lebanon for first time since both countries established independence in 1940s.

2009 March - Jeffrey Feltman, acting assistant US secretary of state for the Near East, visits Damascus with White House national security aide Daniel Shapiro in first high-level US diplomatic mission for nearly four years. Meets Foreign Minister Walid Muallem.

Trading launches on Syria's stock exchange in a gesture towards liberalising the state-controlled economy.

2010 May - US renews sanctions against Syria, saying that it supports terrorist groups, seeks weapons of mass destruction and has provided Lebanon's Hezbollah with Scud missiles in violation of UN resolutions.

Nationwide uprising

2011 March - Security forces shoot dead protestors in southern city of Deraa demanding release of political prisoners, triggering violent unrest that steadily spread nationwide over the following months.

2011 protests

President Assad announces conciliatory measures, releasing dozens of political prisoners, dismissing government, lifting 48-year-old state of emergency.

2011 May - Army tanks enter Deraa, Banyas, Homs and suburbs of Damascus in an effort to crush anti-regime protests. US and European Union tighten sanctions.

2011 June - The IAEA nuclear watchdog decides to report Syria to the UN Security Council over its alleged covert nuclear programme reactor programme. The structure housing the alleged reactor was destroyed in an Israeli air raid in 2007.

Opposition organises

2011 July - President Assad sacks the governor of the northern province of Hama after mass demonstration there, eventually sending in troops to restore order at the cost of scores of lives.

2011 October - New Syrian National Council says it has forged a common front of internal and exiled opposition activists.

2011 November - Arab League votes to suspend Syria, accusing it of failing to implement an Arab peace plan, and imposes sanctions.

Civil war

2012 February - Government steps up the bombardment of Homs and other cities.

2012 March - UN Security Council endorses non-binding peace plan drafted by UN envoy Kofi Annan. China and Russia agree to support the plan after an earlier, tougher draft is modified.

Opposition rifts

2012 June - Turkey changes rules of engagement after Syria shoots down a Turkish plane, declaring that if Syrian troops approach Turkey's borders they will be seen as a military threat.

2012 July - Free Syria Army blows up three security chiefs in Damascus and seizes Aleppo in the north.

2012 August - Prime Minister Riad Hijab defects, US President Obama warns that use of chemical weapons would tilt the US towards intervention.

2012 October - Fire in Aleppo destroys much of the historic market as fighting and bomb attacks continue in various cities.

2012 November - National Coalition for Syrian Revolutionary and Opposition Forces formed in Qatar, excludes Islamist militias. Arab League stops short of full recognition.

2012 December - US, Britain, France, Turkey and Gulf states formally recognise opposition National Coalition as "legitimate representative" of Syrian people.

2013 January - Syria accuses Israel of bombing military base near Damascus, where Hezbollah was suspected of assembling a convoy of anti-aircraft missiles bound for Lebanon.

Rise of Islamists

2013 September - UN weapons inspectors conclude that chemical weapons were used in an attack on the Ghouta area of Damascus in August that killed about 300 people, but do not allocate responsibility. Government allows UN to destroy chemical weapons stocks, process complete by June 2014.

2013 December - US and Britain suspend "non-lethal" support for rebels in northern Syria after reports that Islamist rebels seized bases of Western-backed Free Syrian Army.

2014 January-February - UN-brokered peace talks in Geneva fail, largely because Syrian authorities refuse to discuss a transitional government.

2014 March - Syrian Army and Hezbollah forces recapture Yabroud, the last rebel stronghold near the Lebanese border.

2014 June - Islamic State of Iraq and Syria militants declare "caliphate" in territory from Aleppo to eastern Iraqi province of Diyala.

2014 September - US and five Arab countries launch air strikes against Islamic State around Aleppo and Raqqa.

2015 January - Kurdish forces push Islamic State out of Kobane on Turkish border after four months of fighting.

2015 May - Islamic State fighters seize the ancient city of Palmyra in central Syria and proceed to destroy many monuments at pre-Islamic World Heritage site.

Jaish al-Fatah (Army of Conquest) Islamist rebel alliance takes control of Idlib Province, putting pressure on government's coastal stronghold of Latakia.

Russian intervention

2015 September - Russia carries out its first air strikes in Syria, saying they target the Islamic State group, but the West and Syrian opposition say it overwhelmingly targets anti-Assad rebels.

2015 December - Syrian Army allows rebels to evacuate remaining area of Homs, returning Syria's third-largest city to government control after four years.

2016 March - Syrian government forces retake Palmyra from Islamic State with Russian air assistance, only to be driven out again in December.

2016 August - Turkish troops cross into Syria to help rebel groups push back so-called Islamic State militants and Kurdish-led rebels from a section of the two countries' border.

2016 December - Government troops, backed by Russian air power and Iranian-sponsored militias, recapture Aleppo, the country's largest city, depriving the rebels of their last major urban stronghold.

2017 January - Russia, Iran and Turkey agree to enforce a ceasefire between the government and non-Islamist rebels, after talks between the two sides in Kazakhstan.

US intervenes

2017 April - US President Donald Trump orders a missile attack on an airbase from which Syrian government planes allegedly staged a chemical weapons attack on the rebel-held town of Khan Sheikhoun.

2017 May - US decides to arm the YPG Kurdish Popular Protection Units. These fight alongside the main opposition Syrian Democratic Forces, which captures the important Tabqa dam from Islamic State.

2017 June - US shoots down Syrian fighter jet near Raqqa after it allegedly dropped bombs near US-backed rebel Syrian Democratic Forces (SDF).

2017 July - The Lebanese militant group Hezbollah and the Syrian army launch a military operation to dislodge jihadist groups from the Arsal area, near the Lebanese-Syrian border.

2017 October - The Islamic State group is driven from Raqqa, its de-facto capital in Syria.

GEOGRAPHY

Syria lies between latitudes 32° and 38° N, and longitudes 35° and

43° E. It consists mostly of arid plateau, although the northwest part of the country bordering the Mediterranean is fairly green. The Northeast of the country "al-Jazira" and the South "Hawran" are important agricultural areas. The Euphrates, Syria's most important river, crosses the country in the east. It is considered to be one of the fifteen states that comprise the so-called "Cradle of civilization". Its land straddles the "northwest of the Arabian plate".

The climate in Syria is dry and hot, and winters are mild. Because of the country's elevation, snowfall does occasionally occur during winter. Petroleum in commercial quantities was first discovered in the northeast in 1956. The most important oil fields are those of Suwaydiyah, Qaratshui, Rumayian, and Tayyem, near Dayr az–Zawr. The fields are a natural extension of the Iraqi fields of Mosul andKirkuk. Petroleum became Syria's leading natural resource and chief export after 1974. Natural gas was discovered at the field of Jbessa in 1940.

POLITICS AND GOVERNMENT

Syria is formally a unitary republic. The constitutionadopted in 2012 effectively transformed Syria into asemi-presidential republic due to the constitutional right for the election of individuals who do not form part of the National Progressive Front. The President is Head of State and the Prime Minister is Head of Government. The legislature, the Peoples Council, is the body responsible for passing laws, approving government appropriations and debating policy.In the event of a vote of no confidence by a simple majority, the Prime Minister is required to tender the resignation of their government to the President.

The executive branch consists of the president, two vice presidents, the prime minister, and the Council of Ministers (cabinet). The constitution requires the president to be a Muslimbut does not make Islam the state religion.

The constitution gives the president the right to appoint ministers, to declare war and state of emergency, to issue laws (which, except in the case of emergency, require ratification by the People's Council), to declare amnesty, to amend the constitution, and to appoint civil servants and military personnel. According to the 2012 constitution, the president is elected by Syrian citizens in a direct election.

Syria's legislative branch is the unicameral People's Council. Under the previous constitution, Syria did not hold multi-party elections for the legislature, with two-thirds of the seats automatically allocated to the ruling coalition. On 7 May 2012, Syria held its first elections in which parties outside the ruling coalition could take part. Seven new political parties took part in the elections, of which Popular Front for Change and Liberation was the largest opposition party. The armed anti-government rebels, however, chose not to field candidates and called on their supporters to boycott the elections.

The President is currently the Regional Secretary of the Ba'ath party in Syria and leader of the National Progressive Frontgoverning coalition. Outside of the coalition are 14 illegal Kurdish political parties.

Syria's judicial branches include the Supreme Constitutional Court, the High Judicial Council, the Court of Cassation, and theState Security Courts. Islamic jurisprudence is a main source of legislation and Syria's judicial system has elements ofOttoman, French, and Islamic laws. Syria has three levels of courts: courts of first instance, courts of appeals, and the constitutional court, the highest tribunal.

Religious courts handle questions of personal and family law. The Supreme State Security Court (SSSC) was abolished by President Bashar al-Assad by legislative decree No. 53 on 21 April 2011.

The Personal Status Law 59 of 1953 (amended by Law 34 of 1975) is essentially a codified sharia. Article 3(2) of the 1973 constitution declares Islamic jurisprudence a main source of legislation. The Code of Personal Status is applied to Muslims by sharia courts.

As a result of the ongoing civil war, various alternative governments were formed, including the Syrian Interim Government, the Democratic Union Party and localised regions governed by sharia law.

Representatives of the Syrian Interim government were invited to take up Syria's seat at the Arab League on 28 March 2013 and was recognised as the "sole representative of the Syrian people" by several nations including the United States, United Kingdom and France.

Parliamentary elections were held on 13 April 2016 in the government-controlled areas of Syria, for all 250 seats of Syria's unicameral legislature, the Majlis al-Sha'ab, or the People's Council of Syria. Even before results had been announced, several nations, including Germany, the United States and the United Kingdom, have declared their refusal to accept the results, largely citing it "not representing the will of the Syrian people. However, representatives of the Russian Federation have voiced their support of this election's results.

Human rights

The situation for human rights in Syria has long been a significant concern among independent organizations such as Human Rights Watch, who in 2010 referred to the country's record as "among the worst in the world." The US State Department funded Freedom House ranked Syria "Not Free" in its annualFreedom in the World survey.

The authorities are accused of arresting democracy and human rights activists,censoring websites, detaining bloggers, and imposing travel bans.

Arbitrary detention, torture, and disappearances are widespread. Although Syria's constitution guarantees gender equality, critics say that personal statutes laws and the penal code discriminate against women and girls.

Moreover, it also grants leniency for so-called 'Honour killing'. As of 9 November 2011 during the uprising against President Bashar al-Assad, the United Nations reported that of the over 3500 total deaths, over 250 deaths were children as young as 2 years old, and that boys as young as 11 years old have been gang raped by security services officers. People opposing President Assad's rule claim that more than 200, mostly civilians, were massacred and about 300 injured in Hama in shelling by the Government forces on 12 July 2012.

In August 2013 the government was suspected of using chemical weapons against its civilians. US Secretary of State John Kerry said it was "undeniable" that chemical weapons had been used in the country and that President Bashar al-Assad's forces had committed a "moral obscenity" against his own people. "Make no mistake," Kerry said. "President Obama believes there must be accountability for those who would use the world's most heinous weapon against the world's most vulnerable people. Nothing today is more serious, and nothing is receiving more serious scrutiny".

The Emergency Law, effectively suspending most constitutional protections, was in effect from 1963 until 21 April 2011.It was justified by the government in the light of the continuing war with Israel over the Golan Heights.

In August 2014, UN Human Rights chief Navi Pillay criticized the international community over its "paralysis" in dealing with the more than 3-year-old civil war gripping the country, which by April 30, 2014, had resulted in 191,369 deaths with war crimes, according to Pillay, being committed with total impunity on all sides in the conflict. Minority Alawites and Christiansare being increasingly targeted by Islamists and other groups fighting in the Syrian civil war.

Military

The President of Syria is commander in chief of the Syrian armed forces, comprising some 400,000 troops upon mobilization. The military is a conscripted force; males serve in the military upon reaching the age of 18. The obligatory military service period is being decreased over time, in 2005 from two and a half years to two years, in 2008 to 21 months and in 2011 to year and a half. About 20,000 Syrian soldiers were deployed in Lebanon until 27 April 2005, when the last of Syria's troops left the country after three decades.

The breakup of the Soviet Union—long the principal source of training, material, and credit for the Syrian forces—may have slowed Syria's ability to acquire modern military equipment. It has an arsenal of surface-to-surface missiles. In the early 1990s, Scud-C missiles with a 500-kilometer range were procured from North Korea, and Scud-D, with a range of up to 700 kilometers, is allegedly being developed by Syria with the help of North Korea and Iran, according to Zisser.

Syria received significant financial aid from Arab states of the Persian Gulf as a result of its participation in the Persian Gulf War, with a sizable portion of these funds earmarked for military spending.

International disputes

In 1939, while Syria was still a French mandate the French ceded the Sanjak of Alexandretta to Turkey as part of a treaty of friendship in World War II. In order to facilitate this, a faulty election was done in which ethnic Turks who were originally from the Sanjak but lived in Adana and other areas near the border in Turkey came to vote in the elections, shifting the election in favor of secession. Through this, the Hatay Province of Turkey was formed.

The move by the French was very controversial in Syria, and only 5 years later Syria became independent.

Israel unilaterally annexed the Golan Heights in 1981, although the Syrian government continues to demand the return of this territory.

The Syrian occupation of Lebanon began in 1976 as a result of the civil war and ended in April 2006 in response to domestic and international pressure after the assassination of former Lebanese Prime Minister, Rafik Hariri.

Internet and telecommunications

The Telecommunications in Syria are overseen by the Ministry of Communications and Technology. In addition, Syrian Telecom plays an integral role in the distribution of government internet access. The Syrian Electronic Army serves as a pro-government military faction in cyberspace and has been long considered an enemy of the hacktivist groupAnonymous. Because of internet censorship laws, 13,000 internet activists have been arrested between March 2011 and August 2012.

ECONOMY

As of 2015, the Syrian economy relies upon inherently unreliable revenue sources such as dwindling customs and income taxes which are heavily bolstered by lines of credit from Iran. Iran is believed to spend between $6 billion and $20 billion USD a year on Syria during the Syrian Civil War. The Syrian economy has contracted 60% and the Syrian pound has lost 80% of its value, with the economy becoming part state-owned and part war economy. At the outset of the ongoing Syrian Civil War, Syria was classified by the World Bank as a "lower middle income country."In 2010, Syria remained dependent on the oil and agriculture sectors. The oil sector provided about 40% of export earnings. Proven offshore expeditions have indicated that large sums of oil exist on the Mediterranean Sea floor between Syria and Cyprus. The agriculture sector contributes to about 20% of GDP and 20% of employment. Oil reserves are expected to decrease in the coming years and Syria has already become a net oil importer. Since the civil war began, the economy shrank by 35%, and the Syrian pound has fallen to one-sixth of its prewar value. The government increasingly relies on credit from Iran, Russia and China.

The economy is highly regulated by the government, which has increased subsidies and tightened trade controls to assuage protesters and protect foreign currency reserves. Long-run economic constraints include foreign trade barriers, declining oil production, high unemployment, rising budget deficits, and increasing pressure on water supplies caused by heavy use in agriculture, rapid population growth, industrial expansion, and water pollution. The UNDP announced in 2005 that 30% of the Syrian population lives in poverty and 11.4% live below the subsistence level.

Syria's share in global exports has eroded gradually since 2001. The real per capita GDP growth was just 2.5% per year in the 2000–2008 period. Unemployment is high at above 10%. Poverty rates have increased from 11% in 2004 to 12.3% in 2007. In 2007, Syria's main exports include crude oil, refined products, raw cotton, clothing, fruits, and grains. The bulk of Syrian imports are raw materials essential for industry, vehicles, agricultural equipment, and heavy machinery. Earnings from oil exports as well as remittances from Syrian workers are the government's most important sources of foreign exchange.

Political instability poses a significant threat to future economic development.Foreign investment is constrained by violence, government restrictions, economic sanctions, and international isolation. Syria's economy also remains hobbled by state bureaucracy, falling oil production, rising budget deficits, and inflation.

Prior to the civil war in 2011, the government hoped to attract new investment in the tourism, natural gas, and service sectors to diversify its economy and reduce its dependence on oil and agriculture. The government began to institute economic reforms aimed at liberalizing most markets, but those reforms were slow and ad hoc, and have been completely reversed since the outbreak of conflict in 2011.

As of 2012, because of the ongoing Syrian civil war, the value of Syria's overall exports has been slashed by two-thirds, from the figure of US$12 billion in 2010 to only US$4 billion in 2012. Syria's GDP declined by over 3% in 2011, and is expected to further decline by 20% in 2012.

As of 2012, Syria's oil and tourism industries in particular have been devastated, with US$5 billion lost to the ongoing conflict of the civil war. Reconstruction needed because of the ongoing civil war will cost as much as US$10 billion. Sanctions have sapped the government's finance. US and European Union bans on oil imports, which went into effect in 2012, are estimated to cost Syria about $400 million a month.

Revenues from tourism have dropped dramatically, with hotel occupancy rates falling from 90% before the war to less than 15% in May 2012. Around 40% of all employees in the tourism sector have lost their jobs since the beginning of the war.

In May 2015, ISIS captured Syria's phosphate mines, one of the Assad regime's last chief sources of income. The following month, ISIS blew up a gas pipeline to Damascus that was used to generate heating and electricity in Damascus and Homs; "the name of its game for now is denial of key resources to the regime" an analyst stated. In addition, ISIS is closing in on Shaer gas field and three other facilities in the area—Hayan, Jihar and Ebla—with the loss of these western gas fields having the potential to cause Iran to further subsidize the Assad regime.

Petroleum industry

Syria's petroleum industry has been subject to sharp decline. In September 2014, ISIS was producing more oil than the regime at 80,000 bbl/d (13,000 m^3/d) compared to the regime's 17,000 bbl/d (2,700 m^3/d) with the Syrian Oil Ministry stating that by the end of 2014, oil production had plunged further to 9,329 bbl/d (1,483.2 m^3/d); ISIS has since captured a further oil field, leading to a projected oil production of 6,829 bbl/d (1,085.7 m^3/d). In the third year of the Syrian Civil War, the deputy economy minister Salman Hayan stated that Syria's two main oil refineries were operating at less than 10% capacity. Historically, the country produced heavy-grade oil from fields located in the northeast since the late 1960s. In the early 1980s, light-grade, low-sulphur oil was discovered near Deir ez-Zor in eastern Syria. Syria's rate of oil production has decreased dramatically from a peak close to 600,000 barrels per day (95,000 m^3/d) (bpd) in 1995 down to less than 140,000 bbl/d (22,000 m^3/d) in 2012. Prior to the uprising, more than 90% of Syrian oil exports were to EU countries, with the remainder going to Turkey. Oil and gas revenues constituted around 20% of total GDP and 25% of total government revenue.

Transport

Syria has four international airports (Damascus, Aleppo, Lattakia and Kamishly), which serve as hubs for Syrian Air and are also served by a variety of foreign carriers.

The majority of Syrian cargo is carried by Chemins de Fer Syriens (the Syrian railway company), which links up with Turkish State Railways (the Turkish counterpart). For a relatively underdeveloped country, Syria's railway infrastructure is well maintained with many express services and modern trains.

The road network in Syria is 69,873 km long, including 1,103 km of expressways. The country also has 900 km of navigable but not economically significant waterways.

Water supply and sanitation

Syria is a semiarid country with scarce water resources. The largest water consuming sector in Syria is agriculture. Domestic water use stands at only about 9% of total water use. A big challenge for Syria is its high population growth with a rapidly increasing demand for urban and industrial water. In 2006 the population of Syria was 19.4 million with a growth rate of 2.7%.

DEMOGRAPHICS

Most people live in the Euphrates River valley and along the coastal plain, a fertile strip between the coastal mountains and the desert. Overall population density in Syria is about 99 per square kilometre (258 per square mile). According to the *World Refugee Survey 2008*, published by the U.S. Committee for Refugees and Immigrants, Syria hosted a population of refugees and asylum seekers numbering approximately 1,852,300. The vast majority of this population was from Iraq (1,300,000), but sizeable populations fromPalestine (543,400) and Somalia (5,200) also lived in the country. In what the UN has described as "the biggest humanitarian emergency of our era",about 9.5 million Syrians, half the population, have been displaced since the outbreak of the Syrian Civil War in March 2011; 4 million are outside the country as refugees.

Ethnic groups

Syrians are an overall indigenous Levantinepeople, closely related to their immediate neighbours, like Lebanese people,Palestinians, Iraqis, Maltese andJordanians. Syria has a population of approximately 17,065,000 (2014 est.)Syrian Arabs, together with some 600,000Palestinian Arabs, make up roughly 74% of the population (if Syriac Christians are excluded).

The indigenous Christian Western Aramaic-speakers and Assyrians are numbered around 400,000 people, with the Western Aramaic-speakers living all over the country, particularly in major urban centers, while the Assyrians mainly reside in the north and northeast (Homs, Aleppo, Qamishli, Hasakah). Many (particularly the Assyrian group) still retain severalNeo-Aramaic dialects as spoken and written languages, while villagers of Ma'loula, Jubb'adin and Bakh'a still retain Western Aramaic.

The second largest ethnic group in Syria are the Kurds. They constitute about 9% of the population, or approximately 1.6 million people. Most Kurds reside in the northeastern corner of Syria and most speak the Kurmanji variant of the Kurdish language. Syria is also a home to several other ethnic groups mainly the Turkmens (number around 100,000), Circassians (number some 100,000), Greeks, andArmenians (number approximately 100,000), most arrived during the Armenian Genocide. Syria holds the 7th largest Armenian population in the world. They are mainly gathered in Aleppo, Qamishli, Damascus and Kesab.

Syria was once home to a substantial population of Jews, with large communities in Damascus, Aleppo, and Qamishii. Due to a combination of persecution in Syria and opportunities elsewhere, the Jews began to emigrate in the second half of the 19th century to Great Britain, the United States, and Israel. The process was completed with the establishment of the state of Israel in 1948. Today only a few Jews remain in Syria.

The largest concentration of the Syrian diaspora outside the Arab world is in Brazil, which has millions of people of Arab and other Near Eastern ancestries. Brazil is the first country in the Americas to offer humanitarian visas to Syrian refugees. The majority of Arab Argentines are from either Lebanese or Syrian background.

Religion

Sunni Muslims make up about 74% of Syria's population and Sunni Arabs account for 59–60% of the population, most Kurds (9%) and Turkomen (3%) are Sunni, while 13% are Shia (Alawite, Twelvers, and Ismailis combined), 10% Christian (the majority Antiochian Orthodox, the rest including Greek Catholic, Assyrian Church of the East, Armenian Orthodox, Protestants and other denominations), and 3% Druze. Druze number around 500,000, and concentrate mainly in the southern area of Jabal al-Druze. President Bashar al-Assad's family is Alawite and Alawites dominate the government of Syria and hold key military positions. In May 2013, SOHR stated that out of 94,000 killed during the Syrian Civil War, at least 41,000 were Alawites.

Christians (2.5 million), a sizable number of whom are found among Syria's population of Palestinian refugees, are divided into several groups. Chalcedonian Antiochian Orthodox make up 45.7% of the Christian population; the Catholics (Melkite, Armenian Catholic, Syriac Catholic, Maronite, Chaldean Catholic and Latin) make up 16.2%; theArmenian Apostolic Church 10.9%, the Syriac Orthodox make up 22.4%; Assyrian Church of the East and several smaller Christian denominations account for the remainder. Many Christian monasteries also exist. Many Christian Syrians belong to a high socio-economic class.

Languages

Arabic is the official language. Several modern Arabic dialects are used in everyday life, most notably Levantine in the west and Mesopotamian in the northeast. Kurdish(in its Kurmanji form) is widely spoken in the Kurdish regions of Syria. Armenian andTurkish (South Azeri dialect) are spoken among the Armenian and Turkmenminorities.

Aramaic was the lingua franca of the region before the advent of Arabic, and is still spoken among Assyrians, and Classical Syriac is still used as the liturgical language of various Syriac Christian denominations. Most remarkably, Western Neo-Aramaic is still spoken in the village of Ma'loula as well as two neighboring villages, 56 km (35 mi) northeast of Damascus. English and French are widely spoken as a second language, but English is more often used.

CULTURE

Syria is a traditional society with a long cultural history. Importance is placed on family, religion, education, self-discipline and respect. Syrians' taste for the traditional arts is expressed in dances such as the al-Samah, the Dabkeh in all their variations, and the sword dance. Marriage ceremonies and the births of children are occasions for the lively demonstration of folk customs.

Arts

The literature of Syria has contributed to Arabic literature and has a proud tradition of oral and written poetry. Syrian writers, many of whom migrated to Egypt, played a crucial role in the nahda or Arab literary and cultural revival of the 19th century. Prominent contemporary Syrian writers include, among others, Adonis, Muhammad Maghout, Haidar Haidar, Ghada al-Samman, Nizar Qabbani and Zakariyya Tamer.

Ba'ath Party rule, since the 1966 coup, has brought about renewed censorship. In this context, the genre of the historical novel, spearheaded by Nabil Sulayman, Fawwaz Haddad,Khyri al-Dhahabi and Nihad Siris, is sometimes used as a means of expressing dissent, critiquing the present through a depiction of the past. Syrian folk narrative, as a subgenre of historical fiction, is imbued with magical realism, and is also used as a means of veiled criticism of the present. Salim Barakat, a Syrian émigré living in Sweden, is one of the leading figures of the genre. Contemporary Syrian literature also encompasses science fiction and futuristic utopiae (Nuhad Sharif, Talib Umran), which may also serve as media of dissent.

Popular culture

The Syrian music scene, in particular that of Damascus, has long been among the Arab world's most important, especially in the field of classical Arab music. Syria has produced several pan-Arab stars, including Asmahan, Farid al-Atrash and singerLena Chamamyan. The city of Aleppo is known for its muwashshah, a form of Andalous sung poetry popularized by Sabri Moudallal, as well as for popular stars like Sabah Fakhri.

Television was first introduced to Syria in 1960, when Syria and Egypt (which adopted television that same year) were part of the United Arab Republic. It broadcast in black and white until 1976. Syrian soap operas have considerable market penetration throughout the eastern Arab world.

Nearly all of Syria's media outlets are state-owned, and the Ba'ath Party controls nearly all newspapers. The authorities operate several intelligence agencies, among them Shu'bat al-Mukhabarat al-'Askariyya, employing a large number of operatives. Since the Syrian Civil War many of Syria's artists, poets, writers and activists have remained incarcerated, including famed cartoonist Akram Raslam.

Sports

The most popular sports in Syria are football, basketball, swimming, and tennis. Damascus was home to the fifth and seventh Pan Arab Games. Many popular football teams are based in Damascus, Aleppo, Homs, Latakia, etc. The Abbasiyyin Stadium in Damascus is home to the Syrian national football team. The team enjoyed some success, having qualified for four Asian Cup competitions. The team had its first international on 20 November 1949, losing to Turkey 7–0. The team was ranked 138th in the world by FIFA as of May 2013.

Cuisine

Linked to the regions of Syria where a specific dish has originated, Syrian cuisine is rich and varied in its ingredients. Syrian food mostly consists of Southern Mediterranean, Greek, and Southwest Asian dishes. Some Syrian dishes also evolved from Turkish and French cooking: dishes like shish kebab, stuffed zucchini/courgette, yabra' (stuffed grape leaves, the word yapra' derýves from theTurkish word 'yaprak' meaning leaf). Drinks in Syria vary, depending on the time of day and the occasion. Arabic coffee, also known as Turkish coffee, is the most well-known hot drink, usually prepared in the morning at breakfast or in the evening. It is usually served for guests or after food. Arak, an alcoholic drink, is also a well-known beverage served mostly on special occasions. More examples of Syrian beverages include Ayran, Jallab, White coffee, and a locally manufactured beer called Al Shark.

EDUCATION

Education is free and compulsory from ages 6 to 12. Schooling consists of 6 years of primary education followed by a 3-year general or vocational training period and a 3-year academic or vocational program. The second 3-year period of academic training is required for university admission. Total enrollment at post-secondaryschools is over 150,000. The literacy rate of Syrians aged 15 and older is 90.7% for males and 82.2% for females.

Since 1967, all schools, colleges, and universities have been under close government supervision by the Ba'ath Party.

There are 6 state universities in Syria and 15 private universities. The top two state universities are University of Damascus (180,000 students) andUniversity of Aleppo. The top private universities in Syria are: Syrian Private University, Arab International University,University of Kalamoon and International University for Science and Technology. There are also many higher institutes in Syria, like the Higher Institute of Business Administration, which offer undergraduate and graduate programs in business.

According to the Webometrics Ranking of World Universities, the top-ranking universities in the country are Damascus University (3540th worldwide), the University of Aleppo (7176th) and Tishreen University (7968th).

HEALTH

In 2010, spending on healthcare accounted for 3.4% of the country's GDP. In 2008, there were 14.9 physicians and 18.5 nurses per 10,000 inhabitants. The life expectancy at birth was 75.7 years in 2010, or 74.2 years for males and 77.3 years for females.

2

History

The history of Syria may cover either events which occurred on the territory of the present Syrian Arab Republic or events which occurred in Greater Syria. This article focuses on the first.

The present Syrian Arab Republic spans territory which was first unified in the 10th century BCE under the Neo-Assyrian Empire, the capital of which was the city of Ashur, from which the name "Syria" most likely derives. This territory was then conquered by various rulers, and settled in by different peoples. Syria is considered to have emerged as an independent country for the first time on 24 October 1945, upon the signing of the United Nations Charter by the Syrian government, effectively ending France's mandate by the League of Nations to "render administrative advice and assistance to the population" of Syria. On 21 February 1958, however, Syria merged with Egypt to create the United Arab Republic after plebiscitary ratification of the merger by both countries' nations, but seceded from it in 1961, thereby recovering its independence. Since 1963, the Syrian Arab Republic has been ruled by the Ba'ath Party, run by the Assad family exclusively since 1970. Currently Syria is fractured between rival forces on the course of the Syrian Civil War.

PREHISTORY

The oldest remains found in Syria date from the Palaeolithic era (c.800,000 BCE). On 23 August 1993 a joint Japan-Syria excavation team discovered fossilized Paleolithic human remains at the Dederiyeh Cave some 400 km north of Damascus. The bones found in this massive cave were those of a Neanderthal child, estimated to have been about two years old, who lived in the Middle Palaeolithic era (ca. 200,000 to 40,000 years ago). Although many Neanderthal bones had been discovered already, this was practically the first time that an almost complete child's skeleton had been found in its original burial state.

Archaeologists have demonstrated that civilization in Syria was one of the most ancient on earth. Syria is part of the Fertile Crescent, and since approximately 10,000 BCE it was one of the centers of Neolithic culture (PPNA) where agriculture and cattle breeding appeared for the first time in the world. The Neolithic period (PPNB) is represented by rectangular houses of the Mureybet culture. In the early Neolithic period, people used vessels made of stone, gyps and burnt lime. Finds of obsidian tools from Anatolia are evidence of early trade relations. The cities of Hamoukar and Emar flourished during the late Neolithic and Bronze Age.

ANCIENT NEAR EAST

The ruins of Ebla, near Idlib in northern Syria, were discovered and excavated in 1975. Ebla appears to have been an East Semitic speaking city-state founded around 3000 BCE. At its zenith, from about 2500 to 2400 BCE, it may have controlled an empire reaching north toAnatolia, east to Mesopotamia and south to Damascus. Ebla traded with the Mesopotamianstates of Sumer, Akkad and Assyria, as well as with peoples to the northwest. Gifts fromPharaohs, found during excavations, confirm Ebla's contact with Egypt. Scholars believe thelanguage of Ebla was closely related to the fellow East Semitic Akkadian language of Mesopotamia and to be among the oldest known written languages.

From the third millennium BCE, Syria was occupied and fought over successively bySumerians, Eblaites, Akkadians, Assyrians, Egyptians, Hittites, Hurrians, Mitanni, Amoritesand Babylonians.

Ebla was probably conquered into the Mesopotamian Akkadian Empire (2335-2154 BCE) by Sargon of Akkad around 2330 BCE. The city re-emerged, as the part of the nation of the Northwest Semitic speaking Amorites, a few centuries later, and flourished through the early second millennium BCE until conquered by the Indo-European Hittites. The Sumerians, Akkadians and Assyrians of Mesopotamia referred to the region as Mar.Tu or *The land of the Amurru* (Amorites) from as early as the 24th century BCE.

Parts of Syria were controlled by the Neo-Sumerian Empire, Old Assyrian Empireand Babylonian Empire between the 22nd and 18th centuries BCE. The region was fought over by the rival empires of the Hittites, Egyptians, Assyriansand Mitanni between the 15th and 13th centuries BCE, with the Middle Assyrian Empire (1365-1050 BCE) eventually left controlling Syria.

When the Middle Assyrian Empire began to deteriorate in the late 11th century BCE,Canaanites and Phoenicians came to the fore and occupied the coast, andArameans and Suteans supplanted the Amorites in the interior, as part of the general disruptions and exchanges associated with the Bronze Age Collapse and the Sea Peoples. During this period the bulk of Syria became known as Eber Nariand Aramea.

From the 10th century BCE the Neo-Assyrian Empire (935-605 BCE) arose, and Syria was ruled by Assyria for the next three centuries, until the late 7th century BCE, and was still known as Eber-Nari and Aram throughout the period. It is from this period that the name *Syria* first emerges, but not in relation to *modern Syria*, but as an Indo-European corruption of*Assyria*, which in fact encompassed the modern regions of northern Iraq, north east Syria, south east Turkey and the northwestern fringe of Iran.

After this empire finally collapsed, Mesopotamian dominance continued for a time with the short lived Neo-Babylonian Empire(612-539 BCE), which ruled the region for 70 or so years.

CLASSICAL ANTIQUITY

Persian Syria

In 539 BCE, Cyrus the Great, King of Achaemenid Persians, took Syria as part of his empire. Due to Syria's location on the Eastern Mediterranean coast, its navy fleet, and abundant forests; Persians showed great interest in easing control while governing the region. Thus, the indigenous Phoenicians paid a much lesser annual tribute which was only 350 talentcompared to Egypt's tribute of 700 talents. Furthermore, Syrians were allowed to rule their own cities in that they continued to adhere their native religions, establish their own businesses, and build colonies all over the Mediterranean coast. Syria'ssatraps used to reside in Damascus, Sidon or Tripoli.

In 525 BCE, Cambyses II managed to conquer Egypt after the Battle of Pelusium. Afterwards, he decided to launch an expedition towards Siwa Oasis and Carthage, but his efforts were in vain as

Phoenicians refused to operate against their kindred.

Later on, Phoenicians contributed dearly to Xerxes I's invasion of Greece. Arwad aided the campaign with its fleet, while land troops helped in constructing a bridge for Xerxes's army to cross the Bosphorus into mainland Greece.

During Artaxerxes III's reign, Sidon, Egyptians, and eleven other Phoenicians cities started to revolt against the Persian rulers. The revolutions were heavily suppressed in that Sidon was burnt with its citizens.

Hellenistic Syria

Persian dominion ended with the conquests of the Macedonian Greek king, Alexander the Great in 333-332 BCE after the Battle of Issus which took place south of the ancient town Issus, close to the present-day Turkish town of Iskenderun. Syria was then incorporated into the Seleucid Empire by general Seleucus who started, with the Seleucid Kings after him, using the title of *King of Syria*. The capital of this Empire (founded in 312 BCE) was situated at Antioch, then a part of historical Syria, but just inside the Turkish border today as well.

A series of six wars, Syrian Wars, were fought between the Seleucid Empire and thePtolemaic Kingdom of Egypt, during the 3rd and 2nd centuries BC over the region then called Coele-Syria, one of the few avenues into Egypt. These conflicts drained the material and manpower of both parties and led to their eventual destruction and conquest by Rome and Parthia. Mithridates II, King of Parthian Empire, extended his control further west, occupying Dura-Europos in 113 BC.

By 100 BC, the once formidable Seleucid Empire encompassed little more than Antioch and some Syrian cities. In 83 BC, after a bloody strife for the throne of Syria, governed by the Seleucids, the Syrians decided to choose Tigranes the Great, King of Armenia, as the protector of their kingdom and offered him the crown of Syria.

Roman Syria

The Roman general Pompey the Great captured Antioch in 64 BCE, turning Syria into a Roman province and ended Armenian rule, establishing the city of Antioch as its capital.

Antioch was the third largest city in the Roman Empire, after Rome and Alexandria, with an estimated population of 500,000 at its zenith, and being a commercial and cultural hub at the region for many centuries later. The largely Aramaic speaking population of Syria during the heyday of the empire was probably not exceeded again until the 19th century. Syria's large and prosperous population made it one of the most important Roman provinces, particularly during the 2nd and 3rd centuries CE.

Syria is significant in the history of Christianity; Paul the Apostle was converted on the Road to Damascus and emerged as a significant figure in the Christian Church atAntioch, from where he set off on many of his missionary journeys. (Acts 9:1–43)

During the Severan dynasty, Syrian nobles administered Rome and even rose to Imperial title, such as the matriarch of the family, Julia Domna, wife of EmperorSeptimius Severus who was born in Emesa (Homs) and belonged to the prestigiousSampsiceramid Priest Kings of Emesa, alongside with her sister, Julia Maesa who resided with her in Rome alongside her two daughters and grandsons. After the ascension of Domna's two sons to the throne and their eventual death, the Severan dynasty was usurped by Macrinus, a prominent figure in Roman court and aPraetorian prefect. Domna's sister, Julia Maesa returned to Emesa, taking her enormous wealth, and her two daughters and grandsons with her. Back in Emesa, her grandson, Elagabalus, ascended as the chief priest of the sun deity Elagabalus. Soldiers from The Gallic Third Legion who were stationed near Emesa, would visit the city occasionally, and were eventually presuaded by Julia Maesa, using her enormous wealth, and the claim that he was Carcalla's bastard to swear fealty to Elagabalus, who later rode to battle against Marcinus, and entered the city of Antioch emerging as emperor, with Marcinus fleeing before being captured near Chalcedon and executed in Cappadocia. Whatsoever, his reign lasted only a short 4 years, filled with sex scandals, eccentricity, decadence, and zealotry. Realizing that the popular support for the emperor was fading, Julia Maesa decided to replace him with her younger grandson, his cousin Severus Alexander, and convinced Elagabalus to name him as his heir and give him the title of *Caesar*, but after revoking his far more popular cousin of his titles and ranks, and reversing his consulships, the Praetorian guard cheered on Alexander, naming him emperor and slaying Elagabalus and his mother. Severus Alexander's rule was longer, and unlike Elagabalus's disastrous rule, was filled with domestic achievements and he earned the popularity and respect of his people, something Elagabalus never had. He ruled for 13 years, before eventually losing the popularity he once had and being slain by the Legio XXII Primigenia.

Another Emperor of Syrian origin was Philip the Arab, born in modern-day Shahba, he reigned from 244 to 249. His reign enjoyed relative stability, he maintaned good relations with the senate, reaffirmed old Roman virtues and traditions, and started many building projects, most popularly in his hometown, renaming it Philippopolis, and raising it to civic status. Whatsoever, the creation of a new city, alongside the massive tribute to the Persians, he had to raise taxes to high levels and stop paying subsidies to the tribes north of theDanube, which were essential to keeping the peace with them. Nonetheless, his reign ended shortly after Decius usurped the throne, killing Philip and emerging as the new emperor.

During the Roman-Sasanian war of the 3d century, the Romans, struggling in the early stages of the Crisis of the Third Century depended on Odaenathus, the King of the Syrian city-state of Palmyra to secure the Roman East from the Persian invaders and to regain lost Roman territories, so Odaenathus rode north leading the Palmyrene army, and regained Armenia, Northern Syria, parts of Asia Minor from the Persians, and even reached the Persian capital of Ctesiphon, thus weakening the Persians and securing the Roman East, before he was murdered by his own nephew, Maeonius.

Years later, Palmyra rose in rebellion against the Roman Empire under the leadership of Zenobia, Odaenathus's widow and Queen Mother of Palmyra, who led her armies to conquer Syria, Asia Minor, Arabia and Lower Egypt in a series of campaigns in which she annexed almost the entire Roman east, all while the Roman Empire was struggling during the Crisis of the Third Century, ruled by incompetent emperors and torn apart by civil war. Whatsoever, the Palmyrene Empire was short lived; once the Roman general Aurelian rose to power, he rode east, defeated Queen Zenobia in battle twice, and rode to Palmyra to reconquer it and subsequently sacked it around 273 AD, which effectively put an end to Palmyrene civilization.

With the decline of the empire in the west, Syria became part of the Eastern Roman, or Byzantine, Empire in 395. The province was subsequently divided into three, smaller provinces. Syria Prima, with the capital remaining at Antioch, and Syria Secunda, with its capital moving to Apamea on the Orontes, and the new province of Theodorias, with Laodice as its capital.

Syria remained one of the most important regions of the Byzantine Empire, and was of strategic importance, being occupiedby the Sassanids between 609 and 628, then recovered by the emperor Heraclius. Whatsoever, Byzantine rule in the region was lost to the Muslims after the battle of Yarmouk and the fall of Antioch.

MEDIEVAL ERA

In 634-640, Syria was conquered by the Muslim Arabs in the form of the Rashidun army led by Khalid ibn al-Walid, resulting in the region becoming part of the Islamic empire. In the mid-7th century, the Umayyad dynasty, then rulers of the empire, placed the capital of the empire in Damascus. Syria was divided into four districts: Damascus, Homs, Palestine and Jordan. The Islamic empire expanded rapidly and at its height stretched from Spain to India and parts of Central Asia; thus Syria prospered economically, being the centre of the empire. Early Umayyad rulers such as Abd al-Malik and Al-Walid I constructed several splendid palaces and mosques throughout Syria, particularly in Damascus, Aleppo and Homs.

There was complete toleration of Christians (mostly ethnic Arameans and in the north east, Assyrians) in this era and several held governmental posts. In the mid-8th century, the Caliphate collapsed amid dynastic struggles, regional revolts and religious disputes. The Umayyad dynasty was overthrown by the Abbasid dynasty in 750, who moved the capital of empire to Baghdad. Arabic — made official under Umayyad rule — became the dominant language, replacing Greek and Aramaic in the Abbasid era. For periods, Syria was ruled from Egypt, under the Tulunids (887-905), and then, after a period of anarchy, the Ikhshidids (941-969). Northern Syria came under the Hamdanids of Aleppo.

The court of Ali Saif al-Daula, 'Sword of the State,' (944-967) was a center of culture, thanks to its nurturing of Arabic literature. He resisted Byzantine efforts to reconquer Syria by skillful defensive tactics and counter-raids into Anatolia. After his death, the Byzantines captured Antioch and Aleppo (969). Syria was then in turmoil as a battleground between the Hamdanids, Byzantines and Damascus-basedFatimids. The Byzantines had conquered all of Syria by 996, but the chaos continued for much of the 11th century as the Byzantines, Fatimids and Buyids of Baghdad engaged in a struggle for supremacy. Syria was then conquered by theSeljuk Turks (1084-1086). After a century of Seljuk rule, Syria was conquered (1175-1185) by Saladin, founder of the Ayyubid dynasty of Egypt.

During the 12th-13th centuries, parts of Syria were held by Crusader states: theCounty of Edessa (1098-1149), the Principality of Antioch (1098-1268) and County of Tripoli (1109-1289). The area was also threatened by Shi'a extremists known as Assassins (*Hassassin*) and in 1260 theMongols briefly swept through Syria. The withdrawal of the main Mongol army prompted the Mamluks of Egypt to invade and conquer Syria. In addition to the sultanate's capital in Cairo, the Mamluk leader, Baibars, made Damascus a provincial capital, with the cities linked by a mail service that traveled by both horses and carrier pigeons. The Mamluks eliminated the last of the Crusader footholds in Syria and repulsed several Mongol invasions.

In 1400, Timur Lenk, or Tamerlane, invaded Syria, defeated the Mamluk army at Aleppo and captured Damascus. Many of the city's inhabitants were massacred, except for the artisans, who were deported to Samarkand. At this time the Christian population of Syria suffered persecution.

By the end of the 15th century, the discovery of a sea route from Europe to the Far East ended the need for an overland trade route through Syria. In 1516, theOttoman Empire conquered Syria.

OTTOMAN ERA

Ottoman Sultan Selim I conquered most of Syria in 1516 after defeating the Mamlukes at theBattle of Marj Dabiq near Aleppo. Syria was part of the Ottoman Empire from 1516 to 1918, although with 2 brief captures by the Iranian Safavids, notably under Shah Ismail I and Shah Abbas. Ottoman rule was not burdensome to the Syrians because the Turks, as Muslims, respected Arabic as the language of the Koran, and accepted the mantle of defenders of the faith. Damascus became the major entrepot for Mecca, and as such it acquired a holy character to Muslims, because of the barakah (spiritual force or blessing) of the countless pilgrims who passed through on the hadj, the pilgrimage to Mecca.

The Ottoman Turks reorganized Syria into one large province or eyalet. The eyalet was subdivided into several districts or sanjaks. In 1549, Syria was reorganized into two eyalets; the Eyalet of Damascus and the new Eyalet of Aleppo. In 1579, the Eyalet of Tripoli which included Latakia, Hama and Homs was established. In 1586, the Eyalet of Raqqa was established in eastern Syria. Ottoman administration was such that it fostered a peaceful coexistence amongst the different sections of Syrian society for over four hundred years. Each religious minority — Shia Muslim, Greek Orthodox, Maronite, Armenian, and Jewish — constituted a millet. The religious heads of each community administered all personal status law and performed certain civil functions as well.

As part of the Tanzimat reforms, an Ottoman law passed in 1864 provided for a standard provincial administration throughout the empire with the Eyalets becoming smaller Vilayets governed by a Wali, or governor, still appointed by the Sultan but with new provincial assemblies participating in administration. The territory of Greater Syria in the final period of Ottoman rule included modern Syria, Lebanon, Israel, Jordan, Palestinian Authority, Gaza Strip and parts of Turkey and Iraq.

During World War I, French diplomat François Georges-Picot and British diplomat Mark Sykes secretly agreed on the post war division of the Ottoman Empire into respective zones of influence in the Sykes-Picot Agreement of 1916. In October 1918, Arab and British troops advanced into Syria and captured Damascus and Aleppo. In line with the Sykes-Picot agreement, Syria became a League of Nations mandate under French control in 1920.

The demographics of this area underwent a huge shift in the early part of the 20th century when Turkish troops along with Kurdish detachments conducted ethnic cleansing of its Christian populations . Some Circassian, Kurdish and Chechens tribes cooperated with the Ottoman authorities in the massacres of Armenian and Assyrian Christians in Upper Mesopotamia, between 1914 and 1920, with further attacks on unarmed fleeing civilians conducted by local Arab militias. Many Assyrians fled to Syria during the genocide and settled mainly in the Jazira area. In 1936, the French forces bombarded Amuda (Tusha Amudi). On 13 August 1937, in a revenge attack, about 500 Kurds from the Dakkuri, Milan, and Kiki tribes attacked the then predominantly Christian Amuda, and burned the town. The town was destroyed and the Christian population, about 300 families, fled to the towns of Qamishli and Hasakah. During the great war, Kurdish tribes attacked and sacked and villages in Albaq District immediately to the north of Hakkari mountains. According to lieutenant Ronald Sempill Stafford, a large numbers of Assyrians and Armenians were killed.

In 1941, the Assyrian community of al-Malikiyah was subjected to a vicious assault. Even though the assault failed, Assyrians were terrorized and left in large numbers, and the immigration of Kurds from Turkey to the area have resulted in a Kurdish majority in Amuda, al-Malikiyah, and al-Darbasiyah. The historically-important Christian city ofNusaybin had a similar fate when its Christian population left after it was ceded to Turkey through the Franco-Turkish Agreement of Ankara in October 1921. The Christian population of the city crossed the border into Syria and settled inQamishli, which was separated by the railway (new border) from Nusaybin. Nusaybin became Kurdish and Qamishli became a Syriac Christian city. Things soon changed, however, with the immigration of Kurds beginning in 1926 following the failure of the rebellion of Saeed Ali Naqshbandi against the Turkish authorities. During the 1920s, waves of Kurds fled their homes in Turkey and settled in northeastern Syria where they were granted citizenship by the French mandate authorities.

MODERN HISTORY

French Mandate

In 1919, a short-lived dependent Kingdom of Syria was established under EmirFaisal I of the Hashemite dynasty, who later became the king of Iraq. In March 1920, the Syrian National Congress proclaimed Faisal as king of Syria "in its natural boundaries" from the Taurus mountains in Turkey to the Sinai desert in Egypt. However, his rule in Syria ended after only a few months following a clash between his Syrian Arab forces and French forces at the Battle of Maysalun. French troops took control of Syria and forced Faisal to flee. Later that year the San Remo conference split up Faisal's kingdom by placing Syria-Lebanon under a French mandate, and Palestine under British control. Syria was divided into three autonomous regions by the French, with separate areas for the Alawis on the coast and the Druze in the south.

Nationalist agitation against French rule led to Sultan al-Atrash leading a revolt that broke out in the Druze Mountain in 1925 and spread across the whole of Syria and parts of Lebanon. The revolt saw fierce battles between rebel and French forces in Damascus, Homs and Hama before it was suppressed in 1927.

The French sentenced Sultan al-Atrash to death, but he had escaped with the rebels to Transjordan and was eventually pardoned. He returned to Syria in 1937 and was met with a huge public reception. Elections were held in 1928 for a constituent assembly, which drafted a constitution for Syria. However, the French High Commissioner rejected the proposals, sparking nationalist protests.

Syria and France negotiated a treaty of independence in September 1936. France agreed to Syrian independence in principle although maintained French military and economic dominance. Hashim al-Atassi, who had been Prime Minister under King Faisal's brief reign, was the first president to be elected under a new constitution, effectively the first incarnation of the modern republic of Syria. However, the treaty never came into force because the French Legislature refused to ratify it. With the fall of France in 1940 during World War II, Syria came under the control of Vichy France until the British and Free French occupied the country in the Syria-Lebanon campaign in July 1941. Syria proclaimed its independence again in 1941, but it was not until 1 January 1944 that it was recognised as an independent republic. There were protests in 1945 over the slow pace of French withdrawal. The French responded to these protests with artillery. In an effort to stop the movement toward independence, French troops occupied the Syrian parliament in May 1945 and cut off Damascus's electricity. Training their guns on Damascus's old city, the French killed 400 Syrians and destroyed hundreds of homes. With casualties mountingWinston Churchill ordered British troops to invade Syria where they escorted French troops to their barracks on June 1. With continuing pressure from the British and Syrian nationalist groups the French were forced to evacuate the last of their troops in April 1946, leaving the country in the hands of a republican government that had been formed during the mandate.

Independence, war and instability

Syria became independent on 17 April 1946. Syrian politics from independence through the late 1960s were marked by upheaval. Between 1946 and 1956, Syria had 20 different cabinets and drafted four separate constitutions.

In 1948, Syria was involved in the Arab-Israeli War, aligning with the other local Arab states who wanted to destroy the state of Israel. The Syrian army entered northern Palestine but, after bitter fighting, was gradually driven back to the Golan Heights by the Israelis. An armistice was agreed in July 1949. A demilitarized zone under UN supervision was established; the status of these territories proved a stumbling-block for all future Syrian-Israeli negotiations. It was during this period that many Syrian Jews, who faced growing persecution and fled Syria as part of Jewish exodus from Arab countries.

The outcome of the war was one of factors behind the March 1949 Syrian coup d'état by Col. Husni al-Za'im, in what has been described as the first military overthrow of the Arab World since the Second World War. This was soon followed by another coup by Col. Sami al-Hinnawi. Army officer Adib Shishakli seized power in the third military coup of 1949. AJabal al-Druze uprising was suppressed after extensive fighting (1953–54). Growing discontent eventually led to another coup, in which Shishakli was overthrown in February 1954. The Arab Socialist Ba'ath Party, founded in 1947, played a part in the overthrow of Shishakli. Veteran nationalist Shukri al-Quwatli was president from 1955 until 1958, but by then his post was largely ceremonial.

Power was increasingly concentrated in the military and security establishment, which had proved itself to be the only force capable of seizing and, perhaps, keeping power.Parliamentary institutions remained weak, dominated by competing parties representing the landowning elites and various Sunni urban notables, whilst the economy was mismanaged and little was done to better the role of Syria's peasant majority.

In November 1956, as a direct result of the Suez Crisis,Syria signed a pact with the Soviet Union, providing a foothold for Communist influence within the government in exchange for planes, tanks, and other military equipment being sent to Syria. This increase in Syrian military strength worriedTurkey, as it seemed feasible that Syria might attempt to retake Ýskenderun, a matter of dispute between Syria and Turkey. On the other hand, Syria and the Soviet Union accused Turkey of massing its troops on the Syrian border. Only heated debates in the United Nations (of which Syria was an original member) lessened the threat of war.

In this context, the influence of Nasserism, Pan-Arab and anti-imperial ideologies created fertile ground for the idea of closer ties with Egypt. The appeal of Egyptian President Gamal Abdal Nasser's leadership in the wake of the Suez Crisis created support in Syria for union with Egypt. On 1 February 1958, Syrian President al-Quwatli and Nasser announced the merging of the two states, creating the United Arab Republic. The union was not a success, however. Discontent with Egyptian dominance of the UAR, led elements opposed to the union under Abd al-Karim al-Nahlawi, to seize power on 28 September 1961. Two days later, Syria re-established itself as the Syrian Arab Republic. Frequent coups, military revolts, civil disorders and bloody riots characterized the 1960s. The 8 March 1963 coup, resulted in installation of the National Council of the Revolutionary Command (NCRC), a group of military and civilian officials who assumed control of all executive and legislative authority. The takeover was engineered by members of the Ba'ath Party led by Michel Aflaq and Salah al-Din al-Bitar. The new cabinet was dominated by Ba'ath members; the moderate al-Bitar became premier. He was overthrown early in 1966 by left-wing military dissidents of the party led by General Salah Jadid.

Under Jadid's rule, Syria aligned itself with the Soviet bloc and pursued hardline policies towards Israel and "reactionary" Arab states especially Saudi Arabia, calling for the mobilization of a "people's war" against Zionism rather than inter-Arab military alliances. Domestically, Jadid attempted a socialist transformation of Syrian society at forced pace, creating unrest and economical difficulties. Opponents of the government were harshly suppressed, while the Ba'ath Party replaced parliament as law-making body and other parties were banned. Public support for his government, such as it was, declined sharply following Syria's defeat in the 1967 Six Day War, when Israel destroyed much of Syria's air force and captured the Golan Heights.

Conflicts also arose over different interpretations of the legal status of the Demilitarized Zone. Israel maintained that it had sovereign rights over the zone, allowing the civilian use of farmland. Syria and the UN maintained that no party had sovereign rights over the zone. Israel was accused by Syria of cultivating lands in the Demilitarized Zone, using armored tractors backed by Israel forces. Syria claimed that the situation was the result of an Israeli aim to increase tension so as to justify large-scale aggression, and to expand its occupation of the Demilitarized Zone by liquidating the rights of Arab cultivators. The Israeli defense minister Moshe Dayan said in a 1976 interview that Israel provoked more than 80% of the clashes with Syria.

Conflict developed between right-wing army officers and the more moderate civilian wing of the Ba'ath Party. The 1970 retreat of Syrian forces sent to aid the PLO during the "Black September" hostilities with Jordan reflected this political disagreement within the ruling Ba'ath leadership. On 13 November 1970, Minister of Defense Hafez al-Assad seized power in a bloodless military overthrow ("The Corrective Movement").

Syria under Hafez al-Assad (1970–2000)

Upon assuming power, Hafez al-Assad moved quickly to create an organizational infrastructure for his government and to consolidate control. The Provisional Regional Command of Assad's Arab Socialist Ba'ath Party nominated a 173-member legislature, the People's Council, in which the Ba'ath Party took 87 seats. The remaining seats were divided among "popular organizations" and other minor parties. In March 1971, the party held its regional congress and elected a new 21-member Regional Command headed by Assad.

In the same month, a national referendum was held to confirm Assad as President for a 7-year term. In March 1972, to broaden the base of his government, Assad formed the National Progressive Front, a coalition of parties led by the Ba'ath Party, and elections were held to establish local councils in each of Syria's 14 governorates. In March 1973, a new Syrian constitution went into effect followed shortly thereafter by parliamentary elections for the People's Council, the first such elections since 1962. The 1973 Constitution defined Syria as a secular socialist state with Islam recognised as the majority religion.

On 6 October 1973, Syria and Egypt initiated the Yom Kippur War by launching a surprise attack on Israel. After intense fighting, the Syrians were repulsed in the Golan Heights. The Israelis pushed deeper into Syrian territory, beyond the 1967 boundary. As a result, Israel continues to occupy the Golan Heights as part of the Israeli-occupied territories. In 1975, Assad said he would be prepared to make peace with Israel in return for an Israeli withdrawal from "all occupied Arab land".

In 1976, the Syrian army intervened in the Lebanese civil war to ensure that the status quo was maintained, and theMaronite Christians remained in power. This was the beginning of what turned out to be a thirty-year Syrian military occupation. Many crimes in Lebanon, including the accused assassinations of Rafik Hariri, Kamal Jumblat and Bachir Gemayel were attributed to the Syrian forces and intelligence services although were not proven to this day. In 1981 Israel declared its annexation of the Golan Heights. The following year, Israel invaded Lebanon and attacked the Syrian army, forcing it to withdraw from several areas. When Lebanon and Israel announced the end of hostilities in 1983, Syrian forces remained in Lebanon. Through extensive use of proxy militias, Syria attempted to stop Israel from taking over southern Lebanon. Assad sent troops into Lebanon for a second time in 1987 to enforce a ceasefire in Beirut.

The Syrian-sponsored Taif Agreement finally brought the Lebanese civil war to an end in 1990. However, the Syrian Army'spresence in Lebanon continued until 2005, exerting a strong influence over Lebanese politics. The assassination of the popular former Lebanese Prime Minister Rafik Hariri, was blamed on Syria, and pressure was put on Syria to withdraw their forces from Lebanon. On 26 April 2005 the bulk of the Syrian forces withdrew from Lebanon although some of its intelligence operatives remained, drawing further international rebuke.

About one million Syrian workers went to Lebanon after the war to find jobs in the reconstruction of the country. In 1994 the Lebanese government controversially granted citizenship to over 200,000 Syrian residents in the country.

The government was not without its critics, though open dissent was repressed. A serious challenge arose in the late 1970s, however, from fundamentalist Sunni Muslims, who rejected the secular values of the Ba'ath program and objected to rule by the Shia Alawis. After the Islamic Revolution in Iran, Muslim groups instigated uprisings and riots in Aleppo, Homs and Hama and attempted to assassinate Assad in 1980.

In response, Assad began to stress Syria's adherence to Islam. At the start of Iran-Iraq war, in September 1980, Syria supported Iran, in keeping with the traditional rivalry between Ba'athist leaderships in Iraq and Syria.

The arch-conservative Muslim Brotherhood, centered in the city of Hama, was finally crushed in February 1982 when parts of the city were hit by artillery fire and leaving between 10,000 and 25,000 people, mostly civilians, dead or wounded. The government's actions at Hama have been described as possibly being "the single deadliest act by any Arab government against its own people in the modern Middle East". Since then, public manifestations of anti-government activity have been limited.

When Iraq invaded Kuwait in 1990, Syria joined the US-led coalition against Iraq. This led to improved relations with the US and other Arab states. Syria participated in the multilateral Southwest Asia Peace Conference in Madrid in October 1991, and during the 1990s engaged in direct negotiations with Israel. These negotiations failed over the Golan Heights issue and there have been no further direct Syrian-Israeli talks since President Hafez al-Assad's meeting with then President Bill Clinton in Geneva in March 2000.

In 1994, Assad's son Bassel al-Assad, who was likely to succeed his father, was killed in a car accident. Assad's brother,Rifaat al-Assad, was "relieved of his post" as vice-president in 1998. Thus, when Assad died in 2000, his second son,Bashar al-Assad was chosen as his successor.

Syria under Bashar al-Assad (2000–present)

Hafez al-Assad died on 10 June 2000, after 30 years in power. Immediately following al-Assad's death, the Syrian Parliament amended the constitution, reducing the mandatory minimum age of the President from 40 to 34. This allowed Bashar Assad to become eligible for nomination by the ruling Ba'ath party. On 10 July 2000, Bashar al-Assad was elected President by referendum in which he ran unopposed, garnering 97.29% of the vote, according to Syrian Government statistics.

The period after Bashar al-Assad's election in the summer of 2000 saw new hopes of reform and was dubbed the Damascus Spring. The period was characterized by the emergence of numerous political forums or salons where groups of like-minded people met in private houses to debate political and social issues. The phenomenon of salons spread rapidly in Damascus and to a lesser extent in other cities. Political activists, such as Riad Seif, Haitham al-Maleh, Kamal al-Labwani, Riyad al-Turk, and Aref Dalila were important in mobilizing the movement. The most famous of the forums were the Riad Seif Forum and the Jamal al-Atassi Forum. Pro-democracy activists mobilized around a number of political demands, expressed in the "Manifesto of the 99". Assad ordered the release of some 600 political prisoners in November 2000. The outlawed Muslim Brotherhood resumed its political activity. In May 2001 Pope John Paul II paid a historic visit to Syria.

However, by the autumn of 2001, the authorities had suppressed the pro-reform movement, crushing hopes of a break with the authoritarian past of Hafez al-Assad. Arrests of leading intellectuals continued, punctuated by occasional amnesties, over the following decade. Although the Damascus Spring had lasted for a short period, its effects still echo during the political, cultural and intellectual debates in Syria today.

Tensions with the USA grew worse after 2002, when the US claimed Damascus was acquiring weapons of mass destruction and included Syria in a list of states that they said made-up an "axis of evil". The USA was critical of Syria because of its strong relationships with Hamas, the Islamic Jihad Movement in Palestine and Hezbollah, which the USA, Israel and EU regard as terrorist groups. In 2003 the US threatened sanctions if Damascus failed to make what Washington called the "right decisions". Syria denied US allegations that it was developing chemical weapons and helping fugitive Iraqis. An Israeli air strike against a Palestinian militant camp near Damascus in October 2003 was described by Syria as "military aggression". President Assad visited Turkey in January 2004, the first Syrian leader to do so. The trip marked the end of decades of frosty relations, although ties were to sour again after 2011. In May 2004, the USA imposed economic sanctions on Syria over what it called its support for terrorism and failure to stop militants entering Iraq. Tensions with the US escalated in early 2005 after the killing of the former Lebanese PM Hariri in Beirut. Washington cited Syrian influence in Lebanon behind the assassination. Damascus was urged to withdraw its forces from Lebanon, which it did by April.

Following 2004 al-Qamishli riots, the Syrian Kurds protested in Brussels, in Geneva, in Germany, at the US and UK embassies, and in Turkey. The protesters pledged against violence in north-east Syria starting Friday, 12 March 2004, and reportedly extending over the weekend resulting in several deaths, according to reports. The Kurds allege the Syrian government encouraged and armed the attackers. Signs of rioting were seen in the towns of Qameshli and Hassakeh.

Renewed opposition activity occurred in October 2005 when activist Michel Kilo and other opposition figures launched theDamascus Declaration, which criticized the Syrian government as "authoritarian, totalitarian and cliquish" and called for democratic reform. Leading dissidents Kamal al-Labwani and Michel Kilo were sentenced to a long jail terms in 2007, only weeks after human rights lawyer Anwar al-Bunni was jailed. Although Bashar al-Assad said he would reform, the reforms have been limited to some market reforms.

Over the years the authorities have tightened Internet censorship with laws such as forcing Internet cafes to record all the comments users post on chat forums. While the authorities have relaxed rules so that radio channels can now play Western pop music, websites such as Wikipedia, YouTube, Facebook and Amazon have been blocked, but were recently unblocked throughout the nation.

Syria's international relations improved for a period. Diplomatic relations with Iraq were restored in 2006, after nearly a quarter century. In March 2007, dialogue between Syria and the European Union was relaunched. The following month saw US House of Representatives Speaker Nancy Pelosi meet President Assad in Damascus, although President Bushobjected. Secretary of State Condoleezza Rice then met with Syrian Foreign Minister Walid Muallem in Egypt, in the first contact at this level for two years.

An Israeli air strike against a site in northern Syria in September 2007 was a setback to improving relations. The Israelis claimed the site was a nuclear facility under construction with North Korean help. 2008 March - When Syria hosted an Arab League summit in 2008, many Western states sent low-level delegations in protest at Syria's stance on Lebanon. However, the diplomatic thaw was resumed when President Assad met the then French President Nicolas Sarkozy in Paris in July 2008. The visit signaled the end of Syria's diplomatic isolation by the West that followed the assassination of Hariri in 2005. While in Paris, President Assad also met the recently elected Lebanese president, Michel Suleiman. The two men laid the foundations for establishing full diplomatic relations between their countries. Later in the year, Damascus hosted a four-way summit between Syria, France, Turkey and Qatar, in a bid to boost efforts towards Middle East peace.

In April 2008, President Assad told a Qatari newspaper that Syria and Israel had been discussing a peace treaty for a year, with Turkey acting as a mediator. This was confirmed in May 2008 by a spokesman for Israeli Prime Minister Ehud Olmert. The status of the Golan Heights, a major obstacle to a peace treaty, was being discussed.

In 2008, an explosion killed 17 on the outskirts of Damascus, the most deadly attack in Syria in several years. The government blamed Islamist militants.

2009 saw a number of high level meetings between Syrian and US government diplomats and officials. US special envoyGeorge J. Mitchell visited for talks with President Assad on Middle East peace. Trading launched on Syria's stock exchange in a gesture towards liberalising the state-controlled economy. The Syrian writer and pro-democracy campaigner Michel Kilo was released from prison after serving a three-year sentence. In 2010, the USA posted its first ambassador to Syria after a five-year break.

The thaw in diplomatic relations came to an abrupt end. In May 2010, the USA renewed sanctions against Syria, saying that it supported terrorist groups, seeks weapons of mass destruction and has provided Lebanon's Hezbollah with Scud missilesin violation of UN resolutions. In 2011 the UN's IAEA nuclear watchdog reported Syria to the UN Security Council over its alleged covert nuclear programme.

Civil War (2011–present)

The Syrian Uprising (later known as the Syrian civil war) is an ongoing internal conflict between the Syrian army and the rebel groups composed by many heterogeneous branches. Encouraged by the Arab Spring, there were pro-reform protests in Damascus and the southern city of Deraa in March 2011. Protestors demanded political freedom and the release of political prisoners. This was immediately followed by a government crackdown whereby the Syrian Army was deployed to quell unrest.

Security forces shot and killed a number of people in Deraa, triggering days of violent unrest that steadily spread nationwide over the following months. There were unconfirmed reports that soldiers who refused to open fire on civilians were summarily executed. The Syrian government denied reports of executions and defections, and blamed militant armed groups for causing trouble. President Assad announced some conciliatory measures: dozens of political prisoners were released, he dismissed the government, and in April he lifted the 48-year-old state of emergency. The government accused protesters of being stirred up by Israeli agents, and in May, army tanks entered Deraa, Banyas, Homs and the suburbs of Damascus in an effort to crush anti-government protests. In June, the government claimed that in 120 members of the security forces had been killed by "armed gangs" in the northwestern town of Jisr al-Shughour. Troops besieged the town, whose inhabitants mostly fled to Turkey. At the same time, President Assad pledged to start a "national dialogue" on reform. He sacked the governor of the northern province of Hama and sent in more troops to restore order.

In July 2011, some of the anti-Assad groups met in Istanbul with a view to bringing the various internal and external opposition groups together. They agreed to form the Syrian National Council. Rebel fighters were joined by army defectors on the Turkish-Syrian border and declared the formation of the Free Syrian Army (FSA). They began forming fighting units to escalate the insurgency from September 2011. From the outset, the FSA was a disparate collection of loosely organized and largely independent units.

In December 2011, Syria agreed to an Arab League initiative allowing Arab observers into the country. Thousand of people gathered in Homs to greet them, but the League suspended the mission in January 2012, citing worsening violence. Twin suicide bomb attacks outside security buildings in Damascus killed 44 people in December 2011. This was the first in a series of bombings and suicide attacks in the Syrian capital that continued throughout 2012. The opposition accuses the government itself of staging the attacks. The government accuses the Western media of turning a blind eye to the rebels' use of al-Qaeda-style terrorist attacks.

As the Syrian army recaptured the Homs district of Baba Amr in March 2012, the UN Security Council endorsed a non-binding peace plan drafted by UN envoy Kofi Annan. However, the violence continued unabated. A number of Western nations expelled senior Syrian diplomats in protest. In May, the UN Security Council strongly condemned both the Syrian government's use of heavy weaponry and the massacre by rebels of over a hundred civilians in Houla, near Homs.

The UN reported that, in the first six months alone, 9,100–11,000 people had been killed during the insurgency, of which 2,470–3,500 were actual combatants and rest were civilians. The Syrian government estimated that more than 3,000 civilians, 2,000–2,500 members of the security forces and over 800 rebels had been killed. UN observers estimated that the death toll in the first six months included over 400 children. Additionally, some media reported that over 600 political prisoners and detainees, some of them children, have died in custody. A prominent case was that of Hamza Al-Khateeb. Syria's government has disputed Western and UN casualty estimates, characterizing their claims as being based on false reports originating from rebel groups.

According to the UN, about 1.2 million Syrians had been internally displaced within the country and over 355,000 Syrian refugees had fled to the neighboring countries of Jordan, Iraq, Lebanon and Turkey during the first year of fighting.

Both sides have been accused of human rights abuses. The United Nations Human Rights Council has found numerous incidents of torture, summary executions and attacks on cultural property. The Syrian government has been accused of committing the majority of war crimes, although independent verification has proven extremely difficult. The conflict has the hallmarks of a sectarian civil war; the leading government figures are Shia Alawites, whilst the rebels are mainly SunniMuslims. Although neither side in the conflict has described sectarianism as playing a major role, the UN Human Rights Council has warned that "entire communities are at risk of being forced out of the country or of being killed." The conflict has increasingly forced minorities to align themselves with one side or another, with Christians, Druze and Armenians largely siding with the government while Turkmen are mostly anti-government. Palestinians have split, while Kurds have fought against both rebels and government forces. Some Christian communities have formed militias to protect their neighborhoods from rebel fighters. International religious freedom groups have been drawing attention to the plight of Syria's Christian minority at the hands of the rebel jihadist elements. Churches have been destroyed, killings and kidnapping reported, and Christians driven out of their homes. Almost the entire Christian population of Homs - 50,000-60,000 people - have fled the city.

The Arab League, the Organisation of Islamic Cooperation, GCC states, the USA and the European Union have condemned the use of violence by the Syrian government and applied sanctions against Syria. China and Russia have sought to avoid foreign intervention and called for a negotiated settlement. They have avoided condemning the Syrian government and disagree with sanctions. China has sought to engage with the Syrian opposition. The Arab League and Organisation of Islamic Cooperation have both suspended Syria's membership.

In June 2012 a number of high-ranking military and political personnel, such as Manaf Tlas and Nawaf al-Fares, fled the country. Nawaf al-Fares stated in a video that this was in response to crimes against humanity by the Assad government. In August 2012, the country's Deputy Prime Minister Qadri Jamil said President Assad's resignation could not be a condition for starting peace negotiations.

Syria-Turkish tension increased in October 2012, when Syrian mortar fire hit a Turkish border town and killed five civilians. Turkey returned fire and intercepted a Syrian plane allegedly carrying arms from Russia. Both countries banned each other's planes from their air space. In the south, the Israeli military fired on Syrian units after alleging shelling from Syrian positions across the Golan Heights.

After heavy fighting, a fire destroyed much of the historic market of Aleppo in October. A UN-brokered ceasefire during the Islamic holiday of Eid al-Adha soon broke down as fighting and bomb attacks continued in several cities. By this time, theSyrian Arab Red Crescent estimated that 2.5 million people had been displaced within Syria, double the previous estimate. According to the anti-Assad Syrian Observatory for Human Rights, almost 44,000 people have died since the insurgency against began. According to a UN report, the humanitarian situation has been "aggravated by widespread destruction and razing of residential areas." "Towns and villages across Latakia, Idlib, Hama and Dara'a governorates have been effectively emptied of their populations," the report said. "Entire neighborhoods in southern and eastern Damascus, Deir al-Zour and Aleppo have been razed. The downtown of Homs city has been devastated."

In November 2012, the National Coalition for Syrian Revolutionary and Opposition Forces, commonly named the 'Syrian National Coalition' was formed at a meeting hosted by Qatar. Islamist militias in Aleppo, including the Al-Nusra and Al-Tawhidgroups, refused to join the Coalition, denouncing it as a "conspiracy". There is also concern over Muslim Brotherhood or Islamist domination of the anti-Assad coalition. Despite this, in December 2012, the USA, the Arab states of the Persian Gulf, Turkey and many EU members moved quickly to recognise the coalition as the "sole legitimate representative of the Syrian people" rather than the former main rebel group, the Syrian National Council. The USA and Persian Gulf stateswanted a reshaped opposition coalition to include more Syrians who were fighting on the ground – as opposed to those who had been in exile for decades – and one that was more broadly representative of all Syria's regions. At the same times, the U.S. has added al-Nusra - one of the most successful rebel military groups - to its terrorist list, citing ties to al-Qaeda.

On 20 December 2012, a UN Independent Commission of Inquiry said that Syria's newest insurgent groups increasingly operate independently of the rebel command and some are affiliated with al-Qaeda. Many of the insurgents are foreign fighters; "Sunnis hailing from countries in the Middle East and North Africa," and are linked to extremist groups.

A sarin gas attack occurred in Syria, near Damascus, on 21 August 2013. The attack is alleged to have been carried out by the Syrian government of Bashar al-Assad according to French and United States' government's intelligence.However, Russia, one of the Syrian government's international supporters, seems unconvinced of the origins of the attack. The attack has led to increased international pressure on the Assad government and threat of internationalmilitary intervention in Syria led by United States armed forces.

On 12 December 2016, the city of Aleppo was fully liberated by Pro-government forces.

MODERN HISTORY OF SYRIA

Ottoman Syria was turned into the short-lived Arab Kingdom of Syria in 1920, which was however soon committed under French Mandate. From 1938 known as a Republic, Syria gained independence in 1946, entering the Arab-Israeli War in 1948, and remaining in a state of political instability during the 1950s and 1960s.

In the context of the Arab Spring of 2011, Bashar al-Assad's government is involved in the ongoing Syrian civil war.

SYRIA UNDER THE MANDATE

Initial civil administration

Following the San Remo conference in April 1920 and the defeat of King Faisal's short-lived monarchy in Syria at the Battle of Maysalun on 24 July 1920, the French general Henri Gouraud established civil administration in the territory. The mandate region was subdivided into six states.

They were the states of Damascus (1920), Aleppo (1920), Alawites (1920), Jabal Druze(1921), the autonomous Sanjak of Alexandretta (1921) (modern-day Hatay), and the State of Greater Lebanon (1920), which later became the modern country of Lebanon.

The drawing of those states was based in part on the sectarian make-up on the ground in Syria. However, nearly all the Syrian sects were hostile to the French mandate and to the division it created. This was best demonstrated by the numerous revolts that the French encountered in all of the Syrian states. Maronite Christians of Mount Lebanon, on the other hand, were a community with a dream of independence that was being realized under the French; therefore, Greater Lebanon was the exception to the newly formed states.

Syrian Federation (1922-24)

In July 1922, France established a loose federation between three of the states: Damascus, Aleppo, and the Alawite under the name of the Syrian Federation (Fédération syrienne). Jabal Druze, Sanjak of Alexandretta, and Greater Lebanon were not parts of this federation, which adopted a new federal flag (green-white-green with French canton). On 1 December 1924, the Alawite state seceded from the federation when the states of Aleppo and Damascus were united into the State of Syria.

Great Syrian revolt

In 1925, a revolt in Jabal Druze led by Sultan Pasha el Atrash spread to other Syrian states and became a general rebellion in Syria. France tried to retaliate by having the parliament of Aleppo declare secession from the union with Damascus, but the voting was foiled by Syrian patriots.

Republic of Syria

On 14 May 1930, the State of Syria was declared the Republic of Syria and a new constitution was drafted. Two years later, in 1932, a new flag for the republic was adopted. The flag carried three red stars that represented the three districts of the republic (Damascus, Aleppo, and Deir ez Zor).

1936 Independence treaty

In 1936, the Franco-Syrian Treaty of Independence was signed, a treaty that would not be ratified by the French legislature. However, the treaty allowed Jabal Druze, the Alawite (now called Latakia), and Alexandretta to be incorporated into the Syrian republic within the following two years. Greater Lebanon (now the Lebanese Republic) was the only state that did not join the Syrian Republic. Hashim al-Atassi, who was Prime Minister under King Faisal's brief reign (1918–1920), was the first president to be elected under a new constitution adopted after the independence treaty.

Separation of Hatay

In September 1938, France again separated the Syrian district of Alexandretta and transformed it into the Republic of Hatay. The Republic of Hatay joined Turkey in the following year, in June 1939. Syria did not recognize the incorporation of Hatay into Turkey and the issue is still disputed until the present time.

WORLD WAR II AND THE FOUNDING OF THE UN

With the fall of France in 1940 during World War II, Syria came under the control of the Vichy Government until the British and Free

French invaded and occupied the country in July 1941. Syria proclaimed its independence again in 1941 but it wasn't until 1 January 1944, that it was recognized as an independent republic.

On 27 September 1941, France proclaimed, by virtue of, and within the framework of the Mandate, the independence and sovereignty of the Syrian State. The proclamation said "the independence and sovereignty of Syria and Lebanon will not affect the juridical situation as it results from the Mandate Act. Indeed, this situation could be changed only with the agreement of the Council of the League of Nations, with the consent of the Government of the United States, a signatory of the Franco-American Convention of 4 April 1924, and only after the conclusion between the French Government and the Syrian and Lebanese Governments of treaties duly ratified in accordance with the laws of the French Republic.

Benqt Broms said that it was important to note that there were several founding members of the United Nations whose statehood was doubtful at the time of the San Francisco Conference and that the Government of France still considered Syria and Lebanon to be mandates.

Duncan Hall said "Thus, the Syrian mandate may be said to have been terminated without any formal action on the part of the League or its successor. The mandate was terminated by the declaration of the mandatory power, and of the new states themselves, of their independence, followed by a process of piecemeal unconditional recognition by other powers, culminating in formal admission to the United Nations. Article 78 of the Charter ended the status of tutelage for any member state: 'The trusteeship system shall not apply to territories which have become Members of the United Nations, relationship among which shall be based on respect for the principle of sovereign equality.'"

On 29 May 1945, France bombed Damascus and tried to arrest its democratically elected leaders. While French planes were bombing Damascus, Prime Minister Faris al-Khoury was at the founding conference of the United Nations in San Francisco, presenting Syria's claim for independence from the French Mandate. Continuing pressure from Syrian nationalist groups and British pressure forced the French to evacuate their last troops on 17 April 1946.

REPUBLIC OF SYRIA 1946-1963

Syrian independence was acquired in 1946. Although rapid economic development followed the declaration of independence, Syrian politics from independence through the late 1960s was marked by upheaval. The early years of independence were marked by political instability.

In 1948, Syria was involved in the Arab-Israeli War with the newly created State of Israel. The Syrian army was pressed out of the Israeli areas, but fortified their strongholds on the Golan and managed to keep their old borders and occupy some additional territory. In July 1949, Syria was the last Arab country to sign an armistice agreement with Israel.

In March 1949, Syria's national government was overthrown by a military coup d'état led by Hussni al-Zaimy thus ending democratic rule in a coup sponsored by the United States CIA, with the help of agents Miles Copeland and Stephen Meade.

Later that year Zaim was overthrown by his colleague Sami al-Hinnawi. Adib al-Shishakli. The latter undermined civilian rule and led to Shishakli's complete seizure of power in 1951. Shishakli continued to rule the country until 1955, when growing public opposition forced him to resign and leave the country. The national government was restored, but again to face instability, this time coming from abroad. After the overthrow of President Shishakli in a 1954 coup, continued political maneuvering supported by competing factions in the military eventually brought Arab nationalist and socialist elements to power. Between 1946 and 1956, Syria had 20 different cabinets and drafted four separate constitutions.

During the Suez Crisis of 1956, after the invasion of the Sinai Peninsula by Israeli troops, and the intervention of British and French troops, martial law was declared in Syria. Later Syrian and Iraqi troops were brought into Jordan to prevent a possible Israeli invasion. The November 1956 attacks on Iraqi pipelines were in retaliation for Iraq's acceptance into theBaghdad Pact. In early 1957 Iraq advised Egypt and Syria against a conceivable takeover of Jordan.

In November 1956 Syria signed a pact with the Soviet Union, providing a foothold for Communist influence within the government in exchange for planes, tanks, and other military equipment being sent to Syria. This increase in the strength of Syrian military technology worried Turkey, as it seemed feasible that Syria might attempt to retake Iskenderon, a formerly Syrian city now in Turkey. On the other hand, Syria and the USSR accused Turkey of massing its troops at the

Syrian border. During this standoff, Communists gained more control over the Syrian government and military. Only heated debates in the United Nations (of which Syria was an original member) lessened the threat of war.

. Syria's political instability during the years after the 1954 coup, the parallelism of Syrian and Egyptian policies, and the appeal of Egyptian President Gamal Abdal Nasser's leadership in the wake of the Suez crisis created support in Syria for union with Egypt. On 1 February 1958, Syrian president Shukri al-Kuwatli and Nasser announced the merging of the two countries, creating the United Arab Republic, and all Syrian political parties, as well as the Communists therein, ceased overt activities.

The union was not a success, however. Following a military coup on 28 September 1961, Syria seceded, reestablishing itself as the Syrian Arab Republic. Instability characterised the next 18 months, with various coups culminating on 8 March 1963, in the installation by leftist Syrian Army officers of the National Council of the Revolutionary Command (NCRC), a group of military and civilian officials who assumed control of all executive and legislative authority. The takeover was engineered by members of the Arab Socialist Resurrection Party (Ba'ath Party), which had been active in Syria and other Arab countries since the late 1940s. The new cabinet was dominated by Ba'ath members.

BA'ATHIST REPUBLIC OF SYRIA 1963-TODAY

First Ba'ath government

The Ba'ath takeover in Syria followed a Ba'ath coup in Iraq, the previous month. The new Syrian Government explored the possibility of federation with Egypt and with Ba'ath-controlled Iraq. An agreement was concluded in Cairo on 17 April 1963, for a referendum on unity to be held in September 1963. However, serious disagreements among the parties soon developed, and the tripartite federation failed to materialize. Thereafter, the Ba'ath governments in Syria and Iraq began to work for bilateral unity. These plans foundered in November 1963, when the Ba'ath government in Iraq was overthrown.

In May 1964, President Amin Hafiz of the NCRC promulgated a provisional constitution providing for a National Council of the Revolution (NCR), an appointed legislature composed of representatives of mass organisations — labour, peasant, and professional unions — a presidential council, in which executive power was vested, and a cabinet.

Second Ba'ath government

On 23 February 1966, a group of army officers carried out a successful, intra-party coup, imprisoned President Hafiz, dissolved the cabinet and the NCR, abrogated the provisional constitution, and designated a regionalist, civilian Ba'ath government on 1 March. The coup leaders described it as a "rectification" of Ba'ath Party principles. In June 1967 Israel captured and occupied the Golan. The Six Day War had significantly weakened the radical socialist government established by the 1966 coup.

On 18 September 1970, during the events of Black September in Jordan, Syria tried to intervene on behalf of the Palestinian guerrillas. Hafez al-Assad sent in armored forces equivalent to a brigade, with tanks, some of them allegedly hastily rebranded from the regular Syrian army for the purpose. Other Syrian units were the 5th Infantry Division and Commandos. On 21 September, the Syrian 5th Division broke through the defenses of the Jordanian 40th Armoured Brigade, and pushed it back off the ar-Ramtha crossroads. On 22 September, the Royal Jordanian Air Force began attacking Syrian forces, which were badly battered as a result. The constant airstrikes broke the Syrian force, and on the late afternoon of 22 September the 5th Division began to retreat. The swift Syrian withdrawal was a severe blow to Palestinian guerillas. Jordanian armored forces steadily pounded their headquarters in Amman, and threatened to break them in other regions of the Kingdom as well. Eventually, the Palestinian factions agreed to a cease-fire. King Hussein and Yasser Arafat attended themeeting of the Arab League in Cairo, where the hostilities briefly ended. The Jordanian-Palestinian Civil War shortly resumed, but without Syrian intervention.

By 1970 a conflict had developed between an extremist military wing and a more moderate civilian wing of the Ba'ath Party. The 1970 retreat of Syrian forces sent to aid the PLO during the "Black September" hostilities with Jordan reflected this political disagreement within the ruling Ba'ath leadership.

Ba'ath Party under Hafez al-Assad, 1970–2000

Power takeover

On 13 November 1970, Minister of Defense Hafez al-Assad effected a bloodless military coup, ousting the civilian party leadership and assuming the role of President. Upon assuming power, Hafez al-Assad moved quickly to create an organizational infrastructure for his government and to consolidate control. The Provisional Regional Command of Assad's Arab Socialist Ba'ath Party nominated a 173-member legislature, the People's Council, in which the Ba'ath Party took 87 seats. The remaining seats were divided among "popular organizations" and other minor parties.

In March 1971, the party held its regional congress and elected a new 21-member Regional Command headed by Assad. In the same month, a national referendum was held to confirm Assad as President for a 7-year term. In March 1972, to broaden the base of his government, Assad formed the National Progressive Front, a coalition of parties led by the Ba'ath Party, and elections were held to establish local councils in each of Syria's 14 governorates. In March 1973, a new Syrian constitution went into effect followed shortly thereafter by parliamentary elections for the People's Council, the first such elections since 1962.

October War

On 6 October 1973, Syria and Egypt began the Yom Kippur War (also called the "Ramadan War" or "October War" because Syria and Egypt attacked during Muslim Ramadan holiday) by staging a surprise attack against Israel. Despite the element of surprise, Egypt and Syria lost their initial gains in a three-week-long warfare, and Israel continued to occupy the Golan Heights and the Sinai peninsula.

Intervention in Lebanon

In early 1976, the Lebanese Civil War was going poorly for the Maronite Christians, so the Lebanese President Elias Sarkis officially requested Syria intervene militarily. After receiving their first mandate from Lebanese President, Syria was given a second mandate by the Arab League to intervene militarily in Lebanon.

Syria sent 40,000 troops into the country to prevent the Christians from being overrun, but soon became embroiled in this war, beginning the 30 year Syrian presence in Lebanon. Over the following 15 years of civil war, Syria fought both for control over Lebanon, and as an attempt to undermine Israel in southern Lebanon, through extensive use of Lebanese allies as proxy fighters.

Many saw the Syrian Army's presence in Lebanon as an occupation, especially following the end of the civil war in 1990, after the Syrian-sponsored Taif Agreement. Syria then remained in Lebanon until 2005, exerting a heavy-handed influence over Lebanese politics, that was deeply resented by many.

About one million Syrian workers came into Lebanon after the war ended to find jobs in the reconstruction of the country. Syrian workers were preferred over Palestinian Arabs and Lebanese workers because they could be paid lower wages, but some have argued that the Syrian government's encouragement of citizens entering its small and militarily dominated neighbor in search of work, was in fact an attempt at Syrian colonization of Lebanon. In 1994, under pressure from Damascus, the Lebanese government controversially granted citizenship to over 200,000 Syrians resident in the country.

Muslim Brotherhood uprising and Hama Massacre

On 31 January 1973, Assad implemented the new Constitution which led to a national crisis. Unlike previous constitutions, this one did not require that the president of Syria must be a Muslim, leading to fierce demonstrations in Hama, Homs and Aleppo organized by the Muslim Brotherhood and the *ulama*. They labeled Assad as the "enemy of Allah" and called for a*jihad* against his rule. Robert D. Kaplan has compared Assad's coming to power to "an untouchable becoming maharajah in India or a Jew becoming tsar in Russia—an unprecedented development shocking to the Sunni majority population which had monopolized power for so many centuries." The authoritarian government was not without its critics, a serious challenge arose in the late 1970s from fundamentalist Sunni Muslims, who reject the basic values of the secular Ba'ath program and object to rule by the Alawis whom they consider heretical. From 1976 until its suppression in 1982, the arch-conservative Muslim Brotherhood led an armed insurgency against the government. In response to an attempted uprising by the brotherhood in February 1982, the government crushed the fundamentalist opposition centered in the city of Hama, leveling parts of the city with artillery fire and causing many thousands of dead and wounded. During the rest of Hafez al-Assad's reign, public manifestations of anti-government activity have been very limited.

During Gulf War

Syria's 1990 participation in the U.S.-led multinational coalition aligned against Saddam Hussein marked a dramatic watershed in Syria's relations both with other Arab states and with the Western world. Syria participated in the multilateralMiddle East Peace Conference in Madrid in October 1991, and during the 1990s engaged in direct, face-to-face negotiations with Israel. These negotiations failed, and there have been no further Syrian-Israeli talks since President Hafiz al-Assad's meeting with then President Bill Clinton in Geneva in March 2000.

Internal power struggle

In what has become known as the 1999 Latakia incident, violent protests and armed clashes erupted following the 1998 People's Assembly's Elections. The violent events were an explosion of a long-running feud between Hafez al-Assad and his younger brother Rifaat, who previously attempted to initiate a coup against Hafez in 1984, but was eventually expelled from Syria. Two people were killed in fire exchanges of Syrian police and Rifaat's supporters during police crackdown on Rifaat's port compound in Latakia. According to opposition sources, denied by the government, the clashes in Latakiaresulted in hundreds of dead and injured.

Drought in Syria

From 2006 to 2010, Syria experienced its worst drought in modern history. The drought resulted in a mass migration from the Syrian countryside into urban centers, which notably strained existing infrastructure already burdened by the influx of some 1.5 million refugees from Iraq. The drought itself has been linked to human caused global climate change. It has also been directly linked as a contributing factor to the socieoeconomic conditions that led to initial protests and uprising. Adequate water supply continues to be an issue in the ongoing civil war and the supply is frequently the target of military action.

Under Bashar al-Assad, 2000–present

The Damascus Spring

Hafiz al-Assad died on 10 June 2000, after 30 years in power. Immediately following al-Assad's death, the Parliament amended the constitution, reducing the mandatory minimum age of the President from 40 to 34, which allowed his son, Bashar al-Assad, to become legally eligible for nomination by the ruling Ba'ath party. On 10 July 2000, Bashar al-Assad was elected President by referendum in which he ran unopposed, garnering 97.29% of the vote, according to Syrian government statistics.

Bashar, who speaks French and English and has a British-born wife, was said to have "inspired hopes" for reform, and a "Damascus Spring" of intense political and social debate took place from July 2000 to August 2001. The period was characterized by the emergence of numerous political forums or salons where groups of like minded people met in private houses to debate political and social issues. The phenomenon of salons spread rapidly in Damascus and to a lesser extent in other cities. Political activists, such as, Riad Seif, Haitham al-Maleh, Kamal al-Labwani, Riyad al-Turk, and Aref Dalila were important in mobilizing the movement. The most famous of the forums were the Riad Seif Forum and theJamal al-Atassi Forum. The Damascus Spring ended in August 2001 with the arrest and imprisonment of ten leading activists who had called for democratic elections and a campaign of civil disobedience.

International and internal tensions

On 5 October 2003, Israel bombed a site near Damascus, claiming it was a terrorist training facility for members of Islamic Jihad. Islamic Jihad said the camp was not in use; Syria said the attack was on a civilian area.

The Israeli action was condemned by European governments. The German Chancellor said it "cannot be accepted" and the French Foreign Ministry said "The Israeli operation... constituted an unacceptable violation of international law and sovereignty rules." The Spanish UN Ambassador Inocencio Arias called it an attack of "extreme gravity" and "a clear violation of international law."

The United States Congress passed the Syria Accountability Act in December 2003, with the goal of ending what the U.S. sees as Syrian involvement in Lebanon, Iraq, terrorism, and weapons of mass destruction through international sanctions.

Ethnic tensions increased in Syria, following an incident in a football stadium in Al Qamishli, 30 people were killed and more than 160 were injured in days of clashes starting from 12 March. Kurdish sources indicated that Syrian security forces used live ammunition against civilians after clashes broke out at a football match between

Kurdish fans of the local team and Arabsupporters of a visiting team from the city of Deir al-Zor.

The international press reported that nine people were killed on 12 March. According to Amnesty International hundreds of people, mostly Kurds, were arrested after the riots. Kurdishdetainees were reportedly tortured and ill-treated. Some Kurdish students were expelled from their universities, reportedly for participating in peaceful protests.

In June 2005, thousands of Kurds demonstrated in Qamishli to protest the assassination of Sheikh Khaznawi, a Kurdish cleric in Syria, resulting in the death of one policeman and injury to four Kurds. Renewed opposition activity occurred in October 2005 when activist Michel Kilo launched with leading opposition figures theDamascus Declaration, which criticized the Syrian government as "authoritarian, totalitarian and cliquish" and called for democratic reform.

On 6 September 2007 a Syrian facility was bombed in the Deir ez-Zor region. While no one claimed responsibility for this act, Syria accused Israel, which in turn declared that the indicated site was a nuclear facility with a military purpose. Syria denied the claim.

On 26 October 2008 helicopter-borne CIA paramilitary officers and United States Special Operations Forces carried out a raid to the Syrian territory from Iraq The Syrian government called the event a "criminal and terrorist" attack on its sovereignty, alleging all of the reported eight fatalities were civilians.

An unnamed U.S. military source, however, alleged that the target was a network of foreign fighters who travel through Syria to join the Iraqi insurgency against the United States-led Coalition in Iraq and the Iraqi government.

Syrian civil war

The Syrian civil war is an ongoing internal violent conflict in Syria. It is a part of the wider Arab Spring, a wave of upheaval throughout the Arab World. Public demonstrations across Syria began on 26 January 2011 and developed into a nationwide uprising. Protesters demanded the resignation of President Bashar al-Assad, the overthrow of his government, and an end to nearly five decades of Ba'ath Party rule.

Since spring 2011, the Syrian government deployed the Syrian

Army to quell the uprising, and several cities were besieged, though the unrest continued. According to some "witnesses", soldiers, who refused to open fire on civilians, were summarily executed by the Syrian Army.

The Syrian government denied reports of defections, and blamed armed gangs for causing trouble. Since early autumn 2011, civilians and army defectors began forming fighting units, which began an insurgency campaign against the Syrian Army. The insurgents unified under the banner of the Free Syrian Armyand fought in an increasingly organized fashion; however, the civilian component of the armed opposition lacked an organized leadership.

The uprising has sectarian undertones, though neither faction in the conflict has described sectarianism as playing a major role. The opposition is dominated by Sunni Muslims, whereas the leading government figures are Alawites, affiliated with the Shia Islam. As a result, the opposition is winning support from the Sunni Muslim states, whereas the government is publicly supported by the Shia dominated Iran and the Lebanese Hizbullah.

According to various sources, including the United Nations, up to 13,470–19,220 people have been killed, of which about half were civilians, but also including 6,035–6,570 armed combatants from both sides and up to 1,400 opposition protesters.

Many more have been injured, and tens of thousands of protesters have been imprisoned. According to the Syrian government, 9,815–10,146 people, including 3,430 members of the security forces, 2,805–3,140 insurgents and up to 3,600 civilians, have been killed in fighting with what they characterize as "armed terrorist groups."

To escape the violence, tens of thousands of Syrian refugees have fled the country to neighboring Jordan, Iraq and Lebanon, as well toTurkey. The total official UN numbers of Syrian refugees reached 42,000 at the time, while unofficial number stood at as many as 130,000.

UNICEF reported that over 500 children have been killed, Another 400 children have been reportedly arrested and tortured in Syrian prisons.

Both claims have been contested by the Syrian government. Additionally, over 600 detainees and political prisoners have died under torture. Human Rights Watch accused the government and Shabiha of using civilians as human shields when they advanced on opposition held-areas.

Anti-government rebels have been accused of human rights abuses as well, including torture, kidnapping, unlawful detention and execution of civilians, Shabiha and soldiers. HRW also expressed concern at the kidnapping of Iranian nationals.

The UN Commission of Inquiry has also documented abuses of this nature in its February 2012 report, which also includes documentation that indicates rebel forces have been responsible for displacement of civilians.

The Arab League, US, EU states, GCC states, and other countries have condemned the use of violence against the protesters. China and Russia have avoided condemning the government or applying sanctions, saying that such methods could escalate into foreign intervention. However, military intervention has been ruled out by most countries.

The Arab League suspended Syria's membership over the government's response to the crisis, but sent an observer mission in December 2011, as part of its proposal for peaceful resolution of the crisis. The latest attempts to resolve the crisis has been made through the appointment of Kofi Annan, as a special envoy to resolve the Syrian crisis in the Middle East. Some analysts however have posited the partitioning the region into a Sunnite east, Kurdish north and Shiite/Alawite west.

3

Geography

Syria is located in Southwestern Asia, north of the Arabian Peninsula, at the eastern end of the Mediterranean Sea. It is bordered by Turkey to the north,Lebanon and Israel to the west and southwest, Iraq to the east, and Jordan to the south.

It consists of mountain ranges in the west and a steep area inland. In the east is the Syrian Desert and in the south is the Jabal al-Druze Range. The former is bisected by the Euphrates valley. A dam built in 1973 on the Euphrates created a reservoir named Lake Assad, the largest lake in Syria.

The highest point in Syria is Mount Hermon (2,814 m; 9,232 ft) on the Lebanese border. Between the humid Mediterranean coast and the arid desert regions lies a semiarid steep zone extending across three-quarters of the country, which receives hot, dry winds blowing across the desert.

Syria is extensively depleted, with 28 percent of the land arable, 4 percent dedicated to permanent crops, 46 percent utilized as meadows and pastures, and only 3 percent forest and woodland.

Syria is divided into fourteen governorates, or *muhafazat* (singular:*muhafazah*). The governorates are divided into a total of sixty districts, or*manatiq* (sing. *mintaqah*), which are further divided into sub-districts, or *nawahi*(sing. *nahiya*).

The capital Damascus is the second largest city in Syria, and the metropolitan area is a governorate on its own. Aleppo (population 2,301,570) in northern Syria is the largest city. Latakia along with Tartus are Syria's main ports on the Mediterranean Sea.

GEOGRAPHICAL REGIONS

The area includes about 185,180 square kilometers of deserts, plains, and mountains. It is divided into a coastal zone—with a narrow, double mountain belt enclosing a depression in the west—and a much larger eastern plateau. The climate is predominantly dry; about three-fifths of the country has less than 250 millimeters (9.84 in) of rain a year. Fertile land is the state's most important natural resource, and efforts have been made to increase the amount of arable land through irrigation projects.

Coastal plain

Along the Mediterranean, a narrow coastal plain stretches south from the Turkish border to Lebanon. The flatness of this littoral, covered withsand dunes, is broken only by lateral promontories running down from the mountains to the sea. The major ports are Latakia and Tartous. Syria claimed a territorial limit of 35 nautical miles (64.8 km; 40.3 mi) off its Mediterranean coastline. However, in 2003, Syria unilaterally declared its maritime zones, adhering to the 12 nautical miles allowed by the United Nations Law of the Sea.

Upland areas

The Jabal an Nusayriyah, a mountain range paralleling the coastal plain, has an average elevation of just over 1,212 meters above sea level; the highest peak, Nabi Yunis, is about 1,575 meters above sea level. The western slopes catch moisture-laden western sea winds and are thus more fertile and more heavily populated than the eastern slopes, which receive only hot, dry winds blowing across the desert. Before reaching the Lebanese border and the Anti-Lebanon Mountains, the Jabal an Nusayriyah range terminates, leaving a corridor—the Homs Gap—through which run the highway and railroad from Homs to the Lebanese port of Tripoli. For centuries the Homs Gap has been a favorite trade and invasion route from the coast to the country's interior and to other parts of Asia. Eastward, the line of al-Ansariyah mountains is separated from the Jabal az Zawiyah range and the plateau region by the Al Ghab valley, a fertile, irrigated trench crossed by the meanderingOrontes River.

Inland and farther south, the Anti-Lebanon Mountains rise to peaks of over 2,700 meters above sea level on the Syrian-Lebanese frontier and spread in spurs eastward toward the plateau region. The eastern slopes have little rainfall and vegetation and merge eventually with the desert. In the southwest, the lofty Mount Hermon (Jabal ash Shaykh), also on the border between Syria and Lebanon, descends to the Hawran Plateau that receives rain-bearing winds from the Mediterranean. All but the lowest slopes of Mount Hermon are uninhabited, however. Volcanic cones, some of which reach over 900 meters, intersperse the open, rolling, once-fertile Hawran Plateau south of Damascus and east of the Anti-Lebanon Mountains. Southwest of the Hawran lies the high volcanic region of the Jabal al-Druze range home of the country's Druze population. This is part of the Harrat ash Shaam volcanic field that stretches all the way to Saudi Arabia. Northeast of Jabal al-Druze is a large lava field called Al-Safa that stands out in satellite views.

Eastern plateau

The entire eastern plateau region is intersected by a low chain of mountains, the Jabal ar Ruwaq, the Jabal Abu Rujmayn, and the Jebel Bishri, extending northeastward from the Jabal Al Arab to the Euphrates. South of these mountains lies a barren desert region known as the Hamad. North of the Jabal ar Ruwaq and east of the city of Homs is another barren area known as the Homs Desert, which has a hard-packed dirt surface.

Northeast of the Euphrates, which originates in the mountains of Turkey and flows diagonally across Syria into Iraq, is the fertile Jazira region. This region is watered by two tributaries to the Euphrates, the Balikh and the Khabur. The area underwent irrigation improvements during the 1960s and 1970s, and it provides substantial cereal and cotton crops. Oil and natural gas discoveries in the extreme northeastern portion of the Jazira have significantly enhanced the region's economic potential.

WATER

The country's waterways are of vital importance to its agricultural development. The longest and most important river is the Euphrates, which represents more than 80 percent of Syria's water resources. Its main left-bank tributaries, the Balikh and the Khabur, are small perennial rivers that both rise in the Syro-Turkish border region. The right-bank tributaries of the Euphrates are mostly small seasonal streams called wadis. In 1973, Syria completed construction of the Tabqa Dam on the Euphrates River upstream from the town of Raqqa. The dam created a reservoir named Lake Assad (Buhayrat al Assad), a body of water about 80 kilometers long and averaging eight kilometers in width.

Throughout the arid plateau region east of Damascus, oases, streams, and a few interior rivers that empty into swamps and small lakes provide water for local irrigation. Most important of these is the Barada, a river that rises in the Anti-Lebanon Mountains and disappears into the desert.

The Barada creates the Al Ghutah Oasis, site of Damascus. This verdant area, some 370 square kilometers, has enabled Damascus to prosper since ancient times. In the mid-1980s, the size of Al Ghutah was gradually being eroded as suburban housing and light industry from Damascus encroached on the oasis.

Areas in the Jazira have been brought under cultivation with the waters of the Khabur River (Nahr al Khabur). The Sinn, a minor river in Latakia Governorate, is used to irrigate the area west of the Jabal an Nusayriyah, about 32 kilometers southwest of the port of Latakia. In the south the springs that feed the upper Yarmouk River are diverted for irrigation of the Hawran. Underground water reservoirs that are mainly natural springs are tapped for both irrigation and drinking. The richest in underground water resources is the Al Ghab region, which contains about 19 major springs and underground rivers that have a combined yield of thousands of liters per minute.

CLIMATE

The most striking feature of the climate is the contrast. Between the humid Mediterranean coast and the arid desert regions lies a semiarid steppe zone extending across three-quarters of the country and bordered on the west by the Anti-Lebanon Mountains and the Jabal an Nusayriyah, on the north by the Turkish mountain region, and on the southeast by the Jabal al Arab, Jabal ar Ruwaq, Jabal Abu Rujmayn, and the Jabal Bishri ranges.

Rainfall in this area is fairly abundant, annual precipitation ranging between 750 and 1,000 millimeters (30 and 40 in). Most of the rain, carried by winds from the Mediterranean, falls between November and May. The annual mean temperatures range from 7 °C (45 °F) in January to 27 °C (81 °F) in August. Because the high ridges of the Jabal an Nusayriyah catch most of the rains from the Mediterranean, the Al Ghab depression, located east of these mountains, is in a relatively arid zone with warm, dry winds and scanty rainfall. Frost is unknown in any season, although the peaks of the Jabal an Nusayriyah are sometimes snow-covered.

Farther south, rain-bearing clouds from the Mediterranean pass through the gap between the Jabal an Nusayriyah and the Anti-Lebanon Mountains, reaching the area of Homs and, sometimes, the steppe region east of that city. Still farther to the south, however, the Anti-Lebanon Mountains bar the rains from the Mediterranean, and the area, including the capital city of Damascus, becomes part of the semiarid climatic zone of the steppe, with precipitation averaging less than 200 millimeters (8 in) a year and with temperatures from 4 °C (39 °F) in January to 40 °C (104 °F) in July and August. The vicinity of the capital is, nevertheless, verdant and cultivable because of irrigation from the Barada River by aqueducts built during Roman times.

In the southeast, the humidity decreases, and annual precipitation falls below 100 millimeters (4 in). The scanty amounts of rain, moreover, are highly variable from year to year, causing periodic droughts. In the barren stony desert south of the Jabal ar Ruwaq, Jabal Abu Rujmayn, and Jabal Bishri ranges, temperatures in July often exceed 45 °C (113 °F). Sandstorms, common during February and May, damage vegetation and prevent grazing. North of the desert ranges and east of the Al Ghab depression lie the vast steppes of the plateau, where cloudless skies and high daytime temperatures prevail during the summer, but frosts, at times severe, are common from November to March. Precipitation averages 250 millimeters (10 in) a year but falls below 200 millimeters (8 in) in a large belt along the southern desert area. In this belt, only the Euphrates and Khabur rivers provide sufficient water for settlement and cultivation.

Resources and land use

Natural resources: petroleum, phosphates, chrome and manganese ores, asphalt, iron ore, rock salt, marble, gypsum, hydropower

Land use:

arable land: 24.8%

permanent crops: 4.47%

other: 70.73% (2005)

Irrigated land: 13.560 km^2(2003)

Total renewable water resources: 46.1 cu km (1997)

Area and boundaries

Area:

total: 185,180 km²

land: 183,630 km²

water: 1,550 km²

note: includes 1,295 km² of Israeli-occupied territory

Land boundaries:

total: 2,253 km

border countries: Iraq 605 km, Israel 76 km, Jordan 375 km, Lebanon 375 km, Turkey 822 km

Coastline: 193 km

Maritime claims:

contiguous zone: 41 nautical miles (75.9 km; 47.2 mi)

territorial sea: 35 nautical miles (64.8 km; 40.3 mi)

Elevation extremes:

lowest point: unnamed location near Lake Tiberias (Sea of Galilee) -200 m

highest point: Mount Hermon 2,814 m

Environmental concerns

Natural hazards: dust storms, sandstorms, earthquakes

Environment - current issues: deforestation; overgrazing; soil erosion; desertification; water pollution from dumping of raw sewage and wastes from petroleum refining; inadequate supplies of potable water

4

Government and Politics

HISTORY OF THE GOVERNMENT OF SYRIA

Between the years of 1936 and 1946, Syrianegotiated, demanded, and planned for its independence from France. From 1946 through the 1960's, the country experienced political unrest and several successful military coups. During this time, the government was changed to a wide range of systems, everything from multi-partyism to nationalism. Since in 1961, the country has been ruled by the Syrian Ba'ath party and has experienced decades of international conflict and internal violence. Since 1971 till his death in 2000, Hafez al-Assad was the Ba'ath Party President of the country. Upon the death of Hafez, his son, Bashar, ran for the presidency with no political opponents. He continues to be President today.

Current Government Of Syria

Syria is considered a unitary republic with a semi-presidential style of government. However, the controlling parties practice a highly authoritarian regime with most of the political power in the hands of the al-Assad family. The President appoints members to the Council of Ministers, issues laws, amends the Constitution, declares war, and approves government 5-year plans. As per the Constitution, the President serves a 7-year term and may be re-elected one additional time. In addition to the office of the President, the government also consists of the People's Council and the Council of Ministers. The government is divided into the three branches of executive, legislative, and judicial.

Executive Body Of The Government Of Syria

The Council of Ministers represents the executive body of the government. It is made up of the Prime Minister, deputies, and ministers. In 2011, the entire Council resigned, and the President appointed new members. The Prime Minister is the official head of government. It is the responsibility of the executive branch to administer the law as dictated by the legislative branch.

Legislative Branch Of The Government Of Syria

The legislative body of the Syrian government is the People's Council. This department consists of 250 members. These members are elected to serve 4-year terms. The two main political parties represented by the People's Council are the National Progressive Front and the Popular Front for Change and Liberation. The year 2012 marked the first time the members were made up of more than one political party.

Judiciary Of Syria

The judicial branch of Syria is made up of several types of courts including civil, criminal, military, security, and religious. Religious courts handle family law, such as divorce cases. The legal codes are mainly based on French law.

This branch is overseen by the High Judicial Council which is made up of the President and senior civil judges. Together, they appoint and dismiss judges of lower courts. The highest court in Syria is the Court of Cassation which rules on judicial issues. The High Constitutional Court decides on questions about the constitutionality of laws, bills, and regulations.

Constitution of 2012

The Constitution provides the basic outline for government functions and places great emphasis on pan-Arab nationalism. As a result of the Civil War of 2011 to 2012, the Constitution was amended.

The new Constitution requires the President to be Muslim but does not define a state religion. It also removed the article that once gave the Ba'ath party total political control. The new amendment states that the government is based on pluralism and that decisions can only be made based on democratically voting. In addition, the new Constitution limits presidential terms to 7 years with a 2-term limit.

POLITICS OF SYRIA

Politics in the Syrian Arab Republic takes place in the framework of a semi-presidential republic with multiparty representation. President Bashar al-Assad's family and his Arab Socialist Ba'ath Party have remained dominant forces in the country's politics since a 1970 coup.

Until the early stages of the Syrian uprising, the president had broad and uncheckeddecree authority under a long-standing state of emergency. The end of this emergency was a key demand of the uprising, and decrees are now subject to approval by the People's Council, the country's legislature. The Ba'ath Party is Syria's ruling party and the previous Syrian constitution of 1973 stated that "the Arab Socialist Ba'ath Party leads society and the state." At least 167 seats of the 250-member parliament were guaranteed for the National Progressive Front, which is a coalition of the Ba'ath Party and several other much smaller allied parties. The newSyrian constitution of 2012 introduced multi-party system based on the principle of political pluralism without guaranteed leadership of any political party. The Syrian army and security services maintained a considerable presence in the neighbouringLebanese Republic from 1975 until 24 April 2005.

Background

Hafez al-Assad took power in 1970. After his death in 2000 his son, Bashar al-Assad (B-a-A), succeeded him as President. A surge of interest in political reform took place after Bashar al-Assad assumed power in 2000. Human-rights activists and other civil-society advocates, as well as some parliamentarians, became more outspoken during a period referred to as the "Damascus Spring" (July 2000-February 2001). Assad also made a series of appointments of reform-minded advisors to formal and less formal positions and is included a number of similarly oriented individuals in his Cabinet.

Neo-Ba'athism

The Ba'ath platform is proclaimed succinctly in the party's slogan: "Unity, freedom, and socialism." The party is both socialist, advocating state ownership of the means of industrial production and the redistribution of agricultural land (in practice, Syria's nominally socialist economy is effectively a mixed economy, composed of large state enterprises and private small businesses), and revolutionary, dedicated to carrying a pan-Arab revolution to every part of the Arab world. Founded byMichel Aflaq, a Syrian Christian, Salah al-Din al-Bitar, a Syrian Sunni, and Zaki al-Arsuzi, an alawite, the Arab Socialist Ba'ath Party, which was dissolved in 1966 following the 1966 Syrian coup d'état which led to the establishment of one Iraqi-dominated ba'ath movement and one Syrian-led ba'ath movement. The party embraces secularism and has attracted supporters of all faiths in many Arab countries, especially Iraq, Jordan, and Lebanon.

Since August 1990, however, the party has tended to de-emphasize socialism and to stress pan-Arab unity.

Six smaller political parties are permitted to exist and, along with the Ba'ath Party, make up the National Progressive Front(NPF), a grouping of parties that represents the sole framework of legal political party participation for citizens. While created ostensibly to give the appearance of a multi-party system, the NPF is dominated by the Ba'ath Party and does not change the essentially one-party character of the political system. Non-Ba'ath Party members of the NPF exist as political parties largely in name only and conform strictly to Ba'ath Party and government policies. There were reports in 2000 that the government was considering legislation to expand the NPF to include new parties and several parties previously banned; these changes have not taken place. However, one such party- the Syrian Social Nationalist Party- was legalised in 2005.

Traditionally, the parties of the NPF accepted the socialist and Arab nationalist ideology of the government. However, the SSNP was the first party that is neither socialist nor Arab nationalist in orientation to be legalised and admitted to the NPF. This has given rise to suggestions that broader ideological perspectives may be afforded some degree of toleration in the future, but ethnically-based (Kurdish and Assyrian) parties continue to be repressed and a strict ban on religious parties is still enforced.

Syria's Emergency Law was in force from 1963, when the Ba'ath Party came to power, until 21 April 2011 when it was rescinded by Bashar al-Assad (decree 161). The law, justified on the grounds of the continuing war with Israel and the threats posed by terrorists, suspended most constitutional protections.

Government administration

The previous Syrian constitution of 1973 vested the Ba'ath Party (formally the Arab Ba'ath Socialist Party) with leadership functions in the state and society and provided broad powers to the president.

The president, approved by referendum for a 7-year term, was also Secretary General of the Ba'ath Party and leader of the National Progressive Front. During the 2011–2012 Syrian uprising, a new constitution was put to a referendum. Amongst other changes, it abolished the old article 8 which entrenched the power of the Ba'ath party. The new article 8 reads: "The political system of the state shall be based on the principle of political pluralism, and exercising power democratically through the ballot box". In a new article 88, it introduced presidential elections and limited the term of office for the president to seven years with a maximum of one re-election. The referendum resulted in the adoption of the new constitution, which came into force on 27 February 2012.The president has the right to appoint ministers (Council of Ministers), to declare war and states of emergency, to issue laws (which, except in the case of emergency, require ratification by the People's Council), to declare amnesty, to amend the constitution, and to appoint civil servants and military personnel. The late President Hafiz al-Asad was confirmed by unopposed plebiscites five times. His son and current President Bashar al-Asad, was confirmed by an unopposed referendum in July 2000. He was confirmed again on 27 May 2007 with 97.6% of the vote

Along with the National Progressive Front, the president decides issues of war and peace and approves the state's 5-year economic plans. The National Progressive Front also acts as a forum in which economic policies are debated and the country's political orientation is determined.

The Syrian constitution of 2012 requires that the president be Muslim but does not make Islam the state religion. The judicial system in Syria is an amalgam of Ottoman, French, and Islamic laws, with three levels of courts: courts of first instance,courts of appeals, and the constitutional court, the highest tribunal. In addition, religious courts handle questions of personal and family law.

The Ba'ath Party emphasizes socialism and secular Pan-Arabism. Despite the Ba'ath Party's doctrine on building national rather than ethnic identity, the issues of ethnic, religious, and regional allegiances still remain important in Syria.

LEGISLATIVE BRANCH

The People's Council (*Majlis al-Sha'ab*) has 250 members elected for a four-year term in 15 multi-seat constituencies. According to the previous Syrian constitution of 1973 Syria was a one-party state and only one political party, the Arab Socialist Ba'ath Party was legally allowed to hold effective power. Of the 250 seats in the council, 167 were guaranteed for the National Progressive Front (founded in 1972) and 134 of these (as of 2007) were members of the Ba'ath Party. The minor parties in the Progressive Front, were legally required to accept the leadership of the Ba'ath Party. The other parties in the Progressive Front, for example, are not allowed to canvass for supporters in the army or the student body which are "reserved exclusively for the Ba'ath." The new Syrian constitution of 2012 introduced multi-party system without guaranteed leadership of any political party.

POLITICAL PARTIES AND ELECTIONS

The last parliamentary election was on 7 May 2012 and the results were announced on 15 May.

The Baath party won an even larger victory than it did in previous elections. They won a majority of around 60% of the 250 parliamentary seats. Previously, the Baath had a majority of just over 50% of the seats in parliament. If one adds in the independent MPs aligned with the Baath Party, the MPs who support the president make up over 90% of the seats in new parliament. The National Unity List, which is dominated by the Syrian Baath Party, won more than 150 seats in the 250 member parliament. Independent individuals won more than 90 seats. Among the newly established opposition parties (established since August 2011), only one single seat was won, namely a seat in Aleppo won by the Syrian Democratic Party, Ahmad Koussa. In addition three representatives of longstanding opposition parties have been elected to Parliament: Qadri Jamil and Ali Haydar from the Front for Change and Liberation, and Amro Osi from the Initiative of Syrian Kurds.

INTERNATIONAL INVOLVEMENT IN SYRIA WAR

David Cameron stated in response to the video released of David Haines execution that members of the Islamic State are "not Muslims, they are monsters". The British Prime Minister vowed on September 14, 2014,to "drive back, dismantle, and ultimately destroy ISIL and what it stands for". The release of this execution video prompted the British officials to heavily consider increased involvement in the fight to combat the Islamic State. On Monday October 20,Britain authorized surveilance missions over Syria in order to protect their own national interests. These surveilance missions were carried out by unmanned and armed drones and spy planes.

The armed drone operators require special permission from higher-ups in order to use the firepower on their drones. . (The LA Times, September 14 2014) The leader of the Islamic Movement in Israel expressed shame in and verbally attacked the Arab countries who have supported US actions against the Islamic State. Sheikh Raed Salah referred to the US led coalition that includes multiple Arab countries in the region as "a coalition of evil aimed at destroying what is left of Syria and Iraq". Although Salah condemned the actions of the Islamic State he claims that the actions taken by IS do not warrant the response that the US is laying out. (Haaretz, September 13 2014)

According to US diplomats, Israel aided the United States in carrying out air strikes against the Islamic State by providing intelligence information to US forces operating in the region. Israeli satelites over Iraq have provided anti-Islamic State forces with vital information to plan their strategy. The Israeli intelligence community also provided a list of Western citizens who reportedly have travelled to Iraq to join the Islamic State, after analyzing travel record databases. In response to the attacks on the Charlie Hebdo magazine offices in France that left 12 people dead and terrified the country for three days, on January 13 the French Parliament overwhelmingly approved the continuation of air strikes against the Islamic State forces in Syria and Iraq.

The French Prime Minister Manuel Valls urged Parliament to approve the continued engagement of ISIS, saying that "our mission is not over... we are faced with a war against terrorism." The vote to continue fighting ISIS passed 488-1 in the French Parliament and recieved 327 votes in favor with 19 abstaining in the Senate. (Yahoo News, January 13 2015) Top representatives from 21 countries convened in London on January 22 2015 to strategize about how to defeat the Islamic State and deal with the growing threat of "homegrown jihadis" around the world.

The forum was co-hosted by US Secretary of State John Kerry and British Foreign Secretary Phil Hammond, and was the first meeting of the coalition fighting against ISIS since the Charlie Hebdo attacks in early January. A main focus of the meeting was the discussion of how to stop the flow of foreign fighters pouring into Syria and Iraq. At the meeting Kerry announced that the US led coalition had killed 50% of ISIS top commanders, and the number of Islamic State militants killed was in the "single-digit thousands." (Ynet News, January 22, 2015)

The brutal killing of Jordanian First Lt. Moaz al-Kasasbeh and subsequent release of his execution video provoked a strong reaction from Jordan, who's King Abdullah alluded that he may personally take part in the bombing runs of the terrorist group (he was trained as a pilot in the Jordanian Air Force). King Abdullah declared that "the only problem we're going to have is running out of fuel and bullets," and quoted the Clint Eastwood film "Unforgiven", stating that "Any man I see out there, I'm gonna kill him." Less than 12 hours after the video of Kasabeh's execution was released, Jordan executed two of their own captured terrorists whose release had been demanded by ISIS. Jordanpromised "swift retribution" for the killing, and during the following days the Jordanian Air Force carried out bombing raids against the Islamic State, killing more than 100 fighters and damaging many of their fighting positions. The killing of Kasabeh brought condemnation by many Islamic scholars, including the head of Sunni Islam's most prestigious higher learning institution, Egypt's Al-Azhar University. Ahmed al-Tayeb, the "grand Imam" of Al-Azhar University, recommended "the Koran-prescribed punishment of death" for the ISIS fighters, which amounts to either crucifixion or the cutting off of their arms. The Jordainain military conducted aggressive and devastating air-strikes against the Islamic State in retalliation for the brutal killing of captured Jordanian pilot Moaz al-Kasasbeh during the first week of February 2015. Jordanian officials promised swift retribution for the murder, and carried out more than 56 air strikes against ISIS positions during the weekend of February 7.

The United Arab Emirates sent a squad of F-16 fighter jets to Jordan that same weekend in attempts to boost the military effort. Earlier in the campaign the UAE had suspended air support, fearing that there was not an adequate search-and-rescue protocol for downed pilots. The UAE's official news agency released a statement saying that they "reaffirm [their] unwavering and constant solidarity with Jordan." On February 10, 2015, the Jordanian government announced that they had moved thousands of ground troops to the Jordan-Iraq border to prevent ISIS fighters from entering Jordan and as a show of force.

Militants affiliated with the Tripoli Province of Islamic State posted a video of them beheading 21 Egyptian Christians on an unidentified beach in Libya via the Islamic State's official media accounts on

February 15, 2015. The group pledged allegiance to the Islamic State in 2014. The video is very well put together, similar to their other videos, and shows the Christians being marched wearing orange jumpsuits by ISIS fighters wearing black robes and facial coverings. The black masked jihadis then behead all 21 victims after pushing them into the sand. The Egyptian government bombed Islamic militant positions in Derna, Libya the following day in response, which provoked a wave of car-bomb attacks from the militants on the Libyan city of Qubbah in retaliation. The car bombs were detonated at a gas station, killed 40 people, and injured more than 70.

New Zealand officially joined the coalition fight against the Islamic State with the approval of a measure sending ground troops into Iraq on February 23, 2015. Citing a dramatic increase over the past year in New Zealanders who are considered possible terrorist risks, Prime Minister John Key told opposition members to "get some guts!" It was revealed in mid-March 2015 that Iran had provided Iraqi troops fighting ISIS in Tikrit with missiles, rockets, and other smaller munitions. Asserting that "increased military support is a necessity," on April 8, 2015, Swedish Foreign Minister Margot Wallstrom announced that Sweden would be joining the coalition of countries fighting against the Islamic State. In order to help better prepare the Iraqi army, Sweden will send up to 120 troops into Northern Iraq with the task of training members Iraqi infantrymen. Iraqi Prime Minister Haider al-Abadi visited Washington for the first time during his term in April 2015, to explore financial and military support options to aid his country in defeating the Islamic State.

Falling oil revenues left Iraq with a $22 million budget deficit coming into 2015. Al-Abadi called for humanitarian assistance in the areas reclaimed from ISIS, and asked the international community to provide the Iraqi forces weapons and munitions on credit. During meetings with President Obama, Obama stressed that Iran needed to channel it's support for the fight against ISIS through Iraq instead of sporatically funding militias. The President announced a $200 million humanitarian aid package for Iraq, although reportedly during the meetings al-Abadi made no mention of an appeal for help or assistance. Though the aid package was substantial, the White House meeting did not produce any military commitments. Prior to visiting the United States, the Iraqi Prime Minister told reporters that the "Number one (goal of his visit) is a marked increase in the air campaign and the delivery of arms." During his visit al-Abadi also met with 14 Iraqi pilots who were being trained in the United States to fly F-16's. These pilots will hopefully be ready to fly missions against the Islamic State in Iraq in September 2015 (The Wall Street Journal, April 14, 2015).

Australian Foreign Minister Julie Bishop travelled to Iran in April 2015, where she signed an intelligence sharing agreement with Iranian officials aimed at combatting the spread of the Islamic State. Bishop was the first Australian Foreign Minister to travel to Iran in over a decade. Officials reached an "informal arrangement whereby we'd share intelligence that would give us information on the Australians who are taking part," according to Bishop (Yahoo News,April 19, 2015). Saudi Arabia announced on April 28, 2015, that they had arrested 93 people within the previous months, accused of plotting terrorist attacks and having ties to the Islamic State.

Saudi officials stated during a press conference that they had thwarted many attacks by arresting these individuals, including a planned attack on the U.S. Embassy in the Saudi Arabian capital. Syrian air strikes killed at least 140 Islamic State fighters in Raqqa during the weekend of May 25, 2015. The Syrian army continued to bomb Islamic State positions in Raqqa during the following week, including the Taqba air base which had been overrun by ISIS fighters in August 2014.

Two top Islamic State commanders were killed by an air-strike in Northern Syria on July 13, but it was unclear whether the strike was carried out by the Syrian Army or the U.S. Air Force. Â The two victims were identified as Abu Osama al-Iraqi, and Amer al-Rafdan, Islamic State leaders in the area. Turkey blocked access to websites that may be used by ISIS sympathizers on July 15, 2015, in an effort to curb the Islamic State's recruitment efforts.

Turkish officials announced on July 23, 2015 that they would begin allowing U.S. bombing runs against the Islamic State to fly out of the strategically located Incirlik air base in Southern Turkey. During the 2003 U.S. invasion of Iraq, the U.S. government spent months negotiating with Turkish officials to let U.S. forces use the Incirlik air base, but they continually refused. This announcement was spurred by the continued spread of the Jihadi organization slowly into Turkey, and follows months of U.S. requests to use the base for military activities.

The deal struck between Turkish and U.S. governments will allow manned and unmanned aircraft to launch from the base and carry out strikes against the Islamic State. This represents a significant shift for the Turkish government, who have been trying to have as little involvement in the conflict as possible. The announcement came during the week following a deadly suicide attack by an Islamic State supporter in Turkey that left 32 people dead and more than 100 wounded. As a part of this deal, the United States and Turkey began negotiating the establishment of a safe zone at the Turkey-Syria border. United States and Turkish forces planned to drive the Islamic State out of a stretch of land between the Euphrates River and Aleppo, which would give the coalition forces a strategic advantage and improve their strike capabilities.

This area will potentially serve as a safe area for Syrian and Turkish refugees displaced by the conflict. For the first time during the conflict, on July 24, 2015, Turkish F-16 fighter jets participated in carrying out bombing runs of ISIS positions in Syria. U.S. strikes against the Islamic State launched out of Incirlik air base in Turkey for the first time during the first week of August 2015.

Speaking about this historic event, Turkish Foreign Minister Mevlut Cavusoglu stated that, "Soon we will together [Turkey and the U.S.] start an extensive battle against Daesh." (New York Times, August 5, 2015). During the second weekend in August, six U.S. F-16 fighter jets arrived at the Incirlik air base, ready to fight against the Islamic State. British Prime Minister David Cameron announced during a press conference on September 7, 2015, that two British jihadis in Syria fighting for the Islamic State had been killed by a drone strike during the previous days. This represents a significant change for the United Kingdom, which had previously only been involved in ISIS bombing missions in Iraq. Cameron staged the press conference to clarify that the strike was necessary and justified.

French President Francois Hollande ordered the French military to prepare for extended air strikes against the Islamic State in Syria on September 9, 2015. The French military began reconnaissance flights over Syria during the following week. Informed by the surveilance gathered, the French Air Force began strike missions against the Islamic State in Syria during the weekend of September 26, 2015. These first strikes were made in conjunction with U.S. forces, and involved six French aircraft.

Russia joined Iraq, Iran, and Syria, in an intelligence and security cooperation agreement aimed at strenghthening the fight against the Islamic State, in late September 2015. The announcement of this security pact took U.S. officials by surprise, as they dealt with multiple setbacks in their campaign against ISIS. Russia carried out their first airstrikes in Syria against the Islamic State on September 29, 2015, allegedly targetting ISIS communications equipment, military vehicles, and ammunition stockpiles.

Russian officials alerted U.S. military commanders of the mission early in the day, and advised them to keep the airspace clear. During a press conference the following day Russian President Vladimir Putin contended that the air engagement was temporary, and he would not be sending any Russian soldiers into Syria. During the following days it was confirmed that the Russian jets had not struck anywhere near any known Islamic State territory, and had instead carried out strikes on U.S. backed and trained rebels fighting against ISIS and Assad. Russia's actions over the following weeks brought to light that they were in fact solely interested in keeping Assad in power and fighting against the insurgency, instead of using their military power to fight ISIS. A Reuters analysis of Russian Defense Ministry data released on October 22, 2015, concluded that 80% of Russian airstrikes in Syria have been on targets unaffiliated with the Islamic State. (Reuters, October 22, 2015) Russian air strikes in Syria made it significantly more difficult for the Red Cross to deliver necessary aid and supplies to citizens, according to an organization spokerperson. The Syrian Observatory for Human Rights reported on October 30, 2015 that in the one month since Russia began it's air campaign they had killed over 400 rebel fighters and ISIS jihadis, but also more ahtn 150 civilians and approximately 50 children. Two U.S. State Department officials testified before the House Foreign Affairs Committee on November 4, 2015, claiming that 85-90% of Russian air strikes in Syria have been against moderate Syrian rebel forces, not the Islamic State. The two testified that Russian air support has done very little in aiding the fight against ISIS. As of November 2015 Russia has four bases established in Syria, with the main one located in Latakia.

News organizations reported on October 13, 2015, that French air strikes in ISIS territory most likely killed a number of French citizens who had gone to the Middle East to join ISIS. Israeli spy satelites kept track of movements of various groups within Syria during the conflict, and helped U.S. forces plan attacks and see more clearly what the Russian military was doing.

The Iraqi government announced in October 2015 that they were to be hiring an additional 10,000 troops to help fight against the

Islamic State in the coming year. Baghdad officials decided to spend less money on major weapons deals in the 2016 budget, and instead hire thousands of new fighters and equip them with the latest weapons and technology.

The Syrian Observatory for Human Rights confirmed on November 6, 2015, that 32-year-old Canadian John Gallagher, who had travelled to Syria to fight against ISIS in May 2015, had been killed by an ISIS suicide bomb. Gallagher fought with the Kurdish Peshmerga and was the second Canadian to be killed in combat with the Islamic State. In response to the devastating terror attacks on French soil on November 13, 2015, the French army carried out it's largest air strikes on ISIS yet on November 15, 2015, dropping 20 bombs on the self-proclaimed capital in Raqqa. During the following week the French aircraft carrier *Charles De Gaulle* made it's way to the Eastern Mediterranean, in preparation for increased air strikes against the ISIS Jihadis.

The *Charles De Gaulle* arrived in the Mediterranean on November 23, 2015, carrying 26 fighter jets and more than doubling French military presence in the region.

The Russian military hit Islamic State targets on November 17, 2015, with one of the largest bombing raids in modern history. Fourteen Tu-22M Backfires, six Tu-95 Bears, and five Tu-160 Blackjacks, the largest combat planes ever built, pounded Idlib and Aleppo destroying 14 strategic ISIS targets during the pre-dawn raid. Germany announced plans to send 1,200 ground troops into Iraq and Syria to join the fight against the Islamic State, in late November 2015. This would represent the largest current overseas deployment of German troops.

INTERNATIONAL COALITIONS AGAINST ISIL

US-led Coalitions

5 September 2014

On the margins of the 4/5 September 2014 NATO summit in Wales, U.S. Secretary of State John Kerry on 5 September invited Ministers of the United Kingdom, France, Germany, Canada, Australia, Turkey, Italy, Poland and Denmark for a separate meeting in which he pressed them to support the fight against ISIL militarily and financially. Those nine countries agreed to do so by supporting anti-ISIL forces in Iraq and Syria with supplies and air support, according to a statement that day of Kerry and U.S. Secretary of Defense Hagel.

3 December 2014

On 3 December 2014, at the NATO headquarters in Brussels, diplomats/(foreign) ministers from 59 countries gathered to plot a way forward against the threat of ISIL. U.S. Secretary of State John Kerry told the gathering, that "defeating the ideology, the funding, the recruitment" of Daesh (ISIL) must be the primary focus of their discussion, more important than airstrikes and other military action.

The countries represented on 3 December were: the 10 countries of the above-mentioned 5 September coalition in Wales; the extra 18 countries of the 15 September France-led coalition in Paris except for China and Russia; and 33 additional countries: Albania, Austria, Bosnia-Herzegovina, Bulgaria, Croatia, Cyprus, Estonia, Finland, Georgia, Greece, Hungary, Iceland, Ireland, Kosovo, Latvia, Lithuania, Luxembourg, Macedonia, Moldova, Montenegro, Morocco, New Zealand, Portugal, South Korea, Romania, Serbia, Singapore, Slovakia, Slovenia, Somalia, Sweden, Taiwan and Ukraine.

They styled themselves as the *Global Coalition to Counter the Islamic State of Iraq and the Levant (ISIL)*, and agreed to a strategy that included:

- exposing ISIL's true nature;
- cutting off ISIL's financing and funding;
- supporting military operations.

France-led Coalition

On 15 September 2014, on the 'International Conference on Peace and Security in Iraq' hosted by the French President François Hollande in Paris, 26 countries were represented: the countries of a US-led coalition that on 5 September in Wales had agreed on a coalition against ISIL except Australia and Poland, and furthermore Bahrain, Egypt, Iraq, Jordan, Kuwait, Lebanon, Oman, Qatar, Saudi Arabia, United Arab Emirates, Belgium, China, Czech Republic, Japan, the Netherlands, Norway, Russia and Spain. They committed themselves to supporting the Iraqi government with military assistance in its fight against ISIL, and they reaffirmed their commitment to UNSC Resolution 2170 of 15 August (condemning all trade with ISIL and urging to prevent all financial donations and all payments of ransoms to ISIL), so reported the French government.

In retaliation for the November 2015 Paris attacks, the French Air Forcesignificantly intensified airstrikes against ISIL targets in Syria, hitting among other the Syrian city of Raqqa, the de facto capital of ISIL.

Russia-led Coalition

At the end of September 2015, Russia, Iraq, Iran and Syria set up a 'joint information center' in Baghdad to "gather, process and analyse current information about the situation in the Middle East – primarily for fighting IS." On 30 September 2015, Russia began its air campaign on the side and in support of the Syrian government.

Russia was also reported to have reached agreements on co-ordiantion of operations in Syria with Jordan and Israel.

AMERICAN-LED INTERVENTION IN IRAQ AND SYRIA (ISIS)

After having started flying manned aircraft over Iraq and sent some troops to Iraq in June, the U.S. in August 2014 began supplying Iraqi KurdishPeshmerga with weapons, humanitarian droppings of food for refugees fleeing from ISIL, and airstrikes against ISIL in Iraq. On 9 August, speaking about U.S. airstrikes in Iraq, President Barack Obamasaid "this is going to be a long-term project." Since then, nine countries, allied with the US, have also executed airstrikes on ISIL in Iraq and various countries contributed military aid to Iraqi and Kurdish ground forces, and humanitarian aid.

16–19 August, according to the U.S., Kurdish and Iraqi forces with the help of U.S. airstrikes took back the Mosul Dam, the largest dam in Iraq. (For further wins and losses of Iraq against ISIL, see Iraq War (2014–present).) President Obama announced on 10 September 2014 that the number of airstrikes in Iraq would increase and that he dispatched 500 more US troops to Iraq.

Military aid to Kurds and Iraqis

On 5 August 2014, Zalmay Khalilzad, the former US ambassador to Iraq and the UN, wrote in the *Washington Post* that the United States is involved in "the direct supply of munitions to the Kurds and, with Baghdad's agreement, the shipment of some Foreign Military Sales (FMS) program weapons to the Kurds." The United States moved from indirectly supplying Kurdistan with small arms through the CIA to directly giving them weapons such asman-portable anti-tank systems. In a coordinated effort led by the United States, many allied countries including NATO members and Middle Eastern partners have supplied or plan to supply Iraqi and/or Kurdish forces with heavy military equipment, small arms, ammunition, non-lethal military gear, and training support.

Building Partner Capacity (BPC)

The Building Partner Capacity (BPC) program is meant to help the Iraqi government to prepare forces for the counter-attack against ISIL and the regaining of its territory. According to the US Department of Defense, by May 2015 a dozen countries had committed themselves to the BPC program: Australia, Belgium, Denmark, France, Germany, Italy, Netherlands, New Zealand, Norway, Spain, United Kingdom and United States, and 6,500 Iraqi forces had been trained by BPC.

Humanitarian efforts

The United States, the United Kingdom, and Australia, supported by international partners, launched a large humanitarian effort to support refugees stranded in northern Iraq. This included air-dropping tens of thousands of meals and thousands of gallons of drinking water to Yazidi refugees stranded in the Sinjar Mountains and threatened by advancing ISIL forces, between 7–14 August 2014, in what was later described as "the first mass air delivery of humanitarian cargo since the outbreak of violence in East Timor in 1999."

Thousands of Yazidis and other Iraqi civilians fled to the area following attacks on their villages and the town of Sinjar throughout late July and early August 2014.

Several human rights and observer organizations in the region reported that those who fled to the mountains were subjected to starvation, and lacked clean drinking water and medical care for several months as ISIL militantssurrounded them. Hundreds of men, women, and children were abducted and killed. In response to the immediate threat to the approximately 30,000 people trapped on the mountain, coalition aircraft commenced humanitarian aid drops. These air drops included basic supplies such as food, water, and shelter and were conducted at low flight levels by coalition transport aircraft under the threat of ISIL surface-to-air attacks.

In direct support of humanitarian aid drops, CF-18s provided top cover for aRoyal Australian Air Force (RAAF) C-130 Hercules transport aircraft on 20 November, ensuring the transport crew was able to safely parachute supplies to waiting refugees below. Canadian fighter jets remained in close proximity to the transport aircraft to protect it from ISIL surface-to-air threats or attacks.

American Military Actions

American Airstrikes

In June 2014, U.S. forces had started undertaking reconnaissance missions over northern Iraq. On 7 August, President Obama gave a live address describing the worsening conditions in Iraq and that the plight of the Yazidis particular had convinced him that U.S. military action was necessary to protect American lives, protect minority groups in Iraq, and to stop a possible ISIL advance on Erbil, the capital of the Kurdish Autonomous Region. On 8 August, the United States started to bomb ISIL targets in Iraq. By 10 August, assisted by these air attacks, Kurdish forces claimed to have recaptured the towns of Mahmour and Gweyr from Islamic State control. Additional Iraqi airstrikes conducted in Sinjar were reported to have killed 45 ISIL militants and injured an additional 60 militants. On 11 August, a spokesman for The Pentagonsaid the airstrikes had slowed down ISIL's advance in northern Iraq, but were unlikely to degrade ISIL's capabilities or operations in other areas.Between 8 and 13 August, U.S. airstrikes and Kurdish ground forces enabled 35,000 to 45,000 of Yazidi refugees to escape or be evacuated from the Sinjar Mountains.

On 16 August, U.S. air power began a close air campaign aimed at supporting the advance of Kurdish fighters moving toward the Mosul Dam. Kurdish sources commented that it was the "heaviest US bombing of militant positions since the start of air strikes". Obama on 17 August defended this usage of U.S. Forces as support of the Iraqi and Kurdish fight in general against ISIL — which indeed went beyond Obama's reasoning for launching airstrikes on 7 August.

On 8 September, the Iraqi Army, with close air support from the U.S., retook the key Haditha Dam, and recaptured the town of Barwana, killing 15 ISIL fighters.

ISIL responded with the public execution of David Haines. By the end of September 2014, the United States had conducted 240 airstrikes in Iraq and Syria, as well as 1,300 tanker refueling missions, totaling 3,800 sorties by all types of aircraft. A tactical arrangement with Kurdish and Iraqi forces, and drone videos are being used to coordinate close air support without needing U.S. troops in ground combat.

On 19 December 2014, US General James Terry announced that

the number of US airstrikes on ISIL had increased to 1,361.

On 25 December 2014, Hassan Saeed Al-Jabouri, the ISIL governor of Mosul, who was also known as Abu Taluut, was killed by a US-led Coalition airstrike in Mosul. It was also reported that the US planned to retake the city of Mosul in January 2015.

On 15 January 2015, it was reported that over 16,000 airstrikes had been carried out by the Coalition. The U.S. Air Force has carried out around 60 percent of all strikes. Among them, F-16s performed 41 percent of all sorties, followed by the F-15E at 37 percent, then the A-10 at 11 percent, the B-1 bomber at eight percent, and the F-22 at 3 percent. The remaining 40 percent has been carried out by the US Navy and allied nations.

On 20 January 2015, the SOHR reported that al-Baghdadi, the leader of ISIL, had been wounded in an airstrike in Al-Qa'im, an Iraqi border town held by ISIL, and as a result, withdrew to Syria.

On 21 January 2015, the US began coordinating airstrikes with a Kurdish launched offensive, to help them begin the planned operation to retake the city of Mosul.

On 21 July 2015, it was reported that nearly 44,000 sorties have flown since August 2014.

American Ground Forces

In July, Obama announced that due to the continuing violence in Iraq and the growing influence of non-state organizations, such as the Islamic State of Iraq and the Levant, the United States would be elevating its security commitment in the region. Approximately 800 U.S. troops secured American installations like the Embassy in Baghdad and the Consulate in Erbil as well as taking control of strategic locations like the Baghdad airport in cooperation with Iraqi troops.

U.S. forces also undertook a mission to "assess and to advise [Iraqi security forces] as they confront [ISIL] and the complex security situation on the ground." Reports from these American units about the capabilities of the Iraqi military have been consistently grim, viewing them as "compromised" by sectarian interests.

On 13 August 2014, the U.S. deployed another 130 military advisers to Northern Iraq and up to 20 U.S. Marines and special forces servicemen landed on Mount Sinjar from V-22aircraft to coordinate the evacuation of Yazidi refugees joining British SAS already in the area.

On 3 September 2014, Obama announced increase of U.S. forces in Iraq to 1,213. On 10 September, Obama gave a speech reiterating that U.S. troops will not fight in combat, but about 500 more troops will be sent to Iraq to help train Iraqi forces.

In early November 2014, Obama announced that he would be doubling the U.S. ground presence inside Iraq to around 3,000 men. By early December 2014, the number of U.S. ground troops in Iraq had increased to 3,100. On 9 December 2014, the United States Senate Committee on Foreign Relations authorized U.S. Military force against ISIL. However, it limits military force to three years, requires the administration to report to Congress every 60 days, and prohibits the deployment of U.S. combat troops, except in specific cases, such as those involving the rescue or protection of U.S. soldiers, or for intelligence operations.

During the early morning hours of 14 December 2014, U.S. ground forces allegedly clashed with ISIL alongside the Iraqi Army and Tribal Forces near the Ain al-Assad Airbase, west of Anbar, in an attempt to repel them from the base of which includes about 100 U.S. advisers in it, when ISIL attempted to overrun the base.

According to a field commander of the Iraqi Army in Anbar province, said that "the U.S. force equipped with light and medium weapons, supported by F-18, was able to inflict casualties against fighters of ISIL organization, and forced them to retreat from the al-Dolab area, which lies 10 kilometers from Ain al-Assad base." Sheikh Mahmud Nimrawi, a prominent tribal leader in the region, added that "U.S. forces intervened because of ISIL started to come near the base, which they are stationed in so out of self-defense," he responded, welcoming the U.S. intervention, and saying "which I hope will not be the last."

This was said to be the first encounter between the United States and the Islamic State, in four years. However, this claim has been stated to be "false" by The Pentagon.

On 5 January 2015, The Pentagon acknowledged that ISIL had been ineffectively mortaring the base.

In late February 2015, another 1,300 US soldiers were deployed to Iraq, increasing the number of US ground troops in Iraq to 4,400.

The Late Naming of Operation Inherent Resolve

Unlike their coalition partners, and unlike previous American combat operations, no name was initially given to the 2014 intervention against ISIL by the U.S. government. The decision to keep the conflict nameless drew considerable media criticism. U.S. Service members remain ineligible for Campaign Medals and other service decorations due to the continuing ambiguous nature of the continuing U.S. involvement in Iraq. On 15 October 2014, the United States Central Command announced that the U.S.-led air campaign against ISIL in Iraq and Syria was henceforth designated as *Operation Inherent Resolve.* The CENTCOM news release noted:

"According to CENTCOM officials, the name INHERENT RESOLVE is intended to reflect the unwavering resolve and deep commitment of the U.S. and partner nations in the region and around the globe to eliminate the terrorist group ISIL and the threat they pose to Iraq, the region and the wider international community. It also symbolizes the willingness and dedication of coalition members to work closely with our friends in the region and apply all available dimensions of national power necessary — diplomatic, informational, military, economic — to degrade and ultimately destroy ISIL."

British Airstrikes

On 12 August 2014, the United Kingdom deployed six Tornado GR4 strike aircraft to RAF Akrotiri inCyprus to help coordinate British humanitarian aid airdrops in Northern Iraq. On 16 August, following the suspension of humanitarian aid airdrops, these aircraft, along with an RC-135 Rivet Joint, were re-tasked to provide aerial surveillance to coalition forces.

In early September, Prime Minister David Cameron began to voice his support for British airstrikes against ISIL in Iraq. On 26 September, Parliament was recalled and MP's debated whether or not to authorise airstrikes. The seven-hour debate resulted in overwhelming support for airstrikes, with 524 votes in favour and 43 votes against.

On 27 September, the first armed reconnaissance mission took place over Northern Iraq. A patrol of two Tornado GR4's left RAF Akrotiri armed with Paveway IV laser-guided bombs. The patrol did not identify any targets requiring immediate air attack and so gathered intelligence for coalition forces instead. The aircraft were supported by a Voyager aerial refueling tanker. On 30 September, the Royal Air Force conducted its first airstrike. A patrol of two Tornado GR4's engaged a heavy weapon position with a Paveway IV laser-guided bomb and an armed pickup truck with a Brimstone air-to-surface missile.

The British contribution to the intervention has steadily increased since it first began on 27 September. On 3 October, two additional Tornado GR4's were deployed to Cyprus to compliment the original six. It was also revealed during the same month that the Royal Navy had been involved in a support role, with air defence destroyer HMS *Defender* providing escort to U.S. Navy aircraft carrierUSS *George H.W. Bush* as she launched aircraft into Iraq and Syria.

Deputy Prime Minister Nick Clegg also disclosed during an interview that there was a nuclear attack submarine armed with Tomahawk cruise missiles deployed to the Persian Gulf. On 16 October, the Ministry of Defence announced it would deploy armed MQ-9 Reaper drones to Iraq to assist with surveillance, however,Defence Secretary Michael Fallon stated that "If strike operations are required then Reaper has the ability to complement the sorties RAF Tornados have already completed". On 7 November, the Ministry of Defence announced it would double the number of Reaper aircraft deployed to the Middle East. The first Reaper drone strike was conducted by the RAF in Bayji, north of Baghdad on 10 November 2014, against a group of ISIL militants which had been laying improvised explosive devices in the area. A single Hellfire missile was used to conduct the strike. As of 2 March 2015, the Reapers had conducted 70 airstrikes in Iraq, whilst the Tornados had conducted 90.

In addition to operating over Iraq, the Royal Air Force has also been operating over Syria in a surveillance role since 21 October 2014, making the UK the first Western country other than the United States to intervene in both countries simultaneously.

According to Defence Secretary Michael Fallon, the UK had conducted a "huge number of missions" over Iraq by 13 December 2014, second only to the United States and five times as many as France. This totaled 6,700 hours of surveillance, reconnaissance, refueling and strike missions by 22 January 2015. On 16 January 2015, during a joint press conference at the White House alongside PresidentBarack Obama, Prime Minister David Cameron stated that the UK was the second-largest contributor to the anti-ISIL coalition, contributing over 100 airstrikes.

The total number of airstrikes conducted by the United Kingdom in Iraq stood at 194 by 23 March 2015. As of 17 September 2015, around 330 ISIL fighters have been killed by British airstrikes, without any civilian casualties.

Australian Airstrikes

On 3 October 2014, Prime Minister Tony Abbott and the Australian Cabinet approved for RAAF Boeing F/A-18F Super Hornet fighter bombers to begin airstrikes against Islamic State militants. Abbott said "It is in our national interest that we do so, it is in the interests of civilisation that we do so. It is in everyone's best interests that the murderous rage of the ISIL death cult be checked and rolled back and that's what we're determined to do."

On 6 October, Air Chief Marshall Mark Binskin announced two Super Hornets had conducted armed combat missions over Iraq although no armaments were expended. An Australian Air task Group KC-30A and an E-7A Wedgetail Airborne Early Warning and Control aircraft have also been flying in support to fighter bombers belonging to coalition forces. The KC-30A performs airborne refueling for coalition aircraft.Binskin said "One of our Super Hornet packages on the first night... had an identified target which it was tracking and that particular target moved into an urban area where the risks of conducting a strike on that target increased to a point where it exceeded our expectations of collateral damage, so they discontinued the attack at that point."

On 9 October, Prime Minister Tony Abbott confirmed that RAAF Super Hornets had been involved in a "strike missions on an ISIL position in Iraq". The aircraft dropped two bombs onto an isolated building which ISIL was using as a command and control center.

As of 17 October, the Royal Australian Air Force had conducted 43 combat sorties over Iraq. Recent strikes had targeted equipment facilities, with "at least two" resulting in ISIL casualties after Australian aircraft had increased the number of missions flown to allow U.S. and coalition forces to assist Kurdish fighters around Kobanî, in northern Syria.

Canadian Airstrikes

The Canadian contribution has been code-named Operation Impact by the Canadian Department of National Defence. Canadian aircraft left for the Middle East to join in airstrikes on 21 October. In total, six CF-18 fighter jets, an Airbus CC-150 Polaris air-to-air refueling tanker and two CP-140 Aurora surveillance aircraft were sent, along with 700 military personnel.

Canadian CF-18 fighter jets completed their first operational flights departing from Kuwait on 31 October. The first Canadian airstrikes began on 2 November. Canada also flew an extra CF-18 to Kuwait to be used as a spare if the need arises, however a maximum of six are authorized to fly with the coalition missions.

On 4 November 2014, Royal Canadian Air Force CF-18s destroyed ISIL construction equipment using GBU-12 bombs. The construction equipment was being used to divert the Euphrates River to deny villages water, and to flood roads, diverting traffic to areas with IEDs.

On 12 November 2014, Canadian jets destroyed ISIL artillery just outside the Northern Iraqi town of Baiji. Airstrikes continued throughout December and into January 2015 totaling 28 strike missions. It was then reported that Canadian special forces troops, which had been highlighting targets for airstrikes, had engaged in fighting after coming under attack.

On 19 January 2015, Canadian special operations forces came under ISIL attack for the first time in Iraq over the last week, and returned sniper fire to "neutralize" the threat. Canadians are "enabling airstrikes from the ground," meaning they are actively finding targets for jets flying overhead.

On 29 January 2015, Canadian special forces in Iraq came under fire from ISIL forces, causing the Canadian troops to return fire, killing some ISIL militants. On 6 March, a Canadian soldier was killed in a friendly fire incident by Kurdish forces while returning to an observation post.

On 8 April 2015, two CF-18s carried out their first airstrike against ISIL in Syria, hitting one of the groups garrisons.

From 2 Nov 2014 to 13 May 2015 the Canadian armed forces struck 80 ISIL fighting positions, 19 ISIL Vehicles, and 10 storage facilities.

On 21 October 2015, Canadian Prime Minister-designate Justin Trudeau informed U.S. President Barack Obama that he intended to withdraw Canadian aircraft from operations over Iraq and Syria but increase training missions on the ground.

French Airstrikes

On 19 September 2014, the French Air Force used its Rafale jets to conduct airstrikes on ISIL targets in Mosul. The airstrikes were approved by French President François Hollande, which indicated that France was committed to fighting ISIL using air power alongside the United States. Hollande mentioned that no ground troops would be used in the conflict. To conduct its airstrikes, France deployed 9 Rafale fighters to the United Arab Emirates, 6 Dassault Mirage 2000 fighters to Jordan, in addition to a Atlantique 2 maritime patrol aircraft, a Boeing E-3 Sentry airborne early warning and control aircraft, and a Boeing KC-135 Stratotanker aerial refueling tanker.

On 23 February 2015, the French Navy also deployed its Task Force 473 carrier strike group to the Persian Gulf with the intent on conducting airstrikes from the aircraft carrier *Charles de Gaulle*. The *Charles de Gaulle* contributed 12 Rafale fighters, 9 Dassault-Breguet Super Étendard strike aircraft, and 2 E-2C Hawkeye airborne early warning and control aircraft. The task force also included the French frigate *Chevalier Paul* (D621), a Rubis-class submarine, a Durance-class tanker, and the British frigate HMS *Kent*. After eight weeks of operations, the task force left the Persian Gulf on its way to India, heralding the end of its contribution to Operation Chammal.

On 5 November 2015, it was announced that the *Charles de Gaulle* would resume operations in Syria to fight ISIL.

On 15 November 2015, after the November 2015 Paris attacks, the French Air Force launched its largest airstrike of the bombing campaign sending 12 planes, including 10 fighters, that dropped 20 bombs in training camps and ammunition facilities in Raqqa, the de facto capital of ISIS.

Dutch Airstrikes

On 24 September 2014, the Dutch government announced its participation in the operations against ISIL in Iraq. Since late 2014, eight F-16s (with two kept in reserve) were deployed to Jordan. Since then, numerous air attacks have been conducted on tactical facilities of ISIL, like camps and command posts. The F-16s also give air support to Iraqi and Kurdish ground forces. In June 2015 the Royal Netherlands Air Force flew its 1000th sortie above Iraq. During the first 9 months of the mission 575 strikes have been carried out.

Morocco Airstrikes

In December 2014 Morocco sent 4 F-16s to bomb ISIL positions, initially in the outskirts of Baghdad and other undisclosed locations. The planes operated under the command of the UAE and suspended operations in February 2015.

Jordanian Airstrikes

After the downed Jordanian pilot, Muath al-Kasasbeh was executed by ISIL by being burned to death, King Abdullah II vowed revenge and temporarily took the lead in the bombing raids on ISIL during February 2015. On 8 February, Jordan claimed that during the course of 3 days, from 5–7 February, their airstrikes alone had killed 7,000 ISIL militants in Iraq and Syria, and also reportedly degraded 20% of the militant group's capability.

US INVOLVEMENT

After the Iraqi Parliament's approval on September 8, 2014, of the new Prime Minister Haider al-Abadi, the United States felt comfortable carrying out increased air strikes and military operations against IS in Iraq because of increased political stability in the country.

On September 10 President Barack Obama addressed the United States in a special speech specifically dedicated to the threat posed by the Islamic State. The President vowed that "we will degrade, and ultimately destroy, ISIS through a comprehensive and sustained counterterrorism strategy". This strategy includes expanding air strikes (as of the speech 150 air strikes had been carried out), and supporting Iraqi and Kurd focres on the ground. The President assured the American people that there is not going to be another large scale ground war against the Islamic State, but troops are being sent in to provide training, equipment, and support to the international troops fighting the terrorists. The United States will also provide assistance to innocent civilians in the combat zones, and continue to do everything in it's power to stop IS funding sources. To read the full statement, please click here. (The White House, September 10 2014)

In response to growing criticism regarding the civilian casualties inflicted by these US led air strikes, the Obamaadministration released a statement on October 1 that the strict "near certainty" operations standards that were imposed by them in the previous year to prevent civilian casualties from drone strikes will not apply to the current situation. The voice of criticism became too loud for the administration to ignore after an estimated dozen civilians were killed by a Tomahawk missile in Syria's Idlib province on September 23. The statement released by the administration details that the "near certainty" policy was only to apply to areas that are outside of the current hot zone of the conflict, when the United States takes military action in areas "outside of direct hostilities". (Yahoo News, October 1, 2014)

Air strikes have been the method of choice for US involvement in the fight against ISIS, but without boots on the ground the West would be fighting a losing battle. A small group of Syrian rebels known as the Mujahideen Army have been given US training and weaponry, and the members say that they can tell the difference. Fifty fighters from the Mujahideen Army were trained in Syria by US forces in September 2014. They learned how to fire mortars and heavy machine guns, and were taught battlefield tactics.

The United States announced plans in late 2014 to arm and train more Syrian rebels to fight against the Islamic State. As of July 2015 there were approximately 7,000 Syrian rebels waiting to be evaluated and trained by the U.S. forces. The United States has made mistakes in past conflicts by arming rebel groups who have turned around and used the weaponry and training against US forces in the future, so the Syrian rebels will be subjected to a very rigorous and thorough testing and evaluation process before they begin their training. According to US officials this screening process will include (but is not limited to) cross-checking potential trainee names with US and foreign intelligence databases, collecting biometric data on the potential trainees, conducting interviews with locals about the general behavior and demeanor of the individuals, and seeking other information from their home communities. The training program is based on a levels system, with continuous and constant evaluations possibly leading to the rebels recieving more specialized training and "moving up" to different weapons and training programs. (The Washington Post, November 28 2014)

On October 3, 2014, the United States State Department and Department of Defense launched seperate informational websites aimed at countering the Islamic State. These sites provide the most up to date public information on the coalition to defeat ISIS, and the military aspects of this operation. The State Department website can be found here, and the Department of Defense site can be found here.

It was revealed in early November 2014 that during the nuclear negotiations between Iran and the P5+1 President Obama wrote a secret letter to Iranian leader Ayatollah Khamenei expressing their mutual interest in defeating the Islamic State. Cooperation between the United States and Iran is extremely rare, and the nuclear negotiations during 2014 represent the most sustained period of diplomacy between the two countries since 1979's Islamic Revolution.

This is the fourth letter that Obama has written to Khamenei, and these suggest that the United States is genuinely interested in pursuing a mutually beneficial relationship with Iran with further cooperation if the nuclear issue is sorted out.

On Friday November 7 President Barack Obama authorized a doubling of the number of US troops in Iraq, bringing the number to 3,100. This announcement of an additional 1,500 troops to be sent into Iraq comes amid a shift in theUnited States strategy in dealing with the Islamic State. President Obama announced that the US was going to be going on the offensive against the Islamic State now that air strikes have degraded some of their capabilities, but stood by the fact that US troops will not be involved in combat against ISIS. These additional troops will serve to advise and assist Iraqi security forces in planning counteroffensives to the brutal Islamic State militants. In order to pay for this, the White House announced that they were asking Congress for an additional $5.6 billion in supplimental funding for 2015.

On January 15, 2015, it was announced that the Pentagon will be sending an additional 400 US military trainers and hundreds of other support personnel to Syria in order to aid the rebel forces in stabalizing Syria and defeating the Islamic State. These military trainers will put the rebel forces through a 6-8 week training cycle, with the hopes that these soldiers will be well equiped to fight the Islamic State due to their grasp on the local terrain and battlefield dynamics.

On February 10, 2015, President Barack Obama submitted a draft Authorization for the Use of Military Force (AUMF) letter to lawmakers. The letter states that ISIS " poses a grave threat to the people and territorial integrity ofIraq and Syria, regional stability, and the national security interests of the United States and its allies and partners," outlines the duration of the authorization, and details the president's power to mobilize the country's armed forces. The draft imposes a three year time limit on military operations, and repeals President Bush's 2002 authorization for the war in Iraq. To read the full draft AUMF, click here.

During the week of February 23, 2015, US military supplies worth $17.9 million flowed into Iraq to arm their security forces in the fight against ISIS. These supplies included over 10,000 M-16 rifles, 250 armored and mine-resistant vehicles, thousands of Kevlar helmets and body armor, and 232 hellfire missiles. American troops will begin training 20,000-25,000 Iraqi security forces in mid-2015 to use this equipment.

It was announced at the end of March 2015 that the US Army's 5th Special Forces Group, who ousted the Taliban inAfghanistan in 2001, would be sent into Jordan to establish an international special operations task force to equip and train Syrian rebels to fight ISIS. This program will be run in tandem with other government rebel training programs inJordan, Syria, and Iraq.

President Obama sent a formal request for Congressional Authorization to fight the Islamic State to Congress in early 2015, and in March it was clear that partisan differences about an issue that was once a bipartisan sticking point were the primary reason that it had not been approved yet. Republicans in Congress believed that the authorization limited the President's authority to send in ground troops and was not enough, and Democrats believed that the request was too much and would get the United States involved in another long, unwinable war in the Middle East. Basic U.S. military operations had been going on against ISIS for months, and according to Secretary of State Kerry, "The president already has statutory authority to act against ISIS. But a clear and formal expression of this Congress's backing at this moment in time would dispel doubts that might exist anywhere that Americans are united in this effort."(New York Times, March 12, 2015)

For the first time since the air campaign began 9 months prior, in the begining of May 2015 the United States admitted that the air strikes that they led against the Islamic State had killed at least two civilians. Global human rights groups alleged that these air strikes had in fact killed hundreds of civilians, but there were no professionals in the area to assess the situations. Airwars, a project run by a team of independent journalists, released a report in early August 2015, containing details of approximately 52 air strikes carried out by the allied coalition forces.

These strikes resulted in the deaths of at least 459 civilians, including 100 children, according to the report. The Syrian Observatory for Human Rights puts the civilian death toll due to U.S. strikes at more than 200.

In the first U.S. executed targetted raid since the begining of the fight against the Islamic State, a small group of American special forces entered Syrian airspace early on May 16, and carried out a home raid that left a senior ISIS official as well as a dozen other ISIS fighters dead. The man killed in the operation, Abu Sayyaf, was described as the "emir of oil and gas" for the Islamic State. The U.S. government spent an extended period of time gathering intelligence on Sayyaf and his whereabouts prior to the execution of the raid.

The United States army approved the assignment to Iraq of approximately 450 military personnel in June 2015. These soldiers will assist the Iraqi army in defeating the Islamic State by providing training and strategic coordination.

In mid-July 2015 it was revealed that the United States military was in talks to build bases to launch surveilance drones from several North African countries in order to better monitor the activities of the Islamic State. Counterterrorism officials stated that having a drone base in a country like Libya would significantly improve one of the U.S.'s major "blind spots" in the battle against ISIS.

Turkish Foreign Minister Mevlut Cavusoglu announced to Reuters on August 24, 2015, that Turkey and the United States, along with Saudi Arabia, Qatar, and Jordan, had reached a comprehensive plan to combat the Islamic State following long and detailed diplomatic talks. The plan involved funding and arming supposed moderate Syrian rebels and providing air cover as they flush the Islamic State out of Syria, while at the same time harshly restricting access to Turkish borders. Hours after the announcement of the conclusion of talks however, White House Spokesman Josh Earnest denied the allegations of an agreement. Earnest stated during his daily press briefing that the negotiations with Turkey and other Mediterranean allies were ongoing and had not reached an agreement yet. Washington announced that the agreement had been completed 4 days later, on August 28, 2015.

A special report published in *The Washington Post* on September 1, 2015, provided a glimpse into the secretive targetted killing program that the CIA and U.S. Special Operations Forces have been running against the Islamic State, seperate from the allied attacks. The program focuses solely on "high-value" targets, and drones flying over Syria participating in this operation were responsible for many strikes on high-profile Islamic State individuals during 2015. These targets included a militant who was linked to two Muslim gunmen who attacked people at a Mohammad drawing contest in Garland, Texas. Despite months of training efforts by U.S. Special Forces, in September 2015 United States security officials embarassingly admitted that there were only "four or five" U.S. trained rebels in Syria fighting against the Islamic State. An additional approximately 100 rebels were receiving training in Turkey at the time of the announcement. The remaining rebels of the 60 that were trained earlier this year had all been captured or killed by the Islamic State. The week after U.S. officials issued this forlorn assessment, 75 more U.S. trained Syrian rebels entered Syria to fight against the Islamic State.

The United States made the decision to suspend the Syrian rebel training program on October 9, 2015, in the wake of continuing dissapointments and news that the rebels had been widely unsuccessful. U.S. Defense Secretary Ash Carter told reporters at a press conference that, "we are looking at different ways to achieve the same strategic objectives," and the administration is still committed to fighting the Islamic State. (CNN, October 9, 2015) Reports during November alleged that the United States spent $2 million training each fighter, according to spending figures and interviews with officials.

The week after officially suspending the Syrian rebel training program, U.S. cargo planes dropped 50 tons of ammunition and other various supplies to rebels in Syria fighting against the Islamic State and Assad's government. According to official sources all supplies were recovered by friendly forces in the Syrian Arab Coalition. United States commandos and Kurdish Peshmerga forces carried out a secretive mission to rescue individuals who were being held hostage by the Islamic State and faced "imminent execution," on October 21, 2015. One U.S. soldier was killed during the operation, which rescued over 70 individuals held hostage by ISIS.

The soldier that was killed was the first American combat death in Iraq since November 2011, and the ensuing firefight with the jihadis marked the first time ever that U.S. forces have stepped into ground combat against ISIS fighters. More than 20 ISIS fighters were killed in the rescue mission, and six were captured. During the following week U.S. Secretary of Defense Ash Carter made it clear that missions like this would become more frequent in the future, as the U.S. re-evaluates it's strategy to combat ISIS. During late October 2015 it became clear that leaders in Washington were heavily considering a push for more active combat roles for U.S. soldiers in the fight against the Islamic State.

The United States announced the authorization of the first sustained deployment of ground troops to Syria on October 30, 2015, as seventeen world powers met to discuss ending the Syrian civil war. According to U.S. officials, President Obama issued an authorization for the deployment of "fewer than 50" U.S. special forces into Northern Syria, who will assist the local fighters battling ISIS and Assad's forces. In addition to ground forces, Washington will be sending A-10 planes as well as F-15 fighter jets to the Incirlik air base in Southern Turkey as part of the new strategy to defeat ISIS.

From October 30 to November 6, 2015, the United States carried out 56 air strikes against ISIS targets, after running only three strikes during the previous 5 days. October 2015 saw only 117 air-strikes inside of Syria total, one of the calmest months of the whole conflict. In addition to the escalation of the air-war in Syria, U.S. Defense Secretary Ashton Carter told ABC News on November 8, 2015, that there could "absolutely" be more U.S. troops on the ground fighting ISIS in the near future. Carter said that, "if we find additional groups that are willing to fight ISIL and are capable and motivated, we'll do more. The President has indicated a willingness to do more, I certainly am prepared to recommend he do more." (ABC News, November 8, 2015)

U.S. airstrikes killed the man known as Jihadi John, who had been featured in ISIS propaganda videos, in Raqqa on November 12, 2015. The next day U.S. airstrikes killed the leader of the ISIS affiliate in Libya, Wisam al Zubaidi.

President Obama vowed that he would intensify all aspects of the U.S. military strategy to defeat ISIS in the wake of the November 13, 2015, Paris terror attacks. Ramped up efforts to attack the oil funding sources of the Islamic State began in mid-October 2015, with the United States carrying out air strikes that destroyed three oil refineries and 116 ISIS oil tankers parked near an Iraqi border crossing during early November. Up until this point in the conflict the United States had been cautious about striking oil facilities and trucks, because they were still technically property of the Syrian people. However, following the Paris attack and an increase in global commitment to defeat ISIS, the United States began air strikes against Syrian oil facilities. During November 2015, the U.S. led coalition carried out over a dozen air strikes against the DayrÂ AzÂ Zawr oil facility and the Abu Kamal oil collection point.

It is estimated that 2/3 of the Islamic State's oil revenues come from within the DayrÂ AzÂ Zawr region, South-East of Raqqa. U.S.

led coalition spokesman Colonel Steve Warren stated during a press conference on November 13, 2015, that, "We realized we needed to re-look how we were targeting these oil facilities... we want them broken longer. Rather than 24 to 48 hours, we're looking at something that would take maybe a year to repair." (Yahoo News, November 16, 2015) On November 20, 2015, U.S. led coalition air strikes destroyed 283 Islamic State fuel trucks. U.S. defense officials estimated that this increased bombing campaign focused on the oil revenues of ISIS, which began in October 2015, reduced their income from oil sales by approximately 30%.

U.S. Presidential candidate Hillary Clinton called for increasing U.S. involvement in the fight against the Islamic State in November 2015, suggesting that the U.S. send special operations forces to assist Syrian rebels and Kurdish militias, expand air strikes, and implement a no-fly-zone with coalition forces over Syria.

Clinton referred to her plan as an "intensification and acceleration" of President Obama's strategy, criticizing him for acting too slowly in arming moderate rebels. Speaking to the Council on Foreign Relations in New York, Clinton stated "it is time to begin a new phase and intensify and broaden our efforts to smash the would-be caliphate and deny ISIS control of territory in Iraq and Syria."(New York Times, November 19, 2015)

MILITARY INTERVENTION AGAINST ISIL

In response to rapid territorial gains made by the Islamic State of Iraq and the Levant (ISIL or ISIS or Daesh, calling itself the Islamic State) militants during the first half of 2014, and internationally condemned brutality, reportedhuman rights abuses and the fear of further spillovers of the Syrian Civil War, many states began to intervene against ISIL in Syria and Iraq, and three states, later, intervened or surveilled on ISIL in Libya.

In mid-June 2014, Iran, according to American and British information, started flying drones over Iraq, and, according to Reuters, Iranian soldiers were in Iraq fighting ISIL. Simultaneously, the United States ordered a small number of troops to Iraq and started flying manned aircraft over Iraq.

In July 2014, according to the International Institute for Strategic Studies, Iran sent Sukhoi Su-25 aircraft to Iraq, and Hezbollah purportedly sent trainers and advisers to Iraq to monitor ISIL's movements. In August 2014, the US began a campaign of airstrikes on ISIL targets in Iraq, and, according to American website *Business Insider*, Iran also began air strikes against ISIL.

Since then, nine countries, allied with the US in some coalition, have also executed airstrikes on ISIL in Iraq; nine countries, including the US, have conducted airstrikes on ISIL in Syria.

TURKISH INTERVENTION

ISIL is suspected of involvement in or responsibility for terrorist attacks in Turkey in May 2013 in Reyhanlý and March 2014 on Turkish police,kidnapping 49 Turkish diplomats in June 2014, the 5 June 2015 Diyarbakýr rally bombing and the 20 July 2015 Suruç bombing killing 32 young activists.

The Turkish government until July 2015 once attacked ISIL militarily, in January 2014. In September 2014 Turkey joined a US-led coalition 'to fight ISIL'.

On 23 July 2015, Turkey allowed the United States to use Ýncirlik and Diyarbakýr air bases in southern Turkey for airstrikes on ISIL. Also on 23 July, after an alleged ISIL attack on a Turkish border outpost in Kilis Province killing one Turkish soldier, the Turkish army with tanks shelled ISIL militants in Syria killing one militant and destroying several ISIL vehicles.

On 24 July 2015, an anonymous report appeared on a Turkish newspaper/website stating that the United States had agreed with Turkey on a 'partial no-fly zone' in northern Syria. While no official statement about the zone has been released, commentators still speculate about the real motives and objectives of Turkey and the US with the supposed 'buffer zone' or 'ISIL-free zone'.

On 24 and 25 July, in a military operation entitled 'Operation Martyr Yalçýn' against both ISIL and the Kurdistan Workers' Party (PKK) deploying at least 70 F-16 fighter jets, Turkey reportedly bombarded at least eight ISIL positions in northern Syria, killing 35 ISIL militants.

IRANIAN INVOLVEMENT IN THE SYRIAN CIVIL WAR

Iran and Syria are close strategic allies, and Iran has provided significant support for the Syrian Government in the Syrian Civil War, including logistical, technical and financial support, as well as training and some combat troops.

Iran sees the survival of the Syrian government as being crucial to its regional interests. Iran's supreme leader, Ali Khamenei, was reported in September 2011 to be vocally in favor of the Syrian government.

In the civil uprising phase of the Syrian civil war, Iran was said to be providing Syria with technical support based on Iran's capabilities developed following the 2009–2010 Iranian election protests. As the uprising developed into the Syrian civil war, there were increasing reports of Iranian military support, and of Iranian training of NDF (National Defence Forces) both in Syria, and in Iran. Iranian security and intelligence services are advising and assisting the Syrian military in order to preserve Bashar al-Assad's hold on power. Those efforts include training, technical support, combat troops. By December 2013 Iran was thought to have approximately 10,000 operatives in Syria. But according to Jubin Goodarzi, assistant professor and researcher of Webster University, Iran aided the Assad regime with a limited number of deployed units and personnel, "at most in the hundreds ... and not in the thousands as opposition sources claimed". Lebanese Hezbollah fighters backed by Iran's government have taken direct combat roles since 2012. In the summer of 2013, Iran and Hezbollah provided important battlefield support for Assad, allowing it to make advances on the opposition.

In 2014, coinciding with the peace talks at Geneva II, Iran has stepped up support for Syrian President Assad. Syrian Opposition Interim Minister of Finance and Economy claimed that the "Iranian government has given more than 15 billion dollars" to Syria as of December 2013. According to the United Nations envoy to Syria, Staffan de Mistura, the Iranian government spends at least $6 billion annually on maintaining Assad's government. Nadim Shehadi, the director of the Fares Center for Eastern Mediterranean Studies at Tufts University, said that his research puts the actual number at $15 billion annually.

From January 2013 onward, the Iranian Revolutionary Guard Corps lost more than 1,100 troops in Syria. 360 of the deaths have been Iranian nationals, mostly officers, including several brigadier generals. The remaining deaths consist of auxiliaries recruited from Afghan and Pakistani immigrants inside Iran, who joined the IRGC in exchange for salaries and citizenship, in an arrangement similar to a Foreign

Legion. The Afghans are recruited largely from refugees inside Iran, and usually had combat experience before joining the IRGC; their status as members of the Iranian military is only vaguely acknowledged and sometimes denied, despite the troops being uniformed fighters led by IRGC officers, trained and equipped in Iran, with state funerals involving uniformed IRGC personnel. Among the dead are 715+ Afghans and at least 66 Pakistanis. Officially, the Afghan auxiliaries are part of the independent Liwa Fatemiyoun group, though news media outside of Iran often simply refers to this organization as the "Fatemiyoun Brigade" or "Fatemiyoun Division" of the IRGC, while the Pakistanis are part of the "Zaynabiyun Brigade".

Background

Iran sees the survival of the Syrian government as being crucial to its interest. Its only consistent ally since the 1979 Islamic revolution, Syria provides a crucial thoroughfare to Hezbollah in Lebanon. Iranian leaders have cited Syria as being Iran's "35th province", with President Bashar al-Assad's Alawite minority led government being a crucial buffer against the influence of Saudi Arabia and the United States.

The Syrian city of Zabadani is vitally important to Assad and to Iran because, at least as late as June 2011, the city served as the Iranian Revolutionary Guard Corps's logistical hub for supplying Hezbollah. Prior to the Syrian war, Iran had between 2,000 and 3,000 IRGC officers stationed in Syria, helping to train local troops and managing supply routes of arms and money to neighboring Lebanon.

In April 2014, Hossein Amir-Abdolahian, Iranian deputy foreign minister said *We aren't seeking to have Bashar Assad remain president for life. But we do not subscribe to the idea of using extremist forces and terrorism to topple Assad and the Syrian government.*

2011

In the civil uprising phase of the Syrian civil war, Iran was said to be providing Syria with technical support based on Iran's capabilities developed following the 2009–2010 Iranian election protests.

In April 2011 U.S. President Barack Obama and U.S. Ambassador to the United Nations Susan Rice accused Iran of secretly aiding Assad in his efforts to quell the protests, and there were reports of Syrian protesters hearing security-force members speaking Persian.

The Guardian reported in May 2011 that the Iranian government was assisting the Syrian government with riot control equipment and intelligence monitoring techniques. According to US journalist Geneive Abdo writing in September 2011, the Iranian government provided the Syrian government with technology to monitor e-mail, cell phones and social media. Iran developed these capabilities in the wake of the 2009 protests and spent millions of dollars establishing a "cyber army" to track down dissidents online. Iran's monitoring technology is believed to be among the most sophisticated in the world, perhaps only second to China.

2012

In May 2012, in an interview with the Iranian Students News Agency which was later removed from its website, the deputy head of Iran's Quds Force said that it had provided combat troops to support Syrian military operations. It was alleged by the Western media that Iran also trained fighters from Hezbollah, a Shia militant group based in Lebanon. Iraq, located between Syria and Iran, was criticized by the U.S. for allowing Iran to ship military supplies to Assad over Iraqi airspace. *The Economist* said that Iran had, by February 2012, sent the Syrian government $9 billion to help it withstand Western sanctions. It has also shipped fuel to the country and sent two warships to a Syrian port in a display of power and support.

In March 2012, anonymous U.S. intelligence officials claimed a spike in Iranian-supplied arms and other aid for the Syrian government. Iranian security officials also allegedly traveled to Damascus to help deliver this assistance. A second senior U.S. official said members of Iran's main intelligence service, the Ministry of Intelligence and Security, were assisting Syrian counterparts in charge of the crackdown.

According to a U.N. panel in May 2012, Iran supplied the Syrian government with arms during the previous year despite a ban on weapons exports by the Islamic Republic.

Turkish authorities captured crates and a truck in February 2012, including assault rifles, machine guns, explosives, detonators, 60mm and 120mm mortar shells as well as other items on its border. It was believed these were destined for the Syrian government.

The confidential report leaked just hours after an article appeared in *The Washington Post* revealing how Syrian opposition fighters started to receive more, and better, weapons in an effort paid for by Persian Gulf Arab states and co-ordinated partly by the US. The report investigated three large illegal shipments of Iranian weapons over the past year and stated "Iran has continued to defy the international community through illegal arms shipments.

Two of these cases involved [Syria], as were the majority of cases inspected by the Panel during its previous mandate, underscoring that Syria continues to be the central party to illicit Iranian arms transfers."More anonymous sources were cited by the UN in May 2012, as it claimed arms were moving both ways between Lebanon and Syria, and alleged weapons brought in from Lebanon were being used to arm the opposition. The alleged spike in Iranian arms was likely a response to a looming influx of weapons and ammunition to the rebels from Gulf states that had been reported shortly before.

On 24 July 2012, Iranian Revolutionary Guards Corp commander Massoud Jazayeri said Iranians would not allow enemy plans to change Syria's political system to succeed. In August 2012 Leon Panetta accused Iran of setting up a pro-Government militia to fight in Syria, and chairman of the joint chiefs of staff General Martin Dempsey compared it to the Mahdi Army of Iraqi Shia leader Muqtada al-Sadr. Panetta said that there was evidence that the Iranian Revolutionary Guards were attempting to "train a militia within Syria to be able to fight on behalf of the regime". 48 Iranians were captured by the FSA in Damascus, and U.S. officials said that the men who were captured were "active-duty Iranian Revolutionary Guard members".

In September 2012, Western intelligence officials stated that Iran had sent 150 senior members of the Iranian Revolutionary Guards to preserve the Assad government, and had also sent hundreds of tons of military equipment (among them guns, rockets, and shells) to the Assad government via an air corridor that Syria and Iran jointly established. These officials believed that the intensification of Iranian support had led to increased effectiveness against the Free Syrian Army by the Assad government.

According to rebel soldiers speaking in October 2012, Iranian Unmanned aerial vehicles had been used to guide Syrian military planes and gunners to bombard rebel positions. CNN reported that the UAV or drones—which the rebels refer to as "wizwayzi" were "easily visible from the ground and seen in video shot by rebel fighters".

Rebels have displayed captured aircraft they describe as Iranian-built drones — brightly colored, pilotless jets. They're accompanied by training manuals emblazoned with the image of Iran's revolutionary leader, the lateAyatollah Ruhollah Khomeini.

2013

In January 2013, a prisoner swap took place between the Syrian Rebels and the Syrian Government authorities. According to reports, 48 Iranians were released by the Rebels in exchange for nearly 2,130 prisoners held by the Syrian Government. Rebels claimed the captives were linked to the Iranian Revolutionary Guard.US State Department spokeswoman Victoria Nuland described the Iranians as "members of the Iranian Revolutionary Guard," calling it "just another example of how Iran continues to provide guidance, expertise, personnel, technical capabilities to the Syrian regime."

Iran reportedly decided in June 2013 to send 4,000 troops to aid the Syrian government forces, described as a "first contingent" by writer/reporter Robert Fisk of *The Independent*, who added that the move underscores a Sunni vs. Shiite alignment in the Middle East. Iran was also reported to have proposed to open a new Syrian front against Israel in the Golan Heights, this coming a day after Egyptian President cut off diplomatic relations with Syria and demanded that Iran support for the pro Syrian-government Hezbollah end. A Syrian official called the severing of relations by Morsi "irresponsible" and said it was part of a move by the U.S. and Israel to exacerbate divisions in the region.

According to American officials questioned by journalist Dexter Filkins, officers from the Quds force have "coordinated attacks, trained militias, and set up an elaborate system to monitor rebel communications" in Syria from late 2012 to 2013. With help from the Hezbollah, and under the leadership of Quds Force general Qassem Soleimani, the al-Assad government has won back strategic territory from rebels in 2013, in particular an important supply route during the Al-Qusayr offensive in April and May.

In the fall of 2013 Iranian Brigadier General Mohammad Jamali-Paqaleh of the Revolutionary Guards was killed in Syria, reportedly while volunteering to defend a Shia shrine. In February, General Hassan Shateri, also of the Revolutionary Guards, had been killed while travelling from Beirut to Damascus.

2014

Iran has stepped up support on the ground for Syrian President Assad, providing hundreds more military specialists to gather intelligence and train troops. This further backing from Tehran, along with deliveries of munitions and equipment from Moscow, is helping to keep Assad in power.

This surge of support was in part a decision strongly promoted by Qasem Soleimani, the head of the Quds force, to exploit the outbreak of infighting between rebel fighters and the al-Qaeda inspiredIslamic State of Iraq and Sham (ISIS).

Former Iranian Revolutionary Guard commander said Iranian forces, said that "top Quds force commanders were tasked with advising and training Assad's military and his commanders", adding that "Revolutionary Guards directed the fighting on the instructions of the Quds Force commanders". In addition there are thousands of Iranian paramilitary Basij volunteer fighters as well as Shi'ites from Iraq. Former Iranian official and a Syrian opposition source also put the count of those auxiliary forces in the thousands.

A Syrian opposition source said in recent months Iranian led forces had begun operating in coastal areas including Tartous and Latakia. They have local ID cards, wear Syrian military fatigues and work with the elite Syrian air force intelligence unit.

2015

Citing two Lebanese sources, Reuters reported on October 1, 2015 that hundreds of Iranian troops arrived in Syria over the previous 10 days and would soon join Syrian government forces and their Lebanese Hezbollah allies in a major ground offensive backed by Russian air strikes. The *Wall Street Journal* reported on October 2, 2015 that Iran's Revolutionary Guard (the IRGC) has had some 7,000 IRGC members and Iranian paramilitary volunteers operating in Iran and was planning to expand its presence in the country through local fighters and proxies. The *Journal* also reported that some experts estimate 20,000 Shiite foreign fighters are on the ground, backed by both Shiite Iran and Hezbollah.

At least 121 IRGC troops, including several commanders, have been killed in the Syrian Civil War since it began.

Key victories were achieved with substantial support provided by the Quds force, namely the al-Ghab plains battles, Aleppooffensives, Dara'aya offensives of 2015 and the al-Qusayr offensives which established government and Hezbollah control over the northern Qalamoun region and the border crossings from Lebanon to Syria. In June 2015, some reports suggested that the Iranian military were effectively in charge of the Syrian government troops on the battlefield.

After the loss of Idlib province to a rebel offensive in the first half of 2015, the situation was judged to have become critical for Assad's survival. High level talks were held between Moscow and Tehran in the first half of 2015 and a political agreement was achieved. On 24 July General Qasem Soleimani visited Moscow to devise the details of the plan forcoordinated military action in Syria.

In mid-September 2015, the first reports of new detachments from the Iranian revolutionary guards arriving in Tartus and Latakia in west Syria were made. With much of the Syrian Arab Army and National Defence Forces units deployed to more volatile fronts, the Russian Marines and Iranian Revolutionary Guard (IRG) have relieved their positions by installing military checkpoints inside the cities of Slunfeh (east Latakia Governorate), Masyaf (East Tartus Governorate) and Ras al-Bassit(Latakia coastal city). There were also further reports of new Iranian contingents being deployed to Syria in early October 2015.

On 1 October 2015, citing two Lebanese sources, Reuters reported that hundreds of Iranian troops had arrived in Syria over the previous 10 days to join Syrian government forces and their Lebanese Hezbollah allies in a major ground offensive backed by Russian air strikes that started on 30 September 2015 and were welcomed as vital by Bashar Assad.

On 8 October 2015, brigadier general Hossein Hamadani, the deputy to General Qasem Soleimani in Syria was killed. On 12 October, two more senior commanders of the Iranian Revolutionary Guard Corps, Hamid Mokhtarband and Farshad Hassounizadeh, were reported by Iranian media to have been killed in Syria. At the end of October 2015, Iran agreed to take part in the Syria peace talks in Vienna.

The talks for the first time brought Iran to the negotiating table with Saudi Arabia, which are said to be engaged in a proxy war in Syria. The talks however were promptly followed by an exchange of sharp rebukes between Iran's and Saudi Arabia's top officials that cast doubt on Iran's future participation in those.

5

Foreign Relations and Policy

FOREIGN RELATIONS OF SYRIA

Ensuring national security, increasing influence among its Arab neighbors, and securing the return of the Golan Heights, have been the primary goals of Syria's foreign policy. At many points in its history, Syria has seen virulent tension with its geographically cultural neighbors, such as Turkey, Israel, Iraq, and Lebanon. Syria enjoyed an improvement in relations with several of the states in its region in the 21st century, prior to the Arab Spring and the Syrian Civil War.

Since the ongoing civil war, Syria has been increasingly isolated from the countries in the region, and the wider international community. Diplomatic relations have been severed with several countries including: Turkey, Saudi Arabia, Canada, France, Italy, Germany, United States, United Kingdom, Belgium, Spain, and the Arab states of the Persian Gulf. Syria was suspended from the Arab League in 2011 and theOrganisation of Islamic Cooperation in 2012. Syria continues to foster good relations with its traditional allies, Iran and Russia. Other countries that presently maintain good relations with Syria include China, North Korea, Angola, Cuba, Venezuela,Bolivia, Ecuador, Nicaragua, Brazil, Guyana, India, South Africa,Tanzania, Pakistan, Armenia, Argentina, Belarus, Tajikistan, Indonesia,Philippines, Uganda, Zimbabwe, and others. From among the Arab League states, Syria continues to have good relations with Iraq, Egypt (after 3 July 2013), Algeria, Kuwait, Lebanon, Oman and Yemen.

MIDDLE EAST

Arab nationalism is a fundamental doctrine of Syrian government policy, and as such it doesn't consider inhabitants of other Arab states as 'foreigners'. Rather the Syrian Arab Republic is considered as part of one vast Arab homeland, *al-watan al-arabi.*

Syria's relations with the Arab world were strained by its support for Iran during the Iran–Iraq War, which began in 1980. With the end of the war in August 1988, Syria began a slow process of reintegration with the other Arab states. In 1989, it joined with the rest of the Arab world in readmitting Egypt to the 19th Arab League Summit at Casablanca.

This decision, prompted in part by Syria's need for Arab League support of its own position in Lebanon, marked the end of the Syrian-led opposition to Egypt and the 1977–79 Sadat initiatives toward Israel, as well as the Camp David Accords. It coincided with the end of the 10-year Arab subsidy to Syria and other front-line Arab countries pledged at Baghdad in 1978. Syria re-established full diplomatic relations with Egypt in 1989. In the 1990–1991 Gulf War, Syria joined other Arab states in the US-led multinational coalition against Iraq. In 1998, Syria began a slow rapprochement with Iraq, driven primarily by economic needs. Syria continues to play an active pan-Arab role, which has intensified as the peace process collapsed in September 2000 with the start of the second Palestinian uprising (Intifada) against Israel. Though it voted in favor of UNSCR 1441 in 2002, Syria was against coalition military action in Iraq in 2003. However, the Syrian government accepted UNSCR 1483 (after being absent for the actual vote), which lifted sanctions on Iraq and established a framework to assist the Iraqi people in determining their political future and rebuilding their economy. Currently, much of the Middle East has condemned Syria's handling of the civil uprising, with only a few countries in the Middle East supporting Syria, most notably Iran, Iraq and Lebanon.

Arab League

Syria has been temporarily suspended from the Arab League since the Syrian civil war. On 26 March 2013, at the Arab league summit in Doha, the League recognised the National Coalition for Syrian Revolutionary and Opposition Forces, as the legitimate representatives of the Syrian people. The National Coalition was henceforth granted Damascus' seat at the summit. This act of recognition was opposed by Algeria, Iraq & Lebanon.

Iran

Syria and Iran are strategic allies. Syria is often called Iran's "closest ally", the Arab nationalism ideology of Syria's ruling Baath party notwithstanding. During the Iran–Iraq War, Syria sided with non-Arab Iran against its enemy Iraq and was isolated by Saudi Arabia and some of the Arab countries, with the exceptions of Libya, Lebanon, Algeria, Sudan andOman. Iran and Syria have had a strategic alliance ever since, partially due to their common animosity towards Saddam Hussein and coordination against the United States and Israel. Syria and Iran cooperate on arms smuggling from Iran to theHezbollah in Lebanon, which borders Israel.

On 16 June 2006 the defence ministers of Iran and Syria signed an agreement for military cooperation against what they called the "common threats" presented by Israel and the United States. Details of the agreement were not specified, however Iranian defense minister Najjar said "Iran considers Syria's security its own security, and we consider our defense capabilities to be those of Syria." The visit also resulted in the sale of Iranian military hardware to Syria. In addition to receiving military hardware, Iran has consistently invested billions of dollars into the Syrian economy. The Syrian leadership, including President Assad himself, belongs predominantly to the Alawite branch of Shi'a Islam. Currently, Iran is involved in implementing several industrial projects in Syria, including cement factories, car assembly lines, power plants, and silo construction. Iran also plans to set up a joint Iranian–Syrian bank in the future.

Iraq

The political states of Iraq and Syria were formed by the United Kingdom and France following the defeat of the Ottoman Empire in World War I. Iraq and Syria are united by historical, social, political, cultural and economic relations, but share a long foreign drawn border. The land known as Mesopotamia is Iraq and eastern Syria and is called such by its inhabitants. Political relations between Iraq and Syria have in the past seen difficulties, however, new diplomatic relations described by both sides as "Historic" were established in November 2006, beginning an era of close cooperation and political friendship between Iraq and Syria.

Israel

Syria has been an active belligerent, with periodic ceasefires and use of proxies, against Israel ever since May 1948, when the Syrian army captured territory from the newly established State of Israel north and south of the Sea of Galilee. Most of this territory was returned to Israel after the signing of the July 1949 Armistice Agreement and declared Demilitarized Zones. However, the exact location of the border between the two states, ownership of portions of territory and the right of Israeli farmers to farm the land in the Demilitarized Zones on the Israeli side of the border remained in dispute and sparked intermittent fighting between Syria and Israel until the 1967 Arab–Israeli War. Through the early 1950s the Syrians gradually retook de facto control of some of the territory ostensibly belonging to Israel (along the foot of part of the western escarpment of the Golan Heights north of the Sea of Galilee, along the north-eastern coast of the Sea of Galilee and the low ground below the southern escarpment of the Golan). In addition to the territorial dispute, small-scale fighting was also sparked by a dispute over Israel's right to pump water from the Jordan River and the Sea of Galilee (actually a fresh-water lake) for use in agricultural irrigation and drinking. From 1964 to 1966 the Syrians attempted to dig a canal that would divert the sources of the Jordan River before they entered Israeli territory — thus drying up that portion of the River and dramatically reducing the water-intake of the Sea of Galilee to prevent Israel from using that water. This led to a period of escalated fighting as the Israelis sought to prevent this diversion project which threatened to severely damage their ability to provide fresh-water to their population and agriculture (attempts to negotiate a solution by UN mediators failed). In fact, escalation of incidents between Israel and Syria in late 1966 and spring 1967 was one of the prime causes leading to the crisis that precipitated the Six Day War.

Syria was an active belligerent in the 1967 Arab–Israeli War, which resulted in Israel's occupation of the Golan Heights and the city of Quneitra. On 19 June, a week after the war ended, Israel offered to return the Golan if Syrian would agree to a full Peace Treaty. However, Syria refused. From 1967 to 1973 there were sporadic bouts of fighting along the new border.

Following the October 1973 Arab–Israeli War, which left Israel in occupation of additional Syrian territory, Syria accepted UN Security Council Resolution 338, which signaled an implicit acceptance of

Resolution 242. Resolution 242, which became the basis for the peace process negotiations begun in Madrid, calls for a just and lasting Middle East peace to include withdrawal of Israeli armed forces from territories (note: not all territories) occupied in 1967; termination of the state of belligerency; and acknowledgment of the sovereignty, territorial integrity, and political independence of all regional states and of their right to live in peace within secure and recognized boundaries.

As a result of the mediation efforts of then US Secretary of State Henry Kissinger, Syria and Israel concluded a disengagement agreement in May 1974, enabling Syria to recover territory lost in the October war and part of the Golan Heights occupied by Israel since 1967, including Quneitra. The two sides have effectively implemented the agreement, which is monitored by UN forces.

In December 1981, the Israeli Knesset voted to extend Israeli law to the part of the Golan Heights over which Israel retained control. The UN Security Council subsequently passed a resolution calling on Israel to rescind this measure. Syria participated in the Middle East Peace Conference in Madrid in October 1991. Negotiations were conducted intermittently through the 1990s, and came very close to succeeding. However, the parties were unable to come to an agreement due to President Bill Clinton's failure to consult with the Syrian President, Hafez al-Assad during the negotiating process, Israeli Prime Minister Ehud Barak's backtracking on the issue of the northeastern shore of the Sea of Galilee and Syria's nonnegotiable demand that Israel withdraw to the positions it held on 4 June 1967 (which meant Israel would relinquish its claim to territory occupied by the Syrians in the early 1950s in contravention to the 1949 Armistice Agreement — including the north-eastern shore of the Sea of Galilee). A major stumbling-block was that in response to Israel's demand that the entire Golan from the Jordan River to the outskirts of Damascus be demilitarized the Syrians demanded that Israel demilitarize all its territory to a similar distance from the new border. This was not acceptable to Israel as it would have effectively left all of northern Israel between the Jordan River and the Mediterranean Sea (more than a quarter of Israel), including the entire length of Israel's border with Lebanon, completely defenceless. The peace negotiations collapsed following the outbreak of the second Palestinian (Intifada) uprising in September 2000, though Syria continues to call for a comprehensive settlement based on UN Security Council Resolutions 242 and 338, and the land-for-peace formula adopted at the 1991 Madrid conference. Tensions between Israel and Syria increased as the Intifada dragged on, primarily as a result of Syria's refusal to stop giving sanctuary to Palestinian militant groups conducting operations against Israel. In October 2003, following a suicide bombing carried out by a member of Palestinian Islamic Jihad in Haifa that killed 20 Israeli citizens, Israeli Defense Forces attacked a suspected Palestinian militant training camp 15 kilometers north of Damascus. This was the first such Israeli attack deep inside Syrian territory since the 1973 war. Syria announced it would respond diplomatically, and asked the UN Security Council to condemn the Israeli action.

In 2004 and 2005 Israel and Syria engaged in private talks discussing an outline peace accord. These were successful at a technical level, but failed to gain adequate political support.

Hostility between Syria and Israel further increased following Israel's execution of Operation Orchard on 6 September 2007. Israel bombed a northern Syrian complex near Dayr az-Zawr which was suspected of holding nuclear materials from North Korea.

In 2008 Syrian President Bashar al-Assad confirmed that talks with Israel have resumed through a third party. The expatriates minister, Buthaina Shaaban has also confirmed that Israel is ready to give up the Golan Heights.

Jordan

Jordanian interest in Syria began in 1921, when the founder of the Emirate of Transjordan, Abdallah, sought to advance into Syria, from which his brother had been expelled by the French, and which he regarded as part of the promised Hashemite kingdom. Even as late as 1946, when both countries gained independence, King Abdallah did not abandon his plan to become king of Syria. Syria considered Abdallah's schemes for an expanded Hashimite kingdom as intervention in its domestic affairs and officially complained to the Arab League.

After the first Gulf War relations between Jordan and Syria had improved. After the Treaty of Peace Between the State of Israel and the Hashemite Kingdom of Jordan in which Jordan established diplomatic ties with Israel, Jordan has been an important transit point for Syrian businessmen doing business in the Palestinian territories.

Jordan has been accepting Syrian military defectors since the Syrian civil war.

Lebanon

Syria plays an important role in Lebanon by virtue of its history, size, power, and economy. Lebanon was part of Ottoman Syria until 1926. The presence of Syrian troops in Lebanon dates to 1976, when President Hafez Al-Assad intervened in theLebanese civil war on behalf of Maronite Christians. Following the 1982 Israeli invasion of Lebanon, Syrian and Israeli forces clashed in eastern Lebanon. The late U.S. Ambassador Philip Habib negotiated a cease-fire in Lebanon and the subsequent evacuation of PLO fighters from West Beirut. However, Syrian opposition blocked implementation of the 17 May 1983 Lebanese-Israeli accord on the withdrawal of Israeli forces from Lebanon. Following the February 1984 withdrawal of the UN Multinational Force from Beirut and the departure of most of Israel's forces from southern Lebanon a year later, Syria launched an unsuccessful initiative to reconcile warring Lebanese factions and establish a permanent cease-fire. Syria actively participated in the March–September 1989 fighting between the Christian Lebanese Forces and Muslim forces allied with Syria. In 1989, Syria endorsed the Charter of National Reconciliation, or "Taif Accord", a comprehensive plan for ending the Lebanese conflict negotiated under the auspices of Saudi Arabia, Algeria, and Morocco.

At the request of Lebanese President Hrawi, the Syrian military took joint action with the Lebanese Armed Forces on 13 October 1990, to oust rebel Gen. Michel Aoun who had defied efforts at reconciliation with the legitimate Government of Lebanon. The process of disarming and disbanding the many Lebanese militias began in earnest in early 1991. In May 1991, Lebanon and Syria signed the treaty of brotherhood, cooperation, and coordination called for in the Taif Accord, which is intended to provide the basis for many aspects of Syrian-Lebanese relations. The treaty provides the most explicit recognition to date by the Syrian Government of Lebanon's independence and sovereignty.

According to the U.S. interpretation of the Taif Accord, Syria and Lebanon were to have decided on the redeployment of Syrian forces from Beirut and other coastal areas of Lebanon by September 1992. Israeli occupation of Lebanon until May 2000, the breakdown of peace negotiations between Syria and Israel that same year, and intensifying Arab/Israeli tensions since the start of the second Palestinian uprising in September 2000 have helped delay full implementation of the Taif Accords. The UN declared that Israel's withdrawal from southern Lebanon fulfilled the requirements of UN Security Council Resolution

425. However, Syria and Lebanon claimed that UNSCR 425 had not been fully implemented because Israel did not withdraw from an area of the Golan Heights called Shebaa Farms, which had been occupied by Israel in 1967, and which Syria now claimed was part of Lebanon. The United Nations does not recognize this claim. However, Lebanese resistance groups such as Hezbollah use it to justify attacks against Israeli forces in that region, creating a potentially dangerous flashpoint along the Lebanon-Israeli border.

In 2005, Syrian troops withdrew from Lebanon after the assassination of Lebanese Sunni Prime Minister Rafik Hariri on 14 February 2005. In December 2008, The Syrian Embassy was opened in Beirut for the first time in history since both countries gained their Independence during the 1940s. In March 2009, Lebanon followed and opened its Embassy in Damascus. On 19 December 2009, Lebanese Prime Minister Saad Al-Hariri visited Syria, and stayed in Damascus for three days meeting with President Bashar Al-Assad & breaking the ice between the two sides.

Saudi Arabia

Saudi Arabia is a member of the Arab League and Syria is an ex-member. Relations between Syria and Saudi Arabia have become severed due to the Syrian Civil War and Saudi Arabia's support for the rebels and their support for the removal ofBashar al-Assad from power. The Saudi monarchy certainly hopes that a new government will emerge and that any government which emerges afterward will be more appeasing to Saudi interests. Many have criticized Saudi Arabia for its support of the Islamic State behind public eye (since both share in their practice of the extremist Islamic sect of Wahabism, and their punishment methods using beheading are identical in their ideology). further distancing itself from the Syrian government. In August 2008, the Saudi Arabian ambassador was called back to Riyadh. Saudi Arabia also closed its embassy in Syria, following the Syrian Civil War.

Turkey

Syrian–Turkish relations have long been strained even though Turkey shares its longest common border with Syria and various other geographic, cultural, and historical links tie the two neighboring states together.

This friction has been due to disputes including the self annexation of the Hatay Province to Turkey in 1939, water disputesresulting from the Southeastern Anatolia Project, and Syria's support for the outlawed Kurdistan Workers' Party (PKK) and the Armenian Secret Army for the Liberation of Armenia (ASALA), but relations have improved greatly since October 1998; when PKK leader Abdullah Öcalan was expelled by Syrian authorities.

Syria currently maintains an embassy in Ankara and two consulates–general in Istanbul and Gaziantep. Turkey has closed its embassy in Damascus and it consulate–general in Aleppo. Both countries are full members of the Union for the Mediterranean and the Organisation of Islamic Cooperation (OIC). Because of the Syrian civil war relations between Syria and Turkey have become increasingly tense. Turkey has been taking in refugees from Syria, although abuse and injustice towards the Syrian refugees has been reported. Relations have further been degraded due to a serious incident that occurred with the Syrian downing of a Turkish military training flight in June 2012. Relations worsened further in May 2013 following a border incident involving two car bombs exploding in the town of Reyhanlý, Hatay Province, Turkey. At least 43 people were killed and 140 more were injured in the attack. The car bombs were left outside Reyhanlý's town hall and post office. The first exploded at around 13:45 local time (10:45 GMT)[40] and the second exploded about 15 minutes later.

The issue that cemented the crack in the relations was Turkey's reportedly confirmed dealings with the Islamic State (an enemy of the Syrian government) in oil and weapons by various sources. A video surfacing of the Islamic State being unopposed by Turkish security as they traveled across the border between Syria, questions more of Turkey's alleged role of simply fighting terrorism. Although large allies such as the United States refuses to acknowledge these facts (because of Turkey's importance as an ally), evidence suggests that this event will not prompt relations between Turkey and Syria to improve in the future.

Turkey closed its embassy in Damascus on 26 March 2012.

EUROPE

Cyprus

Syrian president Bashar al-Assad became the first Syrian head of state to visit Cyprus in November 2010, resulting in the signing of five agreements between the two countries and pledges to work closer together on issues of common interest. The two leaders agreed to enhance cooperation in the sectors of tourism, construction, energy, transport, education, services, and telecommunications, as well as other fields in the public and private sector. The most important agreement signed was on coordinating search and rescue services. In addition, Cyprus and Syria signed agreements on cooperation in Telecommunications and Information Technology Services, Air Services, cultural cooperation for 2009–2011, Social Security and Agriculture. The 7th Protocol for the implementation of the agreement on Tourism Cooperation for the years 2009–2011 was also signed. The two countries also reached an agreement on technical cooperation between the Central Banks of the two countries. After the talks, Christofias awarded al-Assad the Grand Collar of the Order of Makarios III, while the Syrian leader presented Christofias with the National Order of Ummayya with the Grand Sash.

Russia

Russia has an embassy in Damascus and a consulate in Aleppo, and Syria has an embassy in Moscow. As with most of theArab countries, Russia enjoys a historically strong and stable friendly relationship with Syria.

Since 1971, Russia has leased port facilities in Tartus for its naval fleet. Between 1992 and 2008 these facilities were much in disrepair, however, works have commenced concurrent with the 2008 South Ossetia war to improve the port's facilities to support an increased Mediterranean presence of the Russian Navy.

Russia is believed to have sent Syria dozens of Iskander missiles.

Russia has been supporting Syria in the Syrian civil war.

REST OF WORLD

China

Diplomatic relations between both countries were established on 1 August 1956. China has an embassy in Damascusand Syria has an embassy in Beijing.

The total volume of import and export between China and Syria in 2001 was US$223,190,000, of which the Chinese export was US$223,180,000, and import US$10,000. China has helped Syria in building some projects such as textile mill and stadium. China currently has contracted to build a hydraulic power station and a rubber tire factory.

India

India and Syria have historical and cultural links dating back to silk route trade.

Korea

In September 2015, the Syrian government paid tribute to Kim Il-sung in a ceremony for a new park in Damascus named in his honor.

Syria awarded South Korea the following: the 1994 April Command Office Communication Ali 1994 September Minister of Information and Communication Radwan 2000 June Economic Mission of Syria 2007 October President of University of Aleppo.

Pakistan

Both countries were on the silk route through which civilizational exchanges took place for centuries, Islamic missionaries that introduced Islam after 711 AD were from Syria. During the Yom Kippur War of 1973 (usually referred to as the Ramadan war in Pakistan) several Pakistani pilots assisted the Syrian air force. In 2005 Syria and Pakistan agreed on mutual cooperation in the fields of science and technology. Pakistan also supports the Syrian Government since the beginning ofSyrian Civil War

United States

While relations between the two states have long since been tense, the two have maintained diplomatic exchanges. However, relations took an ominous turn in October 2008 with a cross-border raid during the Iraq war to ostensibly fend off the rise of allegedly foreign militants into the Iraq fighting for the Iraqi resistance. As of 2012, the embassy of the United States is suspended due to the Syrian civil war.

As of 21 August 2013, the United States has threatened to strike key Syrian chemical and biological weapons installations in response to a chemical attack that was allegedly carried out by forces loyal to Assad on a rebel stronghold within the capital Damascus. Assad had denied any involvement, however President Obama claims to have intelligence proving otherwise. No proof has been given to the public other than reports from key United States senators and representatives. As of 4 September 2013, the Committee on Foreign Relations approved an attack with a 10-7 vote.

President Trump on April 6, 2017 ordered the first U.S. airstrike on the Syrian air force since the country's civil war began in 2011. US

Navy warships USS Porter and USS Ross in the Mediterranean Sea launched dozens of Tomahawk missiles at Syria's Shayrat air base.

The strikes were in reaction to what Washington says was a sarin poison gas attack by the government of Syrian President Bashar al-Assad that killed at least 70 people in the Idlib region of Syria.

U.S. officials informed Russian forces ahead of the missile strikes, which Russian military were in Syria actively supporting and assisting al-Assad during Syria's civil war, and US air strikes avoided hitting Russian personnel.

Trump, who authorized the launch of 59 Tomahawk missiles from Navy warships in the Mediterranean Sea on an air base near Homs were in direct response to Bashar al-Assad's alleged use of chemical weapons in the town of Idlib on April 4, 2017. Following airstrikes were conducted on April 8, 2017 on the Syrian city that was the site of chemical weapons attack earlier.

MEMBERSHIP IN INTERNATIONAL ORGANIZATIONS

Syria is a member of the Arab Bank for Economic Development in Africa, Arab Fund for Economic and Social Development,Arab League, Arab Monetary Fund, Council of Arab Economic Unity, Customs Cooperation Council, Economic and Social Commission for Western Asia, Food and Agricultural Organization, Group of 24, Group of 77, International Atomic Energy Agency, International Bank for Reconstruction and Development, International Civil Aviation Organization, International Chamber of Commerce, International Development Association, Islamic Development Bank, International Fund for Agricultural Development, International Finance Corporation, International Labour Organization, International Monetary Fund, International Maritime Organization, INTELSAT, INTERPOL, International Olympic Committee, International Organization for Standardization, International Telecommunication Union, League of Red Cross and Red Crescent Societies,Non-Aligned Movement, Organization of Arab Petroleum Exporting Countries, Organisation of Islamic Cooperation, UN, UN Commission on Human Rights, UN Conference on Trade and Development, UN Industrial Development Organization, UN Relief and Works Agency for Palestine Refugees in the Near East, Universal Postal Union, World Federation of Trade Unions, World Health Organization, World Meteorological Organization, and World Tourism Organization. Syria is 1 of only 7

U.N. members which is not a member of the Organization for the Prohibition of Chemical Weapons.

Syria's 2-year term as a nonpermanent member of the UN Security Council ended in December 2003.

Disputes – international:
- Western Golan Heights with Israel;
- dispute with upstream riparian Turkey over Turkish water development plans for the Tigris and Euphrates rivers
- dispute with Turkey concerning the Turkish occupation of North Syria

Illicit drugs: a transit point for opiates and hashish bound for regional and Western markets

FOREIGN RELATIONS OF THE SYRIAN OPPOSITION

The foreign relations of Syrian Opposition refers to the external relations of the self-proclaimed oppositional Syrian Arab Republic, which sees itself as the genuine Syria.

The region of control of Syrian opposition affiliated groups is not well defined. The Turkish government recognizes Syrian opposition as the genuine Syrian Arab Republic and hosts several of its institutions on its territory.

The seat of Syria in the Arab League is reserved for the Syrian opposition since 2014, but not populated.

Foreign relations of the Syrian Opposition

Relations with UN member states

- Turkey - The Turkish government recognizes Syrian opposition as the genuine Syrian Arab Republic and hosts several of its institutions on its territory.

Relations with international organisations

- Arab League - On 6 March 2013, the Arab League granted to the Syrian National Coalition Syria's seat in the Arab League. On 9 March 2014, the pan-Arab group's secretary general Nabil al-Arabi said that Syria's seat at the Arab League would remain vacant until the opposition completes the formation of its institutions.

FOREIGN POLICY

Regional Foreign Relations

In 1987 Syria's policy toward the superpowers and its Middle Eastern neighbors, as well as much of its domestic politics, continued to be affected profoundly by the Arab-Israeli conflict. Because of the Egyptian-Israeli Camp David Agreements, periodic Jordanian-Israeli mutual accommodation, and Israeli domination of southern Lebanon, Syria perceived itself as the last Arab confrontation state to share a border with Israel. Syria believed that the Arab-Israeli conflict had been reduced to a bilateral Syrian-Israeli conflict, in which other parties, including the Palestinians, were marginal.

Recovering the Golan Heights from Israel was the specific motive of Syria's policy, but it was only a part of a broader ambition of regional hegemony. Therefore, Syria's goal was to prevent Jordan, the Palestine Liberation Organization (PLO), or Lebanon from formalizing Syria's isolation by entering into piecemeal settlements with Israel, while Syria simultaneously undermined Egypt's separate peace with Israel. Syria has declared that the Arab nations could extract maximum concessions from Israel only by acting in concert, a policy some regional observers refer to as the "Assad Doctrine." Implicit in the Assad Doctrine is the assumption that Damascus will orchestrate Arab negotiations. Syria's central role in the Arab-Israeli conflict, therefore, is predicated to some extent on the older ideology of Greater Syria, the notion that Syria should dominate its Arab neighbors.

Syria perceived regional politics in bipolar terms, dividing the Arab world into two camps: the rejectionist front of Syrian allies, and the capitulationists who advocated concessions to Israel. However, Syria's categorical classification of the Arab world seemed only to highlight its regional isolation. Syria's only partners in the "Arab Steadfastness and Confrontation Front" were Libya, Algeria, and the People's Democratic Republic of Yemen (South Yemen).

6

Military and Defence

SYRIAN ARMED FORCES

The Syrian Arab Armed Forces are the military forces of the Syrian Arab Republic. They consist of theSyrian Arab Army, Syrian Arab Navy, Syrian Arab Air Force, Syrian Arab Air Defense Force, and several paramilitary forces, such as the National Defence Force. According to the Syrian constitution, the President of Syria is the Commander-in-Chief of the Armed Forces.

The military is a conscripted force; males serve in the military upon reaching the age of 18, but they are exempted from service if they don't have another brother who can take care of their parents. There are many women in the armed forces.

Since the Syrian Civil War, the enlisted members of the Syrian military have dropped by over half from a pre-civil war figure of 325,000 to 150,000 soldiers in the army in December 2014, due to casualties, desertions and draft dodging,reaching between 178,000 and 220,000 soldiers in the army, in addition to 80,000 to 100,000 irregular forces.

Before the start of the Syrian Civil War, the obligatory military service period was being decreased over time. In 2005, it was reduced from two and a half years to two years, in 2008 to 21 months and in 2011 to a year and a half. Since the Syrian Civil War the Syrian government has reportedly engaged in arrest campaigns and enacted new regulations, with even citizens who have completed mandatory conscription being called up for reserve duty.

History

The French Mandate volunteer force, which would later become the Syrian army, was established in 1920 with the threat of Syrian" Arab nationalism in mind. Although the unit's officers were originally all French, it was, in effect, the first indigenous modern Syrian army. In 1925, this force was expanded and designated as the Special Troops of the Levant (Troupes Spéciales du Levant). In 1941, during World War II, the Army of the Levant participated in a futile resistance to the British and Free French invasion that ousted the Vichy French from Syria during the Syria–Lebanon Campaign.

After the Allies takeover, the army came under the control of the Free French and was designated theLevantine Forces (Troupes du Levant). French Mandate authorities maintained a gendarmerie to police Syria's vast rural areas. This paramilitary force was used to combat criminals and political foes of the Mandate government.

As with the Levantine Special Troops, French officers held the top posts, but as Syrian independence approached, the ranks below major were gradually filled by Syrian officers who had graduated from the Homs Military Academy, which had been established by the French during the 1930s. In 1938, the Troupes Spéciales numbered around 10,000 men and 306 officers (of whom 88 were French, mainly in the higher ranks). A majority of the Syrian troops were of rural background and minority ethnic origin, mainly Alawis, Druzes,Kurds, and Circassians.

By the end of 1945, the army numbered about 5,000 and the gendarmerie some 3,500. In April 1946, the last French officers were forced to leave Syria due to sustained resistance offensives; the Levantine Forces then became the regular armed forces of the newly independent state and grew rapidly to about 12,000 by the time of the 1948 Arab"Israeli War, the first of four Arab"Israeli wars between 1948 and 1986.

After the Second World War

The Syrian Armed Forces fought in the 1948 Arab-Israeli War (against Israel), and were involved in a number of military coups. Between 1948 and 1967, a series of military coups destroyed the stability of the government and any remaining professionalism within the armed forces. In March 1949, the chief of staff, General Husni al-Za'im, installed himself as president. Two more military dictators followed by December 1949. General Adib Shishakli then held power until deposed in the 1954 Syrian coup d'etat. Further coups followed, each attended by a purge of the officer corps to remove supporters of the losers from the force.

In 1963, the Military Committee of the Syrian Regional Command of the Arab Socialist Ba'ath Party spent most of its time planning to take power through a conventional military coup. From the very beginning, the Military Committee knew it had to capture al-Kiswah and Qatana, two military camps, seize control of the 70th Armoured Brigade at al-Kiswah, the Military Academy in the city of Homs and the Damascus radio station. While the conspirators of the Military Committee were all young, their aim was not out of reach; the sitting regime had been slowly disintegrating and the traditional elite had lost effective political power over the country. A small group of military officers, including Hafez al-Assad, soon seized control in the March 1963 Syrian coup d'etat. Following the coup, General Amin al-Hafiz discharged many ranking Sunni officers, thereby, Stratfor says, 'providing openings for hundreds of Alawites to fill top-tier military positions during the 1963-1965 period on the grounds of being opposed to Arab unity. This measure tipped the balance in favor of Alawite officers who staged a coup in 1966 and for the first time placed Damascus in the hands of the Alawites.'

The Armed Forces were involved in the 1967 Six Day War (against Israel). Since 1967, most of the Golan Heights territory of southwestern Syria has been under Israeli occupation. They then fought in the late 1960s War of Attrition (against Israel), and the 1970 Black September invasion of Jordan. During the Yom Kippur War of 1973 the Syrian Army launched an invasion of Israel that was only narrowly repulsed. Since 1973 the cease-fire line has been respected by both sides, with very few incidents until the Syrian uprising of 2011 began.

Syria was invited into Lebanon by that country's president in 1976, to intervene on the side of the Lebanese government against a rebellion of PLO and Lebanese forces. The Arab Deterrent Force originally consisted of a Syrian core with participation by some other Arab League states. However the other states withdrew their forces in the late 1970s.

Occupation of Lebanon

Syrian forces, still technically known as the Arab Deterrent Force, lingered in Lebanon throughout the Lebanese civil war(1975–1990). Eventually the Syrians brought most of the nation under their control, as part of a power-struggle with Israel, which occupied areas of southern Lebanon in 1978. Following the end of the Lebanese civil war in 1990, the Syrian occupation of Lebanon continued until 2005, when they were forced out by widespread public protest and international pressure, following the murder of Rafiq al-Hariri. About 20,000 Syrian soldiers were deployed in Lebanon until 27 April 2005, when the last of Syria's troops left the country. Syrian forces have been accused of involvement in that murder, as well as continued meddling in Lebanese affairs, and an international investigation into the Hariri killing and several subsequent bomb attacks has been launched by the UN.

Other engagements

Engagements since 1979 have included the Islamic uprising in Syria (1979–82), notably including the Hama Massacre, the1982 Lebanon War (against Israel), and the dispatch of the 9th Armoured Division to Saudi Arabia in 1990–91, ahead of theGulf War against Iraq. The 9th Armoured Division served as the Arab Joint Forces Command North reserve and saw little action.

Syria's force numbered ~20,000 in strength (the 6th largest contingent) and their involvement was justified domestically as an effort to defend Saudi Arabia. Syria's initial involvement in Operation Desert Shield also rolled into the Allied Operation Desert Storm as Syrian forces did participate in helping dislodge and drive Iraqi forces out of Kuwait City. Total losses sustained were 2 dead and 1 wounded. There were indications the Syrian government had been prepared to double its force to 40,000.

Modernisation

In recent years Syria has relied on Russian arms purchases to obtain modern weapons. Purchases have included anti-tank and air defence systems. In early September 2008, the Syrian government ordered MiG-29SMT fighters, Pantsir S1E air-defence systems,Iskander tactical missile systems, Yak-130 aircraft, and two Amur-1650 submarines from Russia. Russia's Foreign Minister Sergei Lavrov asserted that the sale wouldn't upset the balance of power in the Middle East and were "in line with ..international law."

Russia aims to turn the Russian naval base in Tartus into a permanent naval base. Israel and the United States oppose further arms sales to Syria due to fears that the weapons could fall under the control of Iran or Hezbollah fighters in Lebanon.

Syrian Civil War

Since the Syrian Civil War began, the Armed Forces have been sent to fight insurgents. As the uprising progressed into civil war, several Sunni soldiers began todefect from the Syrian Armed Forces and came together under the banner of theFree Syrian Army. In March 2012, the Syrian government issued new travel restrictions for military-aged males. Under the new restrictions, reported by local Syrian news outlets, all males between 18 and 42 were banned from traveling outside the country. In a late June 2012 interview given by the FSA's *Asharq Al-Awsat* he claimed Riad al-Asaad said that about 20–30 Syrian officers defected to Turkey each day.

Syrian Armed Forces size during the Civil War

Year	Army personnel	Air Force personnel	Total: Army + Air Force
2011	220,000	100,000	320,000
2014	110,000	63,000	173,000

- 2014 – 150,000 military and 60,000 Guard and 50,000 Kurdish army and AIR FORCE, AIR DEFENSE.
- 2015 – 150,000 military and 60,000 Guard and 50,000 Kurdish army and AIR FORCE, AIR DEFENSE.
- 2016 min 3500 volunteers, and the Navy (9000), Military Police (8000), possibly Hezbollah to 10,000 (partly in Syria). and AIR FORCE (40 000-?), AIR DEFENSE (60 000 -?).
- 2011 Total 354 000, (AIR FORCE 40 000, AIR DEFENSE 60 000), + 8000 Military Police + National home guard.
- Reserves for the Army in 2011, an additional 354 000

On 18 July 2012 Syrian Defence Minister Dawoud Rajha, former defence minister Hasan Turkmani, and the president'sbrother-in-law General Assef Shawkat were killed in a bomb attack in Damascus. The Syrian intelligence chief Hisham Bekhityar, and Head of the 4th Army Division Maher Al Assad brother of President Assad were also injured in the same explosion.

Since the start of the Syrian civil war, human rights groups say that the majority of abuses have been committed by the Syrian government's forces, and UN investigations have concluded that the government's abuses are the greatest in both gravity and scale. The branches of the Syrian Armed Forces that have committed war crimes include at least the Syrian Arab Army, Syrian Arab Air Force and the Syrian Military Intelligence. However the Syrian authorities deny these accusations and claim that irregular armed groups with foreign support are behind the atrocities, including Al Qaeda linked Insurgents.

Despite shrinking by nearly half since the beginning of the civil war in 2011, the Armed Forces have become much more flexible and capable, especially in anti-guerilla warfare. Their *modus operandi* switched from traditional Soviet-modeled conventional military forces into a force of smaller groups fighting in close-quarters guerrilla combat with an increasing role for junior officers.

STRUCTURE

With its headquarters in Damascus, the Syrian military consists of air, ground, and naval forces. Active personnel were estimated as 295,000 in 2011, with an additional 314,000 reserves. Paramilitary forces were estimated at 108,000 in 2011.

The majority of the Syrian military are Sunni, but most of the military leadership are Alawites. Alawites make up 12 percent of the Syrian population but are estimated to make up 70 percent of the career soldiers in the Syrian Army. A similar imbalance is seen in the officer corps where some 80 percent of the officers are Alawites. The military's most elite divisions, the Republican Guard and the 4th Armoured Division, which are commanded by Bashar al-Assad's brother Maher, are exclusively Alawite. Most of Syria's 300,000 conscripts were, however, Sunni but that number is speculated to be changing now.

Syrian Army

In 1987, Joshua Sinai of the Library of Congress wrote that the Syrian Arab Armywas the dominant military service, and as such controlled the senior-most posts in the armed forces, and had the most manpower, approximately 80 percent of the combined services. In 1987, Sinai wrote that the major development in force organisation was the establishment of an additional divisional framework based on the special forces and the organisation of ground formations into two corps. In 2010, the International Institute for Strategic Studies estimated army regulars at 220,000, with an additional 280,000 reserves. That figure was unchanged in the 2011 edition of the *Military Balance*, but in the 2013 edition, in the midst of the war, the IISS estimated that army strength was 110,000.

The army's active manpower served in three, all-arms army corps, eight armoured divisions (with one independent armoured brigade), three mechanised divisions, one armoured-special forces division, and ten, independent airborne-special forces brigades. The army had eleven divisional formations reported in 2011, with a fall in the number of armoured divisions reported from the 2010 edition, from eight to seven. The independent armoured brigade had been replaced by an independent tank regiment. However, in addition to the 14th Special Forces Division, the15th Special Forces Division has been identified by Human Rights Watch in 2011.

The former Defense companies were merged into the Syrian Army as the 4th Armoured Division and the Republican Guard. The 4th Armoured Division became one of the Assad government's most trusted security forces.

Syrian Navy

In 1950, the Syrian Navy was established following the procurement of a few naval craft from France. The initial personnel consisted of soldiers who had been sent to French academies of naval training. In 1985, the navy consisted of approximately 4,000 regular and 2,500 reserve officers and men. The navy is under the army's Latakia regional command. The fleet was based in the ports of Latakia, Baniyas, Minat al Bayda, and Tartus. Among the 41 vessel fleet were 2 frigates, 22 missile attack craft (including 10 advanced Osa II missile boats), 2 submarine chasers, 4 mine warfare vessels, 8 gunboats, 6 patrol craft, 4 missile corvettes (on order), 3 landing craft (on order), 1 torpedo recovery vessel and, as part of its coastal defence system, Sepal shore-based, anti-ship missiles with a range of 300 kilometres.

Syrian Air Force

The Syrian Arab Air Force is the aviation branch of the Syrian Armed Forces. It was established in 1948, and saw combat in 1948, 1967, 1973 and in 1982 against Israel. It has seen combat against militant groups on Syrian soil from 2011-2012, during the Syrian civil war. Presently, there are at least 15 Syrian air force bases throughout the country.

Syrian Air Defence Force

In 1987, according to the Library of Congress Country Studies, the Air Defence Command, within the Army Command, but also composed of Air Force personnel, numbered approximately 60,000. In 1987, units included twenty air defence brigades (with approximately ninety-five SAM batteries) and two air defence regiments. The Air Defence Command had command access to interceptor aircraft and radar facilities. Air defences included SA-5 long-range SAM batteries around Damascus and Aleppo, with additional SA-6 and SA-8 mobile SAM units deployed along Syria's side of the Lebanese border and in eastern Lebanon.

At some later point in time, the Air Defence Command was upgraded into a separate, Syrian Air Defense Force.

Paramilitary forces

- As-Sa'iqa - a commando force since merged into the National Defence Forces
- Defense Companies - since merged into the Syrian Arab Army as the 4th Armoured division and the Republican Guard as well as the 14th Airborne Division comprising 5 Special Forces regiments.
- Palestine Liberation Army - a Palestinian Auxiliary, ostensibly returned to Palestine Authority control.
- Republican Guard - since merged into the army.
- Struggle Companies - status unknown.
- National Defence Forces - a part-time volunteer reserve component of the military.
- Local Defence Forces

Role of women in the Armed forces

As the Syrian Civil War progressed and casualties mounted, more and more positions were opened to women. The National Defense Force allows female volunteers into its ranks, mainly in securing checkpoints. The Republican Guard also formed a female section, an all female tank battalion of 800 strong, nicknamed 'Lionesses of Defense', fighting within the limits of Damascus.

WEAPONS, UNIFORMS AND AWARDS

Weapons

The breakup of the Soviet Union — long the principal source of training, material, and credit for the Syrian forces — may have slowed

Syria's ability to acquire modern military equipment. It has an arsenal of surface-to-surface missiles. In the early 1990s, Scud-Cmissiles with a 500-kilometer range were procured from North Korea, and Scud-D, with a range of up to 700 kilometers, is allegedly being developed by Syria with the help of North Korea and Iran, according to Eyal Zisser.

Syria received significant financial aid from Persian Gulf Arab states as a result of its participation in the Persian Gulf War, with a sizable portion of these funds earmarked formilitary spending. In 2005, Russia forgave Syria of three-fourths, or about $9.8 billion, of its $13.4 billion Soviet-era debt. Russia wrote off the debt in order to renew arms sales with Syria. As of 2011, arms contracts with Russia, Syria's main arms supplier, were worth at least $4 billion. Syria has conducted research and produced weapons of mass destruction.

Uniforms (1987)

In 1987, according to a Library of Congress Country Study on Syria, service uniforms for Syrian military officers generally followed the British Army style, although army combat clothing followed the older British model. Each uniform had two coats: a long one for dress and a short jacket for informal wear. Army officer uniforms were khaki in summer, olive in winter. Certain Army and Air Defense personnel (i.e., commandos and paratroops) may have worn camouflage uniforms. Air force officers had two uniforms for each season: a khaki and a light gray for summer and a dark blue and a light gray in winter. Naval officers wore white in summer and navy blue in winter while lower ranks wear the traditional bell bottoms and white blouse. The uniform for naval chief petty officers was a buttoned jacket, similar to that worn by American chief petty officers. Officers had a variety of headgear, including a service cap, garrison cap, and beret (linen in summer and wool in winter). The color of the beret varied by season and according to the officer's unit.

Syrian Commando and Paratroop uniforms consist of lizard or woodland-patterned camouflage fatigues along with combat boots, helmets and bulletproof vests. Headgear consisted of a red or orange beret.

The Syrian military provides NBC uniforms to soldiers in order to remain effective in an environment effected by biological or chemical agents. This uniform consisted of a Russian-made Model ShMS-41 mask similar to those made in the Desert Storm conflict. Previous models of the ShMS used a hose, while the improved "ShmS-41" used a canister-style Respirator.

Rank Insignia (1987)

In 1987, according to a Library of Congress Country Study on Syria, the rank insignia of Syrian commissioned officers were identical for both the army and air force. These were gold on a bright green shoulder board for the army and gold on a bright blue board for the air force. Officer ranks were standard, although the highest is the equivalent of lieutenant general, a rank held in 1986 only by the commander in chief and the minister of defence. Navy officer rank insignia were gold stripes worn on the lower sleeve. The highest-ranking officer in Syria's navy is the equivalent of lieutenant general. Army and air force rank for warrant officers were indicated by gold stars on an olive green shield worn on the upper left arm. Lower noncommissioned ranks were indicated by upright and inverted chevrons worn on the upper left arm.

Awards and decorations

Although some twenty-five orders and medals were authorized, generally only senior officers and warrant officers wear medal ribbons. The following were some important Syrian awards: Order of Umayyads, Medal of Military Honor, the War Medal, Medal for Courage, Yarmuk Medal, Wounded in Action Medal, and Medal of 8 March 1963.

NATIONAL DEFENCE FORCES (SYRIA)

The National Defence Forces (NDF) is a pro-government militia, formed after summer 2012 and organized by the Syrian government during the Syrian Civil War as a part-time volunteer reserve component of the Syrian Armed Forces. The NDF is made of units across various Syrian provinces, each of them consists of local volunteers willing to fight against rebels for various reasons.

Formation

By the beginning of 2013, the Syrian government took steps to formalize and professionalize hundreds of Popular Committee militias under a new group dubbed the National Defence Forces.

The goal was to form an effective, locally based, highly motivated force out of pro-government militias. The NDF, in contrast with the

Shabihaforces, received salaries and military equipment from the government. Since the formation of the NDF, Shabiha members have been incorporated into its structure.

Young and unemployed men join the NDF, which some view as more attractive than the Syrian Army, considered by many of them to be infiltrated by rebels, overstretched and underfunded. A number of recruits say they joined the group because members of their families had been killed by rebel groups. In some Alawite villages almost every military-age male has joined the National Defence Force.

Others, like the Druze people of Al-Suwayda Governorate, join to protect their land from the Islamic State of Iraq and the Levant (ISIL).In late June 2015, the Syrian government began arming citizens of this governorate against ISIL, who were harassing the local population with abductions, executions, and plundering. The locals became a large and powerful NDF contingent in the governorate, including the prominentGolan Regiment.

The creation of the NDF was personally overseen by Iranian Quds Force commander Qasem Suleimani. Syrian security officials stated that they received assistance from Iran and Hezbollah, who both "played a key role in the formalization of the NDF along the model of the Iranian 'Basij' militia". The NDF recruits received training in urban guerilla warfare from Army of the Guardians of the Islamic Revolution (IRGC) and Hezbollah instructors at facilities inside Syria, Lebanon, and Iran, with this partnership remaining in place as of April 2015. Iran has contributed to gathering together existing neighborhood militias into a functioning hierarchy and provided them with better equipment and training. The United States government has also stated that Iran is helping build the group on the model of its own Basij militia, and that some members are being sent for training in Iran.

Role

The force acts in an infantry role, directly fighting against rebels on the ground and running counter-insurgency operations in coordination with the Syrian Army, which provides them with logistical and artillery support.

The force was reported to be 60,000-strong as of June 2013 and grew to 100,000 by August. The NDF is composed mainly of members of the Alawite and Shia sects of Islam and are loyal to Iran and the Assad Government.

Units mostly operate in their local areas, although members can also choose to take part in army operations. Others have claimed that the NDF does most of the fighting because NDF members, as locals, have a strong knowledge of the region. Struggling with reliability and issues with defections, officers of the Syrian Army increasingly prefer the part-time volunteer reserves of the NDF, who they regard as more motivated and loyal, over regular army conscripts to conduct infantry operations. An officer in Homs, who asked not to be identified, said the army was increasingly playing a logistical and directive role, while NDF fighters act as combatants on the ground.

Organization and training

According to a report, as of February 2015 the National Defense Forces are organized under provincial commanders, and loosely overseen by a national coordinator who is reported to be Brigadier-General Ghassan Nassour, although later sources report the name of Hawash Mohammed. Local branches are deemed to act with autonomy and to be not cohesive on the provincial level, although there is little uniformity.

Provincial branches seem to be commanded by a senior officer each.

Since January 2013, the NDF has a 500-strong women's wing called "Lionesses of National Defence", which operates checkpoints in the Homs area. The women are trained to use Kalashnikovs, heavy machine guns and grenades, and taught to storm and control checkpoints.

The period of training can vary from 2 weeks to a month depending on whether an individual is being trained for basic combat, sniping, or intelligence.

7

Economy

The economy of Syria is based on agriculture, oil, industry and services. Its GDP per capita expanded 80% in the 1960s reaching a peak of 336% of total growth during the 1970s. This proved unsustainable for Syria and the economy shrank by 33% during the 1980s. However the GDP per capita registered a very modest total growth of 12% (1.1% per year on average) during the 1990s due to successful diversification. More recently, the International Monetary Fund (IMF) projected real GDP growth at 3.9% in 2009 from close to 6% in 2008. The two main pillars of the Syrian economy used to be agriculture and oil, which together accounted for about one-half of GDP. Agriculture, for instance, accounted for about 25% of GDP and employed 25% of the total labor force. However, poor climatic conditions and severe drought badly affected the agricultural sector, thus reducing its share in the economy to about 17% of 2008 GDP, down from 20.4% in 2007, according to preliminary data from the Central Bureau of Statistics. On the other hand, higher crude oil prices countered declining oil production and led to higher budgetary and export receipts.

Since the outbreak of the Syrian civil war, the Syrian economy has been hit by massive economic sanctions restricting trade with the Arab League, Australia, Canada, the European Union, (as well as the European countries of Albania, Iceland, Liechtenstein,Macedonia, Moldova, Montenegro, Norway, Serbia, andSwitzerland) Georgia, Japan, Turkey, and the United States.These sanctions and the instability associated with the civil war have reversed previous growth in the Syrian economy to a state of decline for the years 2011 and 2012.

According to the UN, total economic damages of the Syrian civil war are estimated at $143 billion as of late 2013.

By July 2013, the Syrian economy had shrunk 45 percent since the start of the Civil War. Unemployment increased fivefold, the value of the Syrian currency decreased to one-sixth its pre-war value, and the public sector lost USD $15 billion. By the end of 2013, the UN estimated total economic damage of the Syrian civil war at $143 billion. The total economic loss from the Syrian Civil War will reach $237 billion by the end of 2015, according to the United Nations Economic and Social Commission for Western Asia, with the Syrian opposition's capture of Nasib border crossing costing the government a further $500–$700 million a year on top of this.

As a result of the war, the six economies of the greater Levant (Turkey, Syria, Lebanon, Jordan, Iraq, and Egypt) taken together have lost close to US$35 billion in output, measured in 2007 prices.

BASIC INFORMATION

During the 1960s, along socialist lines, the government nationalized most major enterprises and adopted economic policies designed to address regional and class disparities. This legacy of state intervention and price, trade, and foreign exchange controls may have hampered economic growth. Syria also has low investment levels, and relatively low industrial and agricultural productivity. Economic reform has been incremental and gradual. In 2001, Syria legalized private banking. In 2004, four private banks began operations. In August 2004, a committee was formed to supervise the establishment of a stock market. Beyond the financial sector, the Syrian Government has enacted major changes to rental and tax laws, and is reportedly considering similar changes to the commercial code and to other laws, which impact property rights. (Ohachq) Syria has produced heavy-grade oil from fields inside in the northeastsince the late 1960s. In the early 1980s, light-grade, low-sulphur oil was discovered near Deir ez-Zor in eastern Syria. This discovery relieved Syria of the need to import light oil to mix with domestic heavy crude in refineries. Recently, Syrian oil production has been about 379,000 barrels per day (bpd). Syria's oil reserves are being gradually depleted and reached 2.5 billion barrels in January 2009. Experts generally agree that Syria will become a net importer of petroleum by the end of the next decade. Recent developments have helped revitalize the energy sector, including new discoveries and the successful development of its hydrocarbon reserves.

According to the 2009 Syria Report of the Oxford Business Group, the oil sector accounted for 23% of government revenues, 20% of exports, and 22% of GDP in 2008. Syria exported roughly 150,000 bpd in 2008, and oil accounted for a majority of the country's export income.

Ad hoc economic liberalization continues to add wealth inequality, impoverishing the average population while enriching a few people in Syria's private sector. In 1990, the government established an official parallel exchange rate to provide incentives for remittances and exports through official channels. This action improved the supply of basic commodities and contained inflation by removing risk premiums on smuggled commodities.

EXTERNAL TRADE AND INVESTMENT

Despite the mitigation of the severe drought that plagued the region in the late 1990s and the recovery of energy export revenues, Syria's economy faces serious challenges. With almost 60% of its population under the age of 20, unemployment higher than the current 9% is a real possibility unless sustained and strong economic growth takes off.

Commerce has always been important to the Syrian economy, which benefited from the country's strategic location along major east-west trade routes. Syrian cities boast both traditional industries such as weavingand dried-fruit packing and modern heavy industry. Given the policies adopted from the 1960s through the late 1980s, Syria refused to join the "global economy". In late 2001, however, Syria submitted a request to the World Trade Organization(WTO) to begin the accession process. Syria had been an original contracting party of the former General Agreement on Tariffs and Trade but withdrew in 1951 because of Israel's joining. Major elements of current Syrian trade rules would have to change in order to be consistent with the WTO. In March 2007, Syria signed an Association Agreement with the European Union that would encourage both sides to negotiate a free trade agreement before 2010.

The bulk of Syrian imports have been raw materials essential for industry, agriculture, equipment, and machinery. Major exports include crude oil, refined products, raw cotton, clothing, fruits, and cereal grains.

Over time, the government has increased the number of transactions to which the more favorable neighboring country exchange rate applies. The government also introduced a quasi-rate for non-commercial transactions in 2001 broadly in line with prevailing black market rates.

Given the poor development of its own capital markets and Syria's lack of access to international money and capital markets, monetary policy remains captive to the need to cover the fiscal deficit. Although in 2003 Syria lowered interest rates for the first time in 22 years and again in 2004, rates remain fixed by law.

Foreign debt

Syria has made progress in easing its heavy foreign debt burden through bilateral rescheduling deals with virtually all of its key creditors in Europe.In December 2004, Syria and Poland reached an agreement by which Syria would pay $27 million out of the total $261.7 million debt. In January 2005, Russia and Syria signed a deal that wrote off nearly 80% of Syria's debt to Russia, approximately •10.5 billion ($13 billion). The agreement left Syria with less than •3 billion (just over $3.6 billion) owed to Moscow. Half of it would be repaid over the next 10 years, while the rest would be paid into Russian accounts in Syrian banks and could be used for Russian investment projects in Syria and for buying Syrian products. This agreement was part of a weapons deal between Russia and Syria. And later that year Syria reached an agreement with Slovakia, and the Czech Republic to settle debt estimated at $1.6 billion. Again Syria was forgiven the bulk of its debt, in exchange for a one time payment of $150 million.

SECTORS OF THE ECONOMY

Agriculture

Agriculture is a high priority in Syria's economic development plans, as the government seeks to achieve food self-sufficiency, increase export earnings, and halt rural out-migration. Thanks to sustained capital investment, infrastructure development, subsidies of inputs, and price supports, Syria has gone from a net importer of many agricultural products to an exporter of cotton, fruits, vegetables, and other foodstuffs. One of the prime reasons for this turnaround has been the government's investment in huge irrigation systems in northern and northeastern Syria. The agriculture sector, as of 2009, employs about 17 percent of the labor force and generates about 21 percent of the gross domestic product, of which livestock accounted for 16 percent and fruit and grains for more than 40 percent.

Most land is privately owned, a crucial factor behind the sector's success. Of Syria's 196,000 km² (72,000 square miles), about 28 percent of it is cultivated, and 21 percent of that total is irrigated. Most irrigated land is designated "strategic", meaning that it encounters significant state intervention in terms of pricing, subsidies, and marketing controls. "Strategic" products such as wheat, barley, and sugar beets, must be sold to state marketing boards at fixed prices, often above world prices in order to support farmers, but at a significant cost to the state budget. The most widely grown arable crop is wheat, but the most important cash crop is cotton; cotton was the largest single export before the development of the oil sector. Nevertheless, the total area planted with cotton has declined because of an increasing problem of water shortage coupled with old and inefficient irrigation techniques. The output of grains like wheat is often underutilized because of poor storage facilities.

Water and energy are among the most pervasive issues facing the agriculture sector. Another difficulty the agricultural sector suffered from is the government's decision to liberalize the prices of fertilizers, which have increased between 100% and 400%. Drought was an alarming problem in 2008; however, the drought situation slightly improved in 2009. Wheat and barley production about doubled in 2009 compared to 2008. In spite of that, the livelihoods of up to 1 million agricultural workers have been threatened. In response, the UN launched an emergency appeal for $20.2 million. Wheat has been one of the crops most affected, and for the first time in 2 decades Syria has moved from being a net exporter of wheat to a net importer. During the civil war which began in 2011, the Syrian government was forced to put out a tender for 100,000metric tonnes of wheat, one of the few trade products not subject to economic sanctions.

Less than 3 percent of Syria's land area is forested, and only a portion of that is commercially useful. Limited forestry activity is centered in the higher elevations of the mountains just inland from the coast, where rainfall is more abundant.

Energy and mineral resources

Mining

Phosphates are the major minerals exploited in Syria. According to estimates Syria is home to around 1,700 million tons of phosphate reserves. Production dropped sharply in the early 1990s when world demand and prices fell, but output has since increased to more than

2.4 million tons. Syria produced about 1.9% of the world's phosphate rock output and was the world's ninth ranked producer of phosphate rock in 2009. Other major minerals produced in Syria include cement, gypsum, industrial sand (silica), marble, natural crude asphalt, nitrogen fertilizer, phosphate fertilizer, salt, steel, and volcanic tuff, which generally are not produced for export.

Oil and natural gas

Syria is a relatively small oil producer, accounting for just 0.5 percent of the global production in 2010. Although Syria is not a major oil exporter by Middle Eastern standards, oil is a major pillar of the economy. According to the International Monetary Fund, oil sales for 2010 were projected to generate $3.2 billion for the Syrian government and account for 25.1% of the state's revenue.

Electrical generation

In 2001 Syria reportedly produced 23.3 billion kilowatt hours (kWh) of electricity and consumed 21.6 billion kWh. As of January 2002, Syria's total installed electric generating capacity was 7.6 gigawatts (GW), with fuel oil and natural gasserving as the primary energy sources and 1.5 GW generated by hydroelectric power. A network totaling 45 GW linking the electric power grids of Syria, Egypt, and Jordan was completed in March 2001. Syria's electric supply capacity is an important national priority, and the government hopes to add 3,000 megawatts of power generating capacity by 2010 at a probable cost of US$2 billion, but progress has been slowed by a lack of investment capital. Power plants in Syria are undergoing intensive maintenance, and four new generating plants have been built. The power distribution network has serious problems, with transmission losses estimated as high as 25 percent of total generated capacity as a result of poor quality wires and transformer stations. A project for the expansion and upgrading of the power transmission network is scheduled for completion in 2005.

As of May 2009 it was reported that the Islamic Development Bank and the Syrian government signed an agreement stating that the bank would provide a •100 million loan for the expansion of Deir Ali power station in Syria.

Nuclear energy

Syria abandoned its plans to build a VVER-440 reactor after the Chernobyl accident. The plans for a nuclear program were revived at the beginning of the 2000s when Syria negotiated with Russia to build a nuclear facility that would include a nuclear power plant and a seawater atomic desalination plant.

Industry and manufacturing

The industrial sector, which includes mining, manufacturing, construction, and petroleum, accounted for 27.3 percent of gross domestic product (GDP) in 2010 and employed about 16 percent of the labor force. The main industrial products are petroleum, textiles, food processing, beverages, tobacco, phosphate rock mining, cement, oil seeds crushing, and car assembly. Syria's manufacturing sector was largely state dominated until the 1990s, when economic reforms allowed greater local and foreign private-sector participation. Private participation remains constrained, however, by the lack of investment funds, input/output pricing limits, cumbersome customs and foreign exchange regulations, and poor marketing.

Because land prices are not controlled by the state, real estate is one of the few domestic avenues for investment with realistic and safe returns. Activity in the construction sector tends to mirror changes in the economy. Investment Law No. 10 of 1991, which opened the country to foreign investment in some areas, marked the beginning of a strong revival, with growth in real terms increasing over 2001 and 2002.

Services

Services accounted for 45.3 percent of gross domestic product (GDP) in 2009 and employed 67 percent of the labor force, including government, in 2008. As of May 2009, it was reported that Damascus office prices are skyrocketing.

Banking and finance

The Syrian government under Assad started its reform efforts by changing the regulatory environment in the financial sector, including the introduction of private banks and the opening of the Damascus Securities Exchange in March 2009. In 2001, Syria legalized private banking and the sector, while still nascent, has been growing. Foreign banks were given licenses in December 2002, in compliance with Law 28 March 2001, which allows the establishment of private and joint-venture banks. Foreigners are allowed up to 49 percent ownership of a bank, but may not hold a controlling stakes. As of January 2010, 13 private banks had opened, including two Islamic banks.

Syria has taken gradual steps to loosen controls over foreign exchange. In 2003, the government canceled a law that criminalized private sector use of foreign currencies, and in 2005 it issued legislation that allowed licensed private banks to sell specific amounts of foreign currency to Syrian citizens under certain circumstances and to the private sector to finance imports. In October 2009, theSyrian Government further loosened its restrictions on currency transfers by allowing Syrians travelling abroad to withdraw the equivalent of up to U.S. $10,000 from their Syrian pound accounts. In practice, the decision allows local banks to open accounts of a maximum of U.S. $10,000 that their clients can use for their international payment cards. The holders of these accounts will be able to withdraw up to U.S. $10,000 per month while travelling abroad.

To attract investment and to ease access to credit, the government allowed investors in 2007 to receive loans and other credit instruments from foreign banks, and to repay the loans and any accrued interest through local banks using project proceeds. In February 2008, the government permitted investors to receive loans in foreign currencies from local private banks to finance capital investments. Syria's exchange rate is fixed, and the government maintains two official rates—one rate on which the budget and the value of imports, customs, and other official transactions are based, and a second set by the Central Bank on a daily basis that covers all other financial transactions. The government passed a law in 2006 which permits the operation of private money exchange companies. However, a small black market for foreign currency is still active.

Still after the opening of the financial sector, the six specialized state banks, the Central Bank of Syria, Commercial Bank of Syria, Agricultural Co-Operative Bank, Industrial Bank, Popular Credit Bank, and Real Estate Bank, are major financial operators. They each extend funds to, and take deposits from, a particular sector. The Central Bank of Syria controls all foreign exchange and trade transactions and gives priority to lending to the public sector. The Industrial Bank also is directed more toward the public sector, although it is under-capitalized. As a result, the private sector often is forced to bank abroad, a process that is more expensive and therefore a poor solution to industrial financing needs. Many business peopletravel abroad to deposit or borrow funds. It is estimated that Syrians have deposited US$6 billion in Lebanese banks. The U.S. sanctions of May 2004 may have increased the role of Lebanese and European banks because a ban on transactions between U.S. financial institutions and the Central Bank of Syria created an increase in demand for intermediary sources for U.S. dollar transfers. The US, EU, Arab league and Turkey all imposed Sanctions on the central bank because of the Syrian Civil War.

Tourism

Non-Arab visitors to Syria reached 1.1 million in 2002, which includes all visitors to the country, not just tourists. The total number of Arab visitors in 2002 was 3.2 million, most from Lebanon, Jordan, Saudi Arabia, and Iraq. Many Iraqi businesspeople set up ventures in Syrian ports to run import operations for Iraq, causing an increased number of Iraqis visiting Syria in 2003–4. Tourism is a potentially large foreign exchange earner and a source of economic growth.Tourism generated more than 6 percent of Syria's gross domestic product in 2000, and more reforms were discussed to increase tourism revenues. As a result of projects derived from Investment Law No. 10 of 1991, hotel bed numbers had increased 51 percent by 1999 and increased further in 2001. A plan was announced in 2002 to develop ecological tourism with visits to desert and nature preserves. Two luxury hotels opened in Damascus at the end of 2004. Since March 2011 tourism in Syria has fallen due to the ongoing civil war.

Labour

Syria has a population of approximately 21 million people, and Syrian government figures place the population growth rate at 2.37%, with 65% of the population under the age of 35 and more than 40% under the age of 15. Each year more than 200,000 new job seekers enter the Syrian job market, but the economy has not been able to absorb them. In 2010, the Syrian labor force was estimated to total about 5.5 million people. An estimated 67 percent worked in the services sectorincluding government, 17 percent in agriculture, and 16 percent in industry in 2008. Government and public sectoremployees constitute about 30% of the total labor force and are paid very low salaries and wages.

According to Syrian Government statistics, the unemployment rate in 2009 was 12.6%; however, more accurate independent sources place it closer to 20%. About 70 percent of Syria's workforce earns less than US$100 per month. Anecdotal evidence suggests that many more Syrians are seeking work over the border in Lebanon than official numbers indicate.In 2002 the Unemployment Commission (UC) was established, tasked with creating several hundred thousand jobs over a five-year period. As of June 2009 it was reported that some 700,000 households in Syria - about 3.5 million people - have no income. Government officials acknowledge that the economy is not growing at a pace sufficient to create enough new jobs annually to match population growth. The UN Development Program announced in 2005 that 30% of the Syrian population lives in poverty and 11.4% live below the subsistence level.

Opportunity cost of conflict

A report by Strategic Foresight Group, an India-based think tank, calculated the opportunity cost of conflict for the Middle East for 1991 — 2010 at US$12 trillion in 2006 dollars. Syria's share in this was US$152 billion, more than four times the projected 2010 GDP of US$36 billion.

The Syrian Center for Policy Research stated in March 2015 that, by then, nearly three million Syrians had lost their jobs because of the civil war, causing the loss of the primary source of income of more than 12 million people; unemployment levels "surged" from 14.9 percent in 2011 to 57.7 percent at the end of 2014. As a result, 4 in 5 Syrians were by then living in poverty, with 30 percent of the population living in "abject poverty" and frequently unable to meet basic household food needs.

AGRICULTURE IN SYRIA

Until the mid-1970s, agriculture in Syria had been the primary economic activity. At independence in 1946, agriculture(including minor forestry and fishing) was the most important sector of the economy, and in the 1940s and early 1950s, agriculture was the fastest growing sector. Wealthy merchants from such urban centers as Aleppo invested in land development and irrigation. Rapid expansion of the cultivated area and increased output stimulated the rest of the economy. However, by the late 1950s, little land that could easily be brought under cultivation remained. During the 1960s, agricultural output stagnated because of political instability and land reform. Between 1953 and 1976, agriculture's contribution to GDPincreased (in constant prices) by only 3.2 percent, approximately the rate of population growth. From 1976 to 1984 growth declined to 2 percent a year. Thus, agriculture's importance in the economy declined as other sectors grew more rapidly.

In 1981, as in the 1970s, 53 percent of the population was still classified as rural, although movement to the cities continued to accelerate. However, in contrast to the 1970s, when 50 percent of the labor force was employed in agriculture, by 1983 agriculture employed only 30 percent of the labor force. Furthermore, by the mid-1980s, unprocessed farm products accounted for only 4 percent of exports, equivalent to 7 percent of non-petroleum exports. Industry, commerce, and transportation still depended on farm produce and related agro-business, but agriculture's preeminent position had clearly eroded. By 1985 agriculture (including a little forestry and fishing) contributed only 16.5 percent to GDP, down from 22.1 percent in 1976.

By the mid-1980s, the Syrian government had taken measures to revitalize agriculture. The 1985 investment budget saw a sharp rise in allocations for agriculture, including land reclamation and irrigation. The government's renewed commitment to agricultural development in the 1980s, by expanding cultivation and extending irrigation, promised brighter prospects for Syrian agriculture in the 1990s.

Water resources

Water is a scarce resource in Syria as it is throughout the Middle East, but Syria is more fortunate than many other countries. Sufficient rainfall supports cultivation in an arc from the southwest, near the border with Israel and Lebanon, extending northward to the Turkish border and eastward along that border to Iraq. The other main area of cultivation, although dependent on irrigation, is along the Euphrates and its major tributaries.

Rainfall is highest along the Mediterranean coast and on the mountains just inland; Syria's limited forestry activities are concentrated in the higher elevations of these mountains. Rainfall diminishes sharply as one moves eastward of the mountains paralleling the coast and southward from the Turkish border. The arc of cultivation from the southwest (and east of the coastal mountains) to the northeast is largely semiarid, having as annual rainfall between 300 and 600 millimeters. Areas south and east of the arc receive less than 300 millimeters of rain annually, classifying the land as arid. Grass and coarse vegetation suitable for limited grazing grow in part of this arid belt, and the rest is desert of little agricultural value.

Rainfall is concentrated between October and May. Without irrigation, cropping is finished by summer, when the climate is very hot and dry. Moreover, the amount of rainfall and its timing varies considerably from year to year, making rain-fed farming extremely risky. When rains are late or inadequate, farmers do not even plant a crop. Successive years of droughtare not uncommon and cause havoc not only for farmers but for the rest of the economy. In the mid-1980s, about two-thirds of agricultural output (plant and animal production) depended on rainfall.

Extension and improvement of irrigation systems could substantially raise agricultural output. For example, in 1985, because of the expansion of irrigation systems, Syria's agricultural output rose 10 percent above the drought-plagued yield of 1984. Yields from irrigated fields have been several times higher than from rain-fed fields, and many irrigated areas could grow more than a single crop a year. Development of irrigation systems, however, is both costly and time consuming.

Syria's major irrigation potential lies in the Euphrates River valley and its two major tributaries, the Balikh and Khabur rivers in the northeast portion of the country. The Euphrates is the largest river in Southwest Asia and it rises in Turkey, where relatively heavy rain- and snowfall provide runoff much of the year. The river flows southeastward across the arid Syrian Plateau into Iraq, where it joins the Tigris River shortly before emptying into the Persian Gulf. In addition to Syria, both Turkey and Iraq use dams on the Euphrates for hydroelectric power, water control, storage, and irrigation. In the mid-1980s, about one half of the annual Euphrates River flow was used by the three nations.

Syrians have long used the Euphrates for irrigation, but, because the major systems were destroyed centuries ago, they make only limited use of the river's flow. In the mid-1980s, the Euphrates River accounted for over 85 percent of the country's surface water resources, but its water was used for only about two-fifths (200,000 hectares) of the land then under irrigated cultivation. In 1984, about 44 percent of irrigated land still used water from wells. Several project studies were conducted after World War II, and, in the 1960s, the Soviet Union agreed to provide financial and technical assistance for the Tabqa Dam, a large hydroelectric power station, and portions of the major Euphrates irrigation project.

The dam, located at al-Thawrah, a short distance upriver from the town of Raqqa, is earth fill, 60 meters high and four and one-half kilometers long. Construction began in 1968, and work was essentially completed by 1978. The Rabqa Dam was closed in 1973, when Lake

Assad, the artificial lake behind the dam, began filling. About 80 kilometers long, Lake Assad averages about 8 kilometers in width and holds nearly 12 billion cubic meters of water. The power plant has eight 100-megawatt turbines for power generation and transmission lines to Aleppo. Until 1983, the power station operated at 65 percent of capacity, generating 2,500 megawatts a year or about 45 percent of Syria's electricity. In 1986, the power station operated at only 30 to 40 percent of capacity because of the low water level in Lake Assad. Provisions were made, however, for future construction to raise the height of the dam, increase the capacity of Lake Assad by about 10 percent, and increase the number of turbines. In 1984, as a result of the disappointing performance of the dam, the government studied the possibility of building a second dam upstream from al-Thawrah between Ash Shajarah, situated on the northern edge of Lake Assad, and Jarabulus, located near the Turkish border. The ultimate goal of the Euphrates irrigation project is to provide 640,000 cultivable hectares by the year 2000, in effect doubling the area of Syria's irrigated land in the mid-1970s. In 1978, observers believed that 20,000 to 30,000 hectares of land had been irrigated and that new housing, roads, and farms had been completed for the 8,000 farmers displaced by the creation of Lake Assad. In the early 1980s, Syrian officials had anticipated the completion of irrigation on about 50,000 to 100,000 hectares in the Euphrates basin, with about 20,000 hectares planned for completion each year after that. The Fourth Five-Year Plan actually called for irrigating an additional 240,000 hectares by the end of the plan. In 1984, however, Syrian government statistics revealed that only 60,000 hectares were actually being irrigated. Ten years after its inception, the Euphrates irrigation project irrigated only about 10 percent of its long-term goal.

A variety of complex, interrelated problems frustrated realization of targeted irrigation goals. Technical problems withgypsum subsoil, which caused irrigation canals to collapse, proved more troublesome than at first anticipated. Large cost overruns on some of the irrigation projects made them much more expensive than planned and created difficulties in financing additional projects. Moreover, these large irrigation projects required several years before returns on the investments began. There was also doubt about whether farmers could be attracted back from urban areas or enticed from more crowded agricultural areas to the sparsely populated Euphrates Valley. Another complication is that the Euphrates flow is insufficient for the irrigation needs of the three countries—Turkey, Iraq, and Syria that share the river. In 1962, talks on allotment of Euphrates water began and continued sporadically throughout the 1970s and early 1980s, but acrimonious relations between Syria and Iraq hampered final agreements. In fact, in 1978 when Syria began filling Lake Assad and water to Iraq was greatly reduced, the two countries almost went to war. In addition, Turkey's use of Euphrates' waters for itsKeban Dam assures that water levels in Lake Assad will remain low. This problem will undoubtedly continue into the 1990s, when Turkey completes construction of the Atatürk Dam.

By 1987, numerous Euphrates irrigation projects and additional irrigation projects throughout the country were proceeding, but what had been accomplished was not clear. Projects initiated in the 1980s included irrigation of 21,000 hectares in the Raqqa area pilot project, 27,000 hectares reclaimed in the Euphrates middle-stage project, and about half of a 21,000-hectare plot reclaimed with Soviet assistance in the Meskanah region. There were also major irrigation schemes involving 130,000 hectares in the Meskanah, Ghab valley, and Aleppo Plains project. In addition, Syria completed a small regulatory dam with three seventy-megawatt turbines approximately twenty- five kilometers downstream from Tabaqah. In the mid-1980s, work continued on the Baath Dam, located twenty-seven kilometers from the Euphrates dam, and the Tishrin Dam on the Kabir ash Shamali River near Latakia evolved from the planning to implementation stage. The government also planned to construct as many as three dams on the Khabur River in northeast Syria and more effectively use the waters of theYarmuk River in southwest Syria. Foreign contractors carried out most of these major development projects. The Soviets and Romanians were particularly active in irrigation schemes as part of their economic aid programs. French, British, Italian, and Japanese firms, the World Bank, and Saudi Arabian and Kuwaiti development assistance funds were deeply involved in financing and implementing these projects.

In the 1980s, there was good potential for expanding and refining irrigation in the western portion of Syria. The government obtained economical results using small impoundments that held winter runoffs to supplement rain-fed cultivation and to provide some summer irrigation. Small storage areas for water from wells and springs permitted additional irrigation. Farmers, however, had not yet turned to sprinkler systems or trickle irrigation, which would considerably reduce the amount of water needed for cultivation.

Land use

The bulk of the country is arid, with little vegetation. In 1984, nearly 20 percent was classified as desert. Another 45 percent of the land was classified as steppe and pasture, although its grazing capacity was very limited — much like land in the American Southwest. Less than 3 percent of the land was forested, with only part of it commercially useful. Cultivatable land amounted to 33 percent of the total area. In 1984, 91.7 percent of the total cultivable area of 6.17 million hectares was cultivated.

Major expansion of the cultivated area occurred in the 1940s and 1950s. Much of the expansion was the result of investment by wealthy urban merchants, many of whom were from the country's religious minorities. Their innovations included large-scale use of farm machinery, pumps, and irrigation where possible, and different tenure arrangements for farm operators than were used in other parts of the country. But the efforts of the merchants of Aleppo and other commercial centers largely exhausted the potential for bringing new land under cultivation. The area of cultivation (6.9 million hectares) and land irrigated (760,000 hectares) peaked in 1963 and has been appreciably smaller since then. In 1984, approximately 5.7 million hectares were under cultivation, with 618,000 irrigated.

Opinions differ as to the causes of the decline of cultivated and irrigated areas after 1963. Some observers say that marginal lands brought under cultivation proved uneconomical after a few years and were abandoned. Others claim that the merchant developers used exploitative techniques that eventually reduced the productivity of the soil. Still other observers blame land-reform measures, which coincided with the decline of the cultivated and irrigated areas. Each view is probably somewhat valid.

In the future, expansion of the cultivated area will be slow and costly. Although the Euphrates irrigation projects will provide water to bring additional land under cultivation, growth will be partly offset by the loss of arable land to urban expansion, roads, and other facilities for a growing population. After the disappointing results of the Euphrates irrigation projects through the mid-1980s, the government began to develop rain-fed agriculture to offset potential setbacks in the Euphrates scheme. Drainage investments also will be required to maintain cultivation on some irrigated areas that currently suffer fromwater logging or excessive salinity.

Land reform

The dynamism of the agricultural sector caused by the opening of new farmland in the north and northeast through investments of wealthy merchants worsened the situation for the poor and often landless rural population. In 1950 the first Syrian constitution placed a limit on the size of farm holdings, but the necessary implementing legislation was not passed until 1958, after the union of Syria and Egypt.

The 1958 agrarian reform laws were similar to those in Egypt and not only limited the size of landholdings but also provided sharecroppers and farm laborers with greater economic and legal security and a more equitable share of crops. The Agricultural Relations Law laid down principles to be observed in administering tenancy leases, protected tenants against arbitrary eviction, and reduced, under a fixed schedule, the share of crops taken by landlords. It also authorized agricultural laborers to organize unions and established commissions to review and fix minimum wages for agricultural workers.

However, by the time Syria withdrew from the merger with Egypt in 1961, opposition from large landowners, administrative difficulties, and severe crop failures during the prolonged 1958- 61 drought had effectively curtailed movement toward land reform. The conservative regime in power from 1961 until March 1963 blocked implementation of the land-reform program in practice by enacting a number of amendments to the original law that substantially raised the ceilings on ownership and opened loopholes.

Shortly after the Baath Party seized power in March 1963, Decree Law 88 of 1963 was promulgated, canceling the actions of the previous regime and reinstating the original agrarian reform laws with important modifications. One of the most significant modifications was lowering the limit on the size of holdings and providing flexibility in accordance with the productivity of the land. The new ceilings on landownership were set at between 15 and 55 hectares on irrigated land and 80 and 300 hectares on rain-fed land, depending on the area and rainfall. Land in excess of the ceilings was to be expropriated within five years. The compensation payable to the former owners was fixed at ten times the average three-year rental value of the expropriated land, plus interest on the principal at the rate of 1.5 percent for forty years.

The expropriated land was to be redistributed to tenants, landless farmers, and farm laborers in holdings of up to a maximum of eight hectares of irrigated land or thirty to forty five hectares of rain-fed land per family. Beneficiaries of the redistribution program were required to form state-supervised cooperatives. The 1963 law reduced the price of redistributed land to the beneficiaries to the equivalent of one-fourth of the compensation for expropriation. The land recipients paid this amount in equal installments to their cooperatives over a twenty-year period to finance such cooperative activities as development, dispensaries, schools, and cultural centers.

By 1975 (the latest available data in early 1987) 1.4 million hectares (68,000 hectares of irrigated land) had been expropriated, primarily in the early years of the program. Distribution moved much more slowly. By 1975, redistributed land had amounted to 466,000 hectares (61,000 hectares of irrigated land) and undistributed land to 351,000 hectares. In addition, there were 254,000 hectares of land that had been allocated to cooperatives, ministries, and other organizations, and 330,000 hectares that were categorized as excluded and sold land. Although it was far from clear what the disposition was in the latter two categories, the statistical data gave the impression that land reform had not transformed the former numerous farm sharecroppers and laborers into landowners. This impression was supported by government data indicating that slightly more than 50,000 family heads (over 300,000 people) had received land under the reform program. In addition, at various times the government offered state farmland for sale to the landless on the same terms as expropriated land, but reported sales were relatively small; farmers apparently chose to lease the land.

Most observers credited land reform measures with liquidating concentration of very large estates and weakening political power of landowners. Some government data of uncertain coverage and reliability indicated that before land reform more than half of agricultural holdings consisted of one hundred hectares or more, but after reform such large holdings amounted to less than 1 percent. The same data showed that smallholdings (seven hectares or less) had increased from about one-eighth before land reform to just over one-half of total holdings after reform, and that 42 percent of holdings were between eight and twenty-five hectares. Other government statistics indicated that holdings of twenty five hectares or less, representing 30 percent of all land under cultivation before 1959, represented 93 percent in 1975. A May 1980 Order in Council mandated additional expropriations and further reduced the size of agricultural holdings. Data from the 1970 census revealed that the average farm holding was about ten hectares, and that one-fifth of the rural population remained landless. Despite the Baath Party's commitment to land reform, the private sector controlled 74 percent of Syria's arable land in 1984.

Role of government

Government involvement in agriculture was minimal prior to Syria's union with Egypt. Although state intervention in the agricultural sector increased following the union, the government avoided playing a direct role in cultivation. In 1984, private farmers tilled 74 percent of the cultivated land, cooperatives 25 percent, and public organizations (essentially state farms) 1 percent.

Government involvement arose indirectly from socialist transformation measures in various parts of the economy and directly from government efforts to fill the void in the countryside caused by land reform. As an example of the former, the Agricultural Cooperative Bank, a private bank established in the eighteenth century but inherited by the socialist regime, in the mid-1960s became the single source for direct production credits to farmers. The bank had limited funds and confined itself almost completely to short-term financing, the bulk of which went to cotton growers. Part of its lending was in kind — primarily seeds, pesticides, and fertilizers at subsidized prices. Although the bank appeared effective, there was insufficient credit through the 1960s and early 1970s for farmers who did not grow cotton and for long-term loans for such needs as machinery or capital improvements. In the mid-1970s, the flow of funds to the bank increased, thus allowing it to expand its lending to the agricultural sector. The bank became an important influence in shaping farmers' production decisions, particularly in cotton.

In the 1960s, government marketing organizations for the major agricultural commodities were established. The Cotton Marketing Organization, as noted, had a complete monopoly. Organizations for tobacco and sugar beets had purchasing monopolies, set the farm purchase prices, and supervised the processing and marketing of their respective commodities. An organization for grains set prices, purchased some of the farmers' surplus, and supervised the marketing of the remainder through private dealers. The government also set prices for several other agricultural commodities, most imports, and many consumer items.

Some economists attributed part of the stagnation in agriculture to the government's pricing of farm produce. Farm prices remained unchanged over long periods and by the 1970s and 1980s were quite low relative to world prices. Some smuggling out of farm products for sale in Turkey, Iraq, and Lebanon resulted as well as some black marketing in controlled commodities. Pricing also was not coordinated to achieve agricultural goals. Although the Ministry of Agriculture attempted to get farmers to increase wheat production, the government's desire to keep basic food costs low for urban consumers imposed low grain prices for farmers. The ministry also urged farmers to shift irrigated areas from cotton to wheat at the same time that the farm price of cotton was raised relative to that of wheat.

Aware of the problems, officials made efforts to improve pricing policy. By 1977 prices paid to farmers had risen substantially and favored grains and some industrial crops over cotton. In fact, the 1977 prices (when converted to dollars at the official exchange rate) paid to farmers for wheat, soybeans, and sugar beets were substantially higher (more than 100 percent for wheat) than the prices paid to American farmers for those products. In 1985 the government again raised procurement prices for a variety of crops. Prices for hard wheat rose by 9 percent, soft wheat by 14 percent, red lentils by 13 percent,white lentils by 18 percent, and barley by 22 percent from the preceding year.

When land reform was introduced, those receiving expropriated or government land were required to join farm cooperatives. Cooperatives were expected to furnish the organization, techniques, credit, and joint use of machinery to replace and expand the functions supplied by the landowners and managers of the large estates. Syrian farmers' individualism and aversion to cooperatives may explain their apparent preference for renting land from the government rather than buying the land and having to join a cooperative. Whether the cause was aversion by farmers or an inability by the government to organize and staff cooperatives, as some economists suggest, the cooperative movement grew slowly until the early 1970s, but accelerated thereafter. In 1976 there were 3,385 agricultural cooperatives with 256,000 members—more than double the number and membership in 1972. By 1984 there were 4,050 agricultural cooperatives with 440,347 members. Statistics do not distinguish between cooperatives for farmers receiving expropriated or government land and voluntary cooperatives of established landowners.

Officials expected cooperatives eventually to mitigate, if not eliminate, two serious agricultural problems. First, farmers tended to specialize in certain crops without practicing crop rotation. Second, substantial amounts of arable land were leftfallow each year. In the 1970s, government extension workers and cooperatives strongly urged farmers to rotate cropping in a pattern that would maintain the fertility of the soil and avoid having cultivable fields left fallow. Cooperatives were also expected to facilitate the use of machinery after land reform reduced the average size of farms, partly by cooperative ownership of equipment and partly by pooling small plots into an economically sized bloc that would then be cultivated as a single unit in the cropping rotation. By 1986 it was not clear how much success cooperatives had achieved in crop rotation or mechanization, but statistics showed an accelerated use of farm equipment by the agricultural sector after the October 1973 War.

Cropping and production

Because only about 16% of the cropped area was irrigated, the output of agriculture (both plant and animal) was heavily dependent on rainfall. The great variation in the amounts and timing of rainfall can immediately cause very substantial shifts in areas planted, yields, and production, but the effect on livestock is less predictable. When drought is unusually severe or prolonged, loss of animals may depress livestock production for several years. In 1984 crop production accounted for 72 percent of the value of agricultural output; livestock and animal products, 28 percent. Livestock alone, not counting products such as milk, wool, and eggs, were 11 percent of the total.

In 1984 crop production amounted to LS13.6 billion. The United States Department of Agriculture (USDA) valued Syrian 1985 production at US $1.1 billion. Grains contributed 15 percent to the value of total crop production in 1984, in contrast to 41 percent in 1974. Industrial crops remained 20 percent of the total. Fruits rose from 15 to 25 percent of the total, and vegetables rose from 16 to 35 percent. In 1984, grain continued to be planted on 66 percent of the cultivated land, consistent with the mid-1970s percentage.

Fluctuations in rainfall resulted in major variations in crop production throughout the 1980s. In 1980, wheat was planted on 1.4 million hectares, yielding 2.2 million tons—the largest wheat harvest since the early 1960s. In 1984, wheat planted on 1.1 million hectares produced only 1.1 million tons. In 1980 and 1984, barley was planted on 1.2 million hectares, but production fell from 1.6 million tons in 1980, the peak year, to 303,500 tons in 1984, revealing the impact of the drought on rain-dependent crops. In 1985 wheat and barley crops rebounded to 1.7 million tons and 740,000 tons, respectively. In 1984, Syria grew a record 60,000 tons of corn.

Earlier stagnation of agricultural output meant primarily stagnation of grain production. Instead of exporting wheat, in the 1980s Syria became a net importer. In 1985 Syria imported 1.4 million tons of wheat, worth more than LS800 million. In addition, cereal imports rose from LS368 million in 1982 to LS.1.6 billion in 1984, amounting to 56 percent of the LS2.85 billion bill for food imports that year.

During the 1970s and 1980s, the government encouraged greater grain production by providing improved high-yield seeds, raising prices paid to farmers, and urging shifts toward wheat growing on some irrigated land formerly planted in cotton. Its intent was to raise grain output at least to self-sufficiency to ease the pressure on the balance of payments. Beginning in the late 1970s, the government showed increased interest in improving rain-fed agriculture and acquired funding from the World Bank, International Fund for Agricultural Development, and the UN Development Program for a US$76.3 million project to expand food production and raise the standard of living in Daraa and As Suwayda provinces. In addition, Syrian agriculture benefited from research projects undertaken by the International Center for Agricultural Research in the Dry Areas' (ICARDA) branch office located near Aleppo. ICARDA helped develop the Sham-1 durum wheat and Sham-2 bread wheatused by Syrian farmers in the mid-1980s and demonstrated through its research the positive effect of phosphate fertilizerson barley crops in dry areas, encouraging the government to consider a change in agricultural strategy.

In the 1980s, vegetables and fruits exhibited the fastest growth rates of the various crops, although they started from a low base. Urbanization and rising incomes spurred cultivation of these products, which were also generally exempt from official price control. Fruits and vegetables were grown primarily in the northwest and coastal plain in irrigated fields and where rainfall and groundwater were greatest. However, Syria lagged considerably behind Lebanon in cultivation of fruits and vegetables in similar terrain, and seasonal fruits were consistently smuggled in from Lebanon in the 1980s.

Cotton

Syria has produced cotton since ancient times, and its cultivation increased in importance in the 1950s and 1960s. Until superseded by petroleum in 1974, cotton was Syria's most important industrial and cash crop, and the country's most important foreign exchange earner, accounting for about one-third of Syria's export earnings. In 1976 the country was the tenth largest cotton producer in the world and the fourth largest exporter. Almost all the cotton was grown on irrigated land, largely in the area northeast of Aleppo. Syrian cotton was medium staple, similar to cotton produced in other developing countries but of lower quality than the extra-long staple variety produced in Egypt. The cotton was handpicked, although mechanical pickers were tried in the 1970s in an attempt to hold down rising labor costs.

Cotton production (cotton lint) rose from 13,000 tons in 1949 to 180,000 tons in 1965. However, land reform and nationalization of the cotton gins precipitated a sharp decline in output in the next few years. Beginning in 1968 and during the 1970s annual lint production hovered around 150,000 tons. However, in 1983 and 1984, Syria enjoyed a record cotton crop of 523,418 tons, and the third highest yield in the world, estimated at 3 tons per hectare. To a large measure, this increase was attributable to the government's raising cotton procurement prices by 44 percent in 1981-82, and by another 20 percent in 1982-83.

Although the area under cotton cultivation has declined since the early 1960s, yields have increased as a result of improved varieties of seed and increasing amounts of fertilizer. The area planted dropped from over 250,000 hectares in the early 1960s to 140,000 hectares in 1980. In response to the jump in procurement prices by 1984, it increased to 178,000 hectares. As domestic consumption of cotton increased in the 1960s and 1970s, the government built several textile mills to gain the value added from exports of fabrics and clothes compared with exports of raw cotton. In the 1980s, cotton exports averaged 120,000 tons, ranging from a low of 72,800 tons to a record of 151,000 tons in 1983. Syria's seed cotton harvest was 462,000 tons in 1985, about 3 percent higher than in 1984. Approximately 110,000 tons of the 1985 harvest were destined for export markets. Major foreign customers in 1985 included the Soviet Union (18,000 tons), Algeria (14,672 tons), Italy (13,813 tons), and Spain (10,655 tons).

The government's goal of expanding and diversifying food production created intense competition for irrigated land and encouraged the practice of double cropping. Because cotton did not lend itself to double cropping, the cultivated cotton area was declining in real terms. However, the area under cultivation and significance of other industrial crops substantially increased during the 1980s. For example, the government initiated policies designed to stimulate sugar beet cultivation to supply the sugar factories built in the 1970s and 1980s. The area under cultivation for sugar beets rose from 22,000 hectares in 1980 to 35,700 hectares in 1984, with sugar beet harvests totaling over 1 million tons in 1984. Syria, however, still imported LS287 million worth of sugar in 1984. USDA estimated that Syria would achieve tobacco self-sufficiency in 1985, with harvests of 12.3 million tons (dry weight) compared with 12.2 million tons in 1984. Although yields per hectare fell slightly in 1985, USDA expected imports to match exports. In 1984 Syria imported 559 tons of tobacco and exported 225 tons. Other important commercial crops included olives and tomatoes.

PETROLEUM INDUSTRY IN SYRIA

The petroleum industry in Syria forms a major part of the economy of Syria. According to the International Monetary Fund, oil sales for 2010 were projected to generate $3.2 billion for the Syrian government and account for 25.1% of the state's revenue.

Syria is a relatively small oil producer, accounting for just 0.5 percent of the global production in 2010. Although Syria isnot a major oil exporter by Middle Eastern standards, oil is a major pillar of the economy.

Geography

Syria is the only significant crude oil producing country in the Eastern Mediterraneanregion, which includes Jordan, Lebanon, Israel and the Palestinian territories. According to the Oil and Gas Journal, Syria had 2,500,000,000 barrels (400,000,000 m³) of petroleum reserves as of 1 January 2010. Syria's known oil reserves are mainly in the eastern part of the country in the Deir ez-Zor Governoratenear its border with Iraq and along the Euphrates River; a number of smaller fields are located in the center of the country. In 2010, Syria produced around 385,000 barrels (61,200 m³) per day of crude oil. Oil production has stabilized after falling for a number of years, and is poised to turn around as new fields come on line. In 2008, Syria produced 5.3 billion cubic metres (1.9×10^{11} cu ft) of natural gas, and two years later in 2010, it increased production to 5.3 m³ (190 cu ft). While much of its oil is exported to Europe, Syria's natural gas is used in reinjection forenhanced oil recovery and for domestic electricity generation.

Although Syria produces relatively modest quantities of oil and gas, its location is strategic in terms of regional security and prospective energy transit routes. The first section of the Arab Gas Pipeline to enter Syria, totalling 600 kilometres (370 mi) through Syria, starts at the Jordan–Syria border in the south, connecting to Tishreen and Deir Ali power stations. This was subsequently extended to connect to Deir Ammar power station in Lebanon and Baniyas in Syria. A further section was planned to continue up to the Turkish border, but the ongoing civil war is expected to further delay this connection.

History

Syrian oil exploration first began in 1933 during the French Mandate, by the Iraq Petroleum Company (a consortium made up of Shell, BP, Exxon-Mobil, Total, and Gulbekian). In 1949 James W. Menhall, an independent oil producer from Illinois, was approached by Syrian President Shukri al-Quwatli to come to Syria to prospect for oil, after the IPC had drilled eleven wells and given up hope of finding any oil in Syria. He was awarded a concession on 17 May 1955 by unanimous vote of the Syrian parliament and started drilling in April 1956. In September 1956, Menhall discovered the Karatchok oil field with over 1 billion barrels of reserves. Six consecutive wells were drilled, each producing in excess of 4,000 barrels (640 m³). Menhall was just commencing preparations to drill the adjoining Rumeilan oil field (with over 500 million barrels of reserves) when, on 5 October 1958, President Nasser of Egypt, as President of the United Arab Republic, expropriated Menhall's concession and confiscated his equipment and three drilling rigs without compensation. The Syrian government, under the Baath Party leadership, has since refused to consider any compensation. The Syrian oil industry took off in 1968, when the Karatchok oil field began production after a pipeline connecting it to the Homs refinery was completed, although Syria did not begin exporting oil until the mid-1980s.

In 2009, Syria's net petroleum exports were estimated to be 148,000 bbl/d (23,500 m³/d). All oil exports are marketed by Sytrol, Syria's state oil marketing firm, which sells most of its volumes under 12-month contracts. Syrian crude oil exports go mostly to the European Union, in particular Germany, Italy, and France, totaling an estimated 137,400 bbl/d (21,840 m³/d) in 2009, according to Eurostat. In 2010, the European Union as a whole spent \$4.1 billion on Syrian oil imports. Local exporters of oil in Syria include the Altoun Group in Maraba Damascus Syria.

Challenges

Alongside the civil war, the oil sector of the economy faces a number of challenges, including a decline in output and production resulting from technological problems and a depletion of oil reserves. Syria's rate of oil production has decreased steadily from a peak close to 610,000 bbl/d (97,000 m^3/d) in 1995 down to approximately 385,000 bbl/d (61,200 m^3/d) in 2010. Meanwhile, consumption is rising, which means that Syria could become a net oil importer within a decade. To counteract this problem, Syria intensified oil exploration efforts.

Syria's upstream oil production and development has traditionally been the mandate of the Syrian Petroleum Company(SPC), an arm of the Syrian Ministry of Petroleum and Mineral Resources. The SPC has undertaken efforts to reverse the trend toward declining oil production and exports by increasing oil exploration and production in partnership with foreign oil companies. The SPC directly controls about half of the country's oil production and takes a 50 percent stake in development work with foreign partners.

Foreign investment is vital for improving production levels, and following the outbreak of the Syrian civil war Western companies are legally prohibited from working in the country. The main foreign producing consortium is the Al-Furat Petroleum Company, a joint venture established in 1985, which currently includes the SPC at 50 percent ownership, Anglo-Dutch Shell at 32 percent, and the remainder held by Himalaya Energy Syria, a consortium of China National Petroleum Company and India's Oil and Natural Gas Corporation. Shell has one of the oldest relationships with Syria dating back to 1949. It produced with its joint venture partners an average 100,000 bbl/d (16,000 m^3/d). As of December 2011 Shell has suspended operations in Syria due to EU sanctions.

Another important consortium is Deir Ez Zor Petroleum Company, owned by SPC and France's Total. Total formed its Syrian operation in 1988 and in 2008 renewed its partnership sharing agreement with Syria during French President Nicolas Sarkozy's visit to Syria, confirming France's continued interest in the company's activities in the country. Prior to the Syrian civil war, Total produced an average 27,000 bbl/d (4,300 m^3/d) from its fields around Deir ez Zour. Since the start of the civil war and the international sanctions applied to Syria, Total suspended operations in the country from December 2011.

A more recent entrant into the Syrian oil sector was the United Kingdom's Gulfsands Petroleum. At the beginning of 2011, its oil fields produced 20,700 bbl/d (3,290 m^3/d). As of February 2012, Gulfsands has suspended its Syria operations and entered into a force majeure due to EU sanctions on the Syrian government prohibiting the trade of oil. Gulfsands dealings in Syria were also hit by EU sanctions due to Syrian tycoon Rami Makhlouf, a cousin of the Syrian presidentformally owning a 5.7 percent stake in the company, with this stake being suspended in August 2011 due to specific sanctions relating to Makhlouf. Other international players include or included: Canada's Suncor, Poland's Kulczyk, US-Egyptian firm IPR, Croatia's INA, Russia's Stroytransgas and Soyuzneftegaz, and Triton Singapore.

Another option to handle the increase in domestic oil consumption besides increasing oil production is to switch power stations from oil-fired to natural gas-fired. Proven natural gas reserves, approximately three-quarters of which are owned by the Syrian Petroleum Company, were estimated at 2.6 trillion cubic meters (9.1 trillion cubic feet) in 2010. A major challenge for the natural gas industry is logistics: reserves are located mainly in northeastern Syria, whereas the population is concentrated in the west and south.

8

Demographics

In 2011, the Syrian population was estimated at roughly 23 million permanent inhabitants, including people with refugee status fromPalestine and Iraq and are an overall indigenous Levantine people. While most modern-day Syrians are commonly described as Arabs by virtue of their modern-day language and bonds to Arab culture and history, they are, in fact, largely a blend of the various Semitic-speaking groups indigenous to the region.

Population

Religion

There has been no Syrian census including a question about religion since 1960, these are thus the last official statistics available: 92.1% Muslims (4,053,349) including 75% Sunnis, 11% Alawis, 3% Druzes; 7.8% Christians (344,621) and 0.1% Jews (4,860). In the next census of 1970, the religion statistics were no longer mentioned.

Languages

Arabic is the official, and most widely spoken, language. Arabic speakers make up 85% of the population (this includes some 500,000 Palestinians). Many educated Syrians also speak English and French. The Kurds, a majority of whom speakKurdish, make up 9% of the population and live mostly in the northeast corner of Syria, as well in pockets all along the northern borders of Syria with Turkey, and demographically dominate the district of Afrin, west of Aleppo, though sizable Kurdish communities live in most major Syrian cities as well. Armenian and Turkmen are spoken among the smallArmenian and

Turkmen populations respectively. Aramaic is still spoken in two forms, the Syriac used by Assyrians andWestern Neo-Aramaic used by a few inhabitants in the villages of Bakh'a, Jubb'adin and Ma'loula. 1,500 people of Greek descent lived in Syria. The majority of them were Syrian citizens.

Disposition

60% of the population live in the Aleppo Governorate, the Euphrates valley or along the coastal plain; a fertile strip between the coastal mountains and the desert.

Overall population density is about 118.3 inhabitants per square kilometre (306/sq mi). Education is free and compulsory from ages 6 to 11. Schooling consists of 6 years of primary education followed by a 3-year general or vocational training period and a 3-year academic or vocational program.

The second 3-year period of academic training is required for university admission. Total enrollment at post-secondary schools is over 150,000. The literacy rate of Syrians aged 15 and older is 86.0% for males and 73.6% for females.

Since 1960, censuses have been conducted in 1960, 1970, 1981, 1994 and 2004.

Civil war's effect on population

More than four million refugees have left the country during the course of the civil war. Most of them fled to neighboring countries such as Turkey, Lebanon, Jordan, and Iraq, as well as European nations like Germany.

The war also affected the birth rate. The annual birth rate in Syria has fallen by more than half since the country plunged into turmoil in March 2011, from about 500,000 births per year before 2011, to about 200,000.

Life expectancy

Prior to the civil war, the life span in Syria was 75.9 years, but that number has since fallen to an estimated 55.7 years.

CIA WORLD FACTBOOK DEMOGRAPHIC STATISTICS

The following demographic statistics are from the CIA World Factbook, unless otherwise indicated.

Population

17,951,639 in 2014, a massive decline due to nearly 4 million Syrian refugeesleaving the country because of the Syrian Civil War and furthermore because of the death in the war. This is a drop of 9.7% from the previous year.

Age structure

0–14 years: 35.2% (male 4,066,109/female 3,865,817)

15–64 years: 61% (male 6,985,067/female 6,753,619)

65 years and older: 3.8% (male 390,802/female 456,336) (2011 est.)

Median age

total

21 years *male*

21.7 years *female*

22.1 years (2011 est.)

Population decline rate

0.797% (2012 est.)

Historical population

Year	Pop.	±%
1937	2,368,000	—
1950	3,252,000	+37.3%
1960	4,565,000	+40.4%
1970	6,305,000	+38.1%
1980	8,704,000	+38.0%
1990	12,116,000	+39.2%
1995	14,186,000	+17.1%

Birth rate

2.35 births/1,000 population (2012 est.)

Death rate

3.67 deaths/1,000 population (July 2012 est.)

Net migration rate

-27.82 migrant(s)/1,000 population (2012 est.)

Sex ratio

at birth: 1.06 male(s)/female

under 15 years: 1.06 male(s)/female

15–64 years: 1.05 male(s)/female

65 years and older: 0.89 male(s)/female

total population: 1.05 male(s)/female (2009 est.)

Life expectancy at birth

total years: 71.19 years

male: 69.8 years

female: 72.68 years (2009 est.)

Nationality

noun: Syrian(s)

adjective: Syrian

Ethnic groups

- Arab 90.3%
- Kurds, Armenians, and Other 9.7%

Religions

- Islam 87% (official; includes Sunni 74% and Alawi, Ismaili, and Shia 13%)
- Christian 10% (includes Orthodox, Uniate, and Nestorian)
- Druze 3%

Languages

- Arabic

Literacy

definition: age 15 and older can read and write

- *total population:* 79.6% (2004 census)
- *male:* 86.0%
- *female:* 73.6%

Urbanization

- *urban population:* 56% of total population (2010)
- *rate of urbanization:* 2.5% annual rate of change (2010-15 est.)

Major urban areas - population

As of 2011:

- *Aleppo*: 3.164 million
- *Damascus* (capital): 2.65 million
- *Homs*: 1.369 million
- *Hama*: 933,000

RELIGION IN SYRIA

Religion in Syria is made of range of faiths and sects. However, membership of a religious community in Syria is ordinarily determined by birth.

According to a research by Michael Izady, 75% of Syrians are Sunni Muslims, 10% are Alawis, 10% are Christians and 3 % are Druze

Not all of the Sunnis are Arabs; Sunni Arabs are about 60-65% Of the population. Most of the Kurds, who make up 9% of the. population are officially Sunni, as are the Turkmens who encompass 1%.

A striking feature of religious life in Syria is the geographic distribution of the religious minorities. Most Christians live in Damascus, Aleppo, Homs, and other large cities along with significant numbers in Al-Hasakah Governorate in northeastern Syria, Tartus andLatakia. Nearly 90 percent of the Alawis live in the coastal area of the country, namely inLatakia Governorate and in Tartus Governorate in the rural areas of the Jabal an Nusayriyah; they constitute over 80 percent of the rural population of the coastal area. The Jabal al-Arab/Jabal al-Druze, a rugged and mountainous region in the southwest of the country, is more than 90 percent Druze inhabited; some 120 villages are exclusively so. The Twelvers Shia's are concentrated in the rural areas of Homs, in addition to two rural towns in Aleppo Governorate, plus some living inDamascus. The Ismailis are concentrated between the Salamiyah region and Masyaf region in Hamah Governorate; approximately 10,000 more inhabit the mountains of Tartus Governorate in a small city called Al-Qadmus. The Jewishcommunity has declined dramatically in the last 20 years. Some estimates that in Damascus remained fewer than 100 Jewish people. But there are some others also in the Aleppo area, as are the Yazidis, some of whom inhabit the Jabal Sam'an and about half of whom live in the vicinity of Amuda in the Al-Jazira.

ISLAM

Sunnis

The largest religious group in Syria is the Sunni Muslims which make up around 74% of the population, of whom about 80% are native Syrian Arabs, with the remainder being Kurds, Turkomans, Circassians, and Palestinians. Sunni Islam sets the religious tone for Syria and provides the country's basic values. Sunnis follow nearly all occupations, belong to all social groups and nearly every political party, and live in all parts of the country. There are only two governorates in which they are not a majority: Al-Suwayda, where Druzes predominate, and Latakia, where Alawis are a majority. In Al Hasakah, Sunnis form a majority, but most of them are Kurds rather than Arabs.

Of the four major schools of Islamic law, represented in Syria are the Shafii school and the Hanafi school, which places greater emphasis on analogical deduction and bases decisions more on precedents set in previous cases than on literal interpretation of the Quran or Sunna. After the first coup d'état in 1949, the waqfs were taken out of private religious hands and put under government control. Civil codes have greatly modified the authority of Islamic laws, and the educational role of Muslim religious leaders is declining with the gradual disappearance of kuttabs, the traditional mosque-affiliated schools. Despite civil codes introduced in the past years, Syria maintains a dual system of sharia and civil courts. According to the International Religious Freedom Report, the government of Syria is increasingly targeting members of faith groups it deemed a threat. It is reported that the Sunni majority is primarily persecuted.

Shi'a

Twelvers/Imamis

The Twelvers/Imamis, numbering about 250,000 or 5.5% of the population of Syria. In Damascus there are Twelvers/Imamis living near to the Shia pilgrimage sites, especially in the al-Amara-quarter which is near to Umayyad Mosque and Sayyidah Ruqayya Mosque, and around Sayyidah Zaynab Mosque. An other important site isBab Saghir Cemetery: The Shia Twelvers in Syria have close links to the Lebanese Shi'a Twelvers. Imami Shias are also found in villages in Idlib, Homs and Aleppoprovinces.

Ismailis (Seveners)

Ismailis (Seveners) are divided into two major groups, the Mustaalis and the Nizaris. The Ismailis of Syria, numbering about 200,000 or 1% percent of the population, are predominantly Nizaris. Originally clustered in Latakia Governorate, the majority of Syrian Ismailis have mainly resettled south of Salamiyah. With the land being granted to the Ismaili community by Abdul Hamid II, sultan of the Ottoman Empire from 1876 to 1909. A few thousand Ismailis live in the mountains west of Hamah, and about 5,000 are in Latakia. The western mountain group is poor and suffers from land hunger and overpopulation — resulting in a drift toward the wealthier eastern areas as well as seasonal migration to the Salamiyah area, where many of them find employment at harvest-time. The wealthier Ismailis of Salamiyah have fertile and well-watered land.

Alawis

The Alawis, numbering about 2,350,562 or 11% of the population of Syria, constitute Syria's largest religious minority. They live chiefly along the coast in Latakia Governorate, where they form over 80 percent of the rural population. For centuries, the Alawis constituted Syria's most repressed and exploited minority. Most worked as indentured servants and tenant farmers or sharecroppers for Sunni landowners. However, after Alawi President Hafez Assad and his family clan came to power in 1970, the living conditions of the Alawis improved considerably. Splits by sectional rivalries - the Alawis lack a single, powerful ruling family - has led, since the 1940s, to the emergence of many individual Alawis who have attained power and prestige as military officers. Although settled cultivators, Alawis gather into kin groups much like those of pastoral nomads. The four Alawi confederations, each divided into tribes, are Kalbiyah, Khaiyatin, Haddadin, and Matawirah.

A third of 250,000 Alawi men of military age have been killed fighting in the Syrian Civil War. The Alawis have suffered as a result of their support for the Assad government against the mainly Sunni Arab opposition.

Druzes

The Syrian Druze community, at 3% of the population, continued to be the overwhelming majority in the Jabal al Arab, a rugged and mountainous region in southwestern Syria. The Druze religion is a tenth-century offshoot of Shia Islam, al-Hakim, the sixth Fatimid caliph of Egypt. However, Druze holds a self-described "unitarian" sentiment, and its members are not considered Muslims by some adherents of mainstream Islam but are legally considered as such in Syria and Lebanon.

Christianity

The Christian communities of Syria, which before 2006 accounted for about 12% of the population, spring from two of the three traditions. The two traditions represented are Roman and Syriac Christianity. These traditions can be distinguished by what books were in their canon of the New Testament. The Roman Tradition includes those churches who existed in the Roman Empire or its satellites, or are derived from Churches that existed in the Roman Empire. These include Oriental Orthodox (Armenian Orthodox and Syriac Orthodox), Eastern Orthodox (such as Greeks or Russians), Roman Catholics, various Eastern Catholic Churches that are under the authority of the Pope, and Protestants. The Syriac Tradition (or Eastern Rite) is represented by the Assyrian Church of the East, Chaldean Catholic and Ancient Church of the East, the members of the Syriac tradition are all Eastern Aramaic-speaking ethnic Assyrians. The total number of Christians before 2011, not including Iraqi refugee Christians, numbered about 2.4 million or 11-12% of the population: 1.1 million Greek Orthodox, 700,000 Syriac Orthodox, 70-100,000 Armenian Christians (Apostolics and Catholics), 400,000 Catholics of various rites and the Church of the East (Assyrian) numbers unknown, and Protestants. Because Protestantism was introduced by missionaries, a small number of Syrians are members of these Western denominations. The Catholics are divided into several groups: Greek Catholics (from a schism in the Greek Orthodox Patriarchate of Antioch in 1724), Latin Rite, Armenian Catholics, Syrian Catholics, Chaldean Catholics and Maronites. The vast majority of Christians belong to the Eastern communions, which have existed in Syria since the earliest days of Christianity. The main Eastern groups are the autonomous Orthodox churches; the Uniate churches, which are in communion with Rome; and the independent Assyrian Church of the East. Even though each group forms a separate community, Christians nevertheless cooperate increasingly, largely because of their fear of the Muslim majority. In 1920 Syria was 25% Christian in a population of 2.5 millions. Christians have emigrated in higher numbers than Muslims and have a lower birth rate.

With the exception of the Armenians and Assyrians, most Syrian Christians are Arameans or Arab Christians. However, many Christians, particularly the Eastern Orthodox, have joined the Arab nationalist movement and some are changing their Aramaic or Westernized names to Arabic ones. More Syrian Christians participate in proportion to their number in political and administrative affairs than do Muslims. Especially among the young, relations between Christians and Muslims are improving.

There are several social differences between Christians and Muslims. For example, Syrian Christians are more highly urbanized than Muslims; many live either in or around Damascus, Aleppo, Hamah, or Latakia, and there are relatively fewer of them in the lower income groups. Proportionately more Christians than Muslims are educated beyond the primary level, and there are relatively more of them in white-collar and professional occupations. The education that Christians receive has differed in kind from that of Muslims in the sense that many more children of Christian parents have attended Western-oriented foreign and private schools. With their higher urbanization, income, and educational levels, the Christians have therefore somewhat the same relation to other Syrians as the Jewish community formerly did before most Jews left for Israel.

The presence of the Christian communities is expressed also by the presence of many monasteries in several parts of the country.

Judaism

Most Jews now living in the Arab World belong to communities dating back to Biblical times or originating as colonies of refugees fleeing the Spanish Inquisition.

Syrian Jews

In Syria, Jews of both origins, numbering altogether fewer than 3,000 in 1987, are found. After a mass emigration in 1992, today fewer than 200 Jews live in Syria, mostly in the capital. Syrian Jews are Arabic-speaking and barely distinguishable from the Arabs around them. In Syria, as elsewhere, the degree to which Jews submit to the disciplines of their religion varies.

The government treats the Jews as a religious community and not as a racial group. Official documents refer to them as musawiyin (followers of Moses) and not yahudin (Jews).

Although the Jewish community continues to exercise a certain authority over the personal status of its members, as a whole it is under considerable restriction, more because of political factors than religious ones. The economic freedom of Jews is limited, and they are under continual surveillance by the police. Their situation, although not good before the June 1967 War, has reportedly deteriorated considerably since then.

The synagogues of the Jewish community have a protected status by the Syrian government.

Israeli Jews

The Golan Heights, which is internationally seen as part of Syria, has been occupied and governed by Israel since the Six-Day War. It has resulted in the region being settled by an influx of Israeli Jews who have become the overall majority. In 2010 the Jewish settlers had expanded to 20,000 living in 32 settlements.

Yazidis

During the fifteenth and sixteenth centuries, the ethno-religious group of the Yazidis, whose religion dates back to pre-Islamic times, migrated from southern Turkey and settled in their present mountainous stronghold – Jabal Sinjar in northeastern Syria and Iraq. Although some are scattered in Iran, Turkey, and the Caucasus, Iraq is the center of their religious life, the home of their amir, and the site (north of Mosul) of the tomb of their most revered saint, Shaykh Adi.

In 1964, there were about 10,000 Yazidis in Syria, primarily in the Jazirah and northwest of Aleppo; population data were not available in 1987. Once seminomadic, most Yazidis now are settled; they have no great chiefs and, although generally Kurdish-speaking or Arabic speaking, gradually are being assimilated into the surrounding Arab population.

Yazidis generally refuse to discuss their faith which, in any case, is known fully to only a few among them. The Yazidi religion has elements of Mesopotamian religions.

Folk spiritual beliefs

In addition to the beliefs taught by the organized religions, many people believe strongly in powers of good and evil and in the efficacy of local saints. The former beliefs are especially marked among the bedouin, who use amulets, charms, and incantations as protective devices against the evil power of jinns (spirits) and the evil eye. Belief in saints is widespread among non-beduin populations. Most villages contain a saint's shrine, often the grave of a local person considered to have led a particularly exemplary life. Believers, especially women, visit these shrines to pray for help, good fortune, and protection. Although the identification of the individual with their religious community is strong, belief in saints is not limited to one religious group. Persons routinely revere saints who were members of other religious communities and, in many cases, members of various faiths pray at the same shrine.

Unorthodox religious beliefs of this kind are probably more common among women than men. Because they are excluded by the social separation of the sexes from much of the formal religious life of the community, women attempt to meet their own spiritual needs through informal and unorthodox religious beliefs and practices, which are passed on from generation to generation.

RELIGION AND LAW

In matters of personal status, such as birth, marriage, and inheritance, the Christian, Jewish, and Druze minorities follow their own legal systems. All other groups, in such matters, come under the jurisdiction of the Muslim code. However, in 2016 the de facto autonomous Federation of Northern Syria - Rojava for the first time in Syrian history introduced and started to promote civil marriage as a move towards a secular open society and intermarriage between people of different religious backgrounds.

Although the faiths theoretically enjoy equal legal status, to some extent Islam is favored. Despite guarantees of religious freedom, some observers maintain that the conditions of the non-Muslim minorities have been steadily deteriorating, especially since the June 1967 war. An instance of this deterioration was the nationalization of over 300 Christian schools, together with approximately 75 private Muslim schools, in the autumn of 1967. Since the early 1960s, heavy emigration of Christians has been noted; in fact, some authorities state that at least 50 percent of the 600,000 people who left during the decade ending in 1968 were Christians. In recent decades, however, emigration was slow until the Syrian Civil War.

9

Culture and Society

CULTURE OF SYRIA

Syria is a traditional society with a long cultural history. Importance is placed on family, religion, education and self-discipline and respect. The Syrian's taste for the traditional arts is expressed in dances such as the al-Samah, the Dabkeh in all their variations and the sword dance. Marriage ceremonies are occasions for the lively demonstration of folk customs.

The scribes of the city of Ugarit (modern Ras Shamra) created a cuneiform alphabet in the 14th century BC. The alphabet was written in the familiar order we use today like the English language, however with different characters.

Archaeologists have discovered extensive writings and evidence of a culture rivaling those of Iraq, and Egypt in and around the ancient city of Ebla (modern Tell Mardikh). Later Syrian scholars and artists contributed to Hellenistic and Romanthought and culture. Cicero was a pupil of Antiochus of Ascalon at Athens; and the writings of Posidonius of Apamea influenced Livy and Plutarch...............................

LITERATURE

Syrians have contributed to Arabic literature and have a proud tradition of oral and written poetry. Syrian writers played a crucial role in the nahda or Arab literary and cultural revival of the 19th century. Prominent contemporary Syrian writers include, among others, Adonis, Muhammad Maghout, Haidar Haidar, Ghada al-Samman, Nizar Qabbani and Zakariyya Tamer.

From 1918 to 1926, while Syria was under French rule, French Romantic influences inspired Syrian authors, many of whom turned away from the traditional models of Arabic poetry.

In 1948, the partitioning of neighbouring Palestine and the establishment of Israel brought about a new turning point in Syrian writing. *Adab al-Iltizam*, the "literature of political commitment", deeply marked by social realism, mostly replaced the romantic trend of the previous decades. Hanna Mina, rejecting art for art's sake and confronting the social and political issues of his time, was arguably the most prominent Syrian novellist of this era. Following the Six-Day War in 1967, *Adab al-Naksa*, the "literature of defeat", grappled with the causes of the Arab defeat.

Ba'ath Party rule, since the 1966 coup, has brought about renewed censorship. In this context, the genre of the historical novel, spearheaded by Nabil Sulayman, Fawwaz Haddad, Khyri al-Dhahabi and Nihad Siris, is sometimes used as a means of expressing dissent, critiquing the present through a depiction of the past.

Syrian folk narrative, as a subgenre of historical fiction, is imbued with magical realism, and is also used as a means of veiled criticism of the present. Salim Barakat, a Syrian émigré living in Sweden, is one of the leading figures of the genre.

Contemporary Syrian literature also encompassesscience fiction and futuristic utopiae (Nuhad Sharif, Talib Umran), which may also serve as media of dissent.

MUSIC

Syria's capital, Damascus, has long been one of the Arab world's centers for cultural and artistic innovation, especially in the field of classical Arab music. Syria has also produced several pan-Arab stars. Asmahan, Farid al-Atrash and singer Lena Chamamyan. The city of Aleppo is known for its muwashshah, a form of Andaloussung poetry popularized by Sabri Moudallal, as well as popular stars like Sabah Fakhri.

Also, Syria was one of the earliest centers of Christian hymnody, in a repertory known as Syrian chant, which continues to be the liturgical music of some of the various Syrian Christians.

There was formerly a distinctive tradition of Syrian Jewish religious music, which still flourishes in the Syrian-Jewish community of New York: see The Weekly Maqam, Baqashot and Pizmonim.

ARCHITECTURE

Traditional Houses of the Old Cities in Damascus, Aleppo and the other Syrian cities are preserved and traditionally the living quarters are arranged around one or more courtyards, typically with a fountain in the middle supplied by spring water, and decorated with citrus trees, grape vines, and flowers.

Outside of larger city areas such as Damascus, Aleppo or Homs, residential areas are often clustered in smaller villages. The buildings themselves are often quite old (perhaps a few hundred years old), passed down to family members over several generations. Residential construction of rough concrete and blockwork is usually unpainted, and the palette of a Syrian village is therefore simple tones of grays and browns.

MEDIA

Television in Syria was formed in 1960, when Syria and Egypt (which adopted television that same year) were part of theUnited Arab Republic. It broadcast in black and white until 1976. The Arab League officially asked the satellite operatorsArabsat and Nilesat to stop broadcasting Syrian media in June 2012.

There was a private sector presence in the Syrian cinema industry until the end of the 1970s, but private investment has since preferred the more lucrative television serial business. Syrian soap operas, in a variety of styles (all melodramatic, however), have considerable market penetration throughout the eastern Arab world.

The authorities operate several intelligence agencies among them Shu'bat al-Mukhabarat al-'Askariyya, employing a large number of operatives.

CUISINE

Syrian cuisine is rich and varied in its ingredients and is linked to the regions of Syria where a specific dish has originated. Syrian food mostly consists of Southern Mediterranean, Greek, and Southwest Asian dishes. Some Syrian dishes also evolved from Turkish and French cooking. Dishes like shish kebab, stuffed zucchini/courgette, yabra' (stuffed grape leaves, the word yapra' derýves from theTurkish word 'yaprak' meaning leaf).

The main dishes that form Syrian cuisine are kibbeh, hummus, tabbouleh, fattoush,labneh, shawarma, mujaddara, shanklish, pastýrma, sujuk and baklava. Baklava is made of filo pastry filled with chopped nuts and soaked in honey. Syrians often serve selections of appetizers, known as meze, before the main course. za'atar,minced beef, and cheese manakish are popular hors d'œuvres. The Arabic flatbreadkhubz is always eaten together with meze.

Syrians are also well known for their cheese. The very popular string cheese jibbneh mashallale is made of curd cheese and is pulled and twisted together. Syrians also make cookies/biscuits to usually accompany their cheese called ka'ak. These are made of farina and other ingredients, rolled out, shaped into rings and baked. Another form of a similar cookie is filled with crushed dates mixed with butter, to accompany jibbneh mashallale.

SPORTS

The most popular sports in Syria are football, basketball, swimming, and tennis.Damascus was home to the fifth and seventh Pan Arab Games. Many popular football teams are based in Damascus, Aleppo, Homs, Latakia, etc.

The Abbasiyyin Stadium in Damascus is home to the Syrian national football team. The team enjoyed some success, having qualified for four Asian Cup competitions. The team's first international was on 20 November 1949, losing to Turkey 7–0. The team was ranked 115th in the world by FIFA as of November 2011.

CULTURE NAME

Orientation

*Identification.*Syria is the name that was given to the region by the Greeks and Romans and probably derives from the Babylonian*suri.*Arabs traditionally referred to Syria and a large, vaguely defined surrounding area as*Sham,*which translates as "the northern region," "the north," "Syria," or "Damascus." Arabs continued to refer to the area as*Sham*up until the twentieth century. That name still is used to refer to the entire area of Jordan, Syria, Lebanon, Israel, and the West Bank and has become a symbol of Arab unity.

*Location and Geography.*Syria borders Turkey to the north, Iraq to the east, Israel and Jordan to the south, and Lebanon and the Mediterranean Sea to the west. It is 71,000 square miles (183,900 square kilometers) in area. One-third of the land is arable, and one-third is pasturable. The terrain is mostly desert, and home to drought resistant plants such as myrtle, boxwood, and wild olive. There is little wildlife. Remote areas have wolves, hyenas, and foxes; the desert has lizards, eagles, and buzzards. Most of the population is concentrated in the western region of the country, near the Mediterranean. Damascus, the capital and the largest city, is located at the foot of the Anti-Lebanon Mountains along the small Barada River. It has a favorable location in a fertile area close to the desert and has historically served as a refueling stop and commercial center for traders making trips through the desert. Inland of this area is a range of limestone mountains, the Jabal al-Nusayriya. The Gharb Depression, a dry but fertile valley, lies between this range and other mountains to the east. TheEuphratesRiver and several of its tributaries pass through Syria, supplying more than 80 percent of the country's water. There are two natural lakes: Arram in the crater of an extinct volcano in the Golan Heights and Daraa along the Jordanian border. There are several artificial lakes created by dams that supply irrigation and electrical power. Most of the country has a desertlike climate, with hot, dry summers and milder winters. What little rain there is falls in the winter, mainly along the coast.

*Demography.*The population in 2000 was 16,673,282 (not including the 35,150 people living in the Israeli-occupied Golan Heights, of whom 18,150 are Arabs and 17,000 are Israelis). The country is 90.3 percent Arab. Kurds are estimated to constitute between 3 and 9 percent of the population. Also represented are Turks; Armenians, most of whom fled Turkey between 1925 and 1945; and small numbers of Circassians, Assyrians, and Jews. The Bedoins are Arabs, but form a distinct group. They were originally nomadic, but many have been forced to settle in towns and villages.

*Linguistic Affiliation.*Arabic is the official language, and 90 percent of the population speaks it. The Syrian dialect is very similar to Jordanian and Egyptian and varies little from Modern Standard Arabic, the standardized form used in communications throughout the Arab world. Kurdish, Armenian, and Circassian also are spoken. Kurdish is spoken mostly in the northeast, but even there it is rarely heard, as speaking it is viewed as a gesture of dissent. Some ancient languages are still spoken in parts of the country, including Maalua, Aramaic, and Syriac. As a result of colonial influence, French and English (French in particular) are understood and used in interactions with tourists and other foreigners.

*Symbolism.*The coat of arms displays a hawk, which is the emblem of Muhammad, the founder of the Islamic faith. The flag consists of three horizontal stripes: red on top, white in the middle, and black on the bottom. In the white section are two green stars, symbolizing Islam.

History and Ethnic Relations

*Emergence of the Nation.*The modern-day nation emerged from*Sham,*an area that historically included Jordan, Israel, and Lebanon. Between 2700 and 2200B.C.E., this area was home to the Ebla kingdom. Later, the country's strategic location helped its coastal towns rise to prominence as Phoenician trading posts. It was conquered by the Persians around 500B.C.E., and by the Greeks in 333B.C.E.The Romans took over in 64B.C.E., and established a fortress at Palmyra whose remains still stand in the desert. Muslim Arabs conquered Damascus in 635C.E.Beginning in 1095, Syria was a target of the Crusades, but the Arabs ultimately defeated the Christian invaders. The Turkish Ottoman Empire took control in 1516 and ruled the area for four hundred years. That era came to an end in 1920 with the end of World War I, when the French took control of Syria and Lebanon. The French drew a straight-line border to separate this territory from British-ruled Transjordan. Syria had experienced a brief period of independence from 1918–1920, and was dissatisfied with French rule, which ignored the will of the people and did little for the country as a whole. There was a brief insurrection in 1925 and 1926, which the French put down by bombing Damascus.

Syria held its first parliamentary elections in 1932. All the candidates were hand-picked by the French, but once elected, they declined the constitution France had proposed for the country. Anti-French sentiment grew when France turned over control of the Syrian province of Alexandretta to Turkey. It was exacerbated by the promise of independence in 1941, which was not delivered until five years later. After independence, civilian rule was short-lived, and the early 1950s saw a succession of coups, after which Syria formed the United Arab Republic with Egypt in 1958. This represented an effort to keep the Arab states more powerful than Israel, but it disintegrated in 1961, when Syria came to resent the concentration of power in Egypt. The disbanding was followed by further political instability. The situation was worsened by the Six Day War against Israel in 1967 and the Black September disagreement with Jordan in 1970.

Hafez al-Assad, the leader of a radical wing of the Arab Socialist party, the Baath, seized control in 1971. He cracked down hard on dissent and in 1982 killed thousands of members of the theMuslim Brotherhoodopposition organization. However, his tight-reined rule averted the civil war and political anarchy that plagued Middle Eastern countries such as Lebanon.

In 1992, he won his fourth consecutive bid for election with 99.9 percent of the vote. During the Gulf War in the early 1990s, the country aligned itself with the anti-Iraq coalition, thus winning the approval of the United States and removing itself from the United States' government's list of nations supporting international terrorism. Hafez al-Assad died in June 2000. The younger of his two sons, Bashar, assumed his father's position.

*National Identity.*Syrians tend to identify primarily with their religious group or sect; however, as the majority of the country is Sunni Muslim, this creates a strong feeling of cultural unity. Modern-day Syria is in part the result of geographic lines drawn by the French in 1920, and there is still a strong pan-Arab sympathy that defines national identity beyond the current borders. The current map was also redrawn in 1967, when Israel took the Golan Heights, a previously Syrian territory, and the national identity is based in part on the concept of defending and reclaiming this land.

*Ethnic Relations.*Syria is ethnically fairly homogeneous (80 percent of the population is Arab). Religious differences are tolerated, and minorities tend to retain distinct ethnic, cultural, and religious identities. The Alawite Muslims (about a half-million people) live in the area of Latakia.

TheDruze, a smaller group that resides in the mountainous region of Jebel Druze, are known as fierce soldiers. The Ismailis are an even smaller sect, that originated in Asia. The Armenians from Turkey are Christian. The Kurds are Muslim but have a distinct culture and language, for which they have been persecuted throughout the Middle East.

The Circassians, who are Muslim, are of Russian origin and generally have fair hair and skin. The nomadic Beduoin lead a lifestyle that keeps them largely separated from the rest of society, herding sheep and moving through the desert, although some have settled in towns and villages. Another group that remains on the outside of society both politically and socially, is the roughly 100,000 Palestinian refugees, who left their homeland in 1948 after the founding of Israel.

Urbanism, Architecture, and the Use of Space

The focal point of any Middle Eastern city is the*souk,*or marketplace, a labyrinthine space of alleys, stalls, and tiny shops that also include ancient mosques and shrines. Traditionally, the residential quarters of a city were divided along ethnic and religious lines. Today, this system has been largely replaced by divisions along class lines, with some wealthier neighborhoods and some poorer ones. Damascus is an ancient city, and along withAleppo, one of the oldest continuously inhabited places in the world.

The Great Omayyad Mosque, which dates back to the early days of Islam, is one of its oldest and most famous buildings. It formerly served as a Byzantine church honoring Saint John the Baptist and was constructed on the site of an old temple to pre-Islamic gods. The walls are lined with marble and overlaid with golden vines.

Six hundred gold lamps hang from the ceiling. The city is home to ruins as well as intact buildings that date back thousands of years. These structures are located in the area called the Old City. Damascus is also a city of cars, highways, and tall modern buildings made of reinforced concrete.

Aleppo, although smaller, is equally ancient. It is geographically protected by its elevation and rocky terrain, and traces its history back to its days as a fort. Today Aleppo is the nation's second largest urban center and most industrialized city. It engages in silk weaving and cotton printing as well as the tanning of animal hides and the processing of produce. Other cities include Latakia, the country's main port, and Homs and Tartus, both of which have oil refineries.

In villages, houses present a closed front to the outside world, symbolizing the self-contained family unit. They are small, usually with one to three rooms, and are built around an enclosed central courtyard. Traditional rural houses in the northwest are mud structures that are shaped like beehives. In the south and east, most houses are made of stone. The nomadic Bedouin, who live mainly in the south and east, sleep in tents that are easily transportable.

In 1960, 30 percent of the population lived in cities; in 1970, that proportion was 46 percent; and by 1988, the number had climbed to half. Most of this growth has been concentrated in Damascus. The rapid spread of that city into nearby farmland has resulted in traffic congestion, overtaxed water supplies, pollution, and housing shortages. Many older buildings have been taken down to make room for roads and newer structures. The outskirts of the city have become overrun with quickly and shoddily constructed homes that sometimes have electricity but rarely have running water or sewage facilities.

Food and Economy

*Food in Daily Life.*Wheat is the main crop and one of the staple foods. Vegetables, fruits, and dairy products also are eaten. Lamb is popular, but most people cannot afford to eat meat on a regular basis. Islam proscribes the consumption of pork, and other meats must be specially prepared in a method called*halal*cooking. In middle-class and wealthier homes, meals are like those eaten in other Middle Eastern countries: roast or grilled chicken or lamb with side dishes of rice, chickpeas, yogurt, and vegetables. A*mezzeh*is a midday meal composed of up to twenty or thirty small dishes. These dishes can include*hummous*, a puree of chickpeas and*tahini*(groundsesame paste);*baba ganouj,*aneggplantpuree; meat rissoles;stuffed grape leaves;*tabouleh*(a salad of cracked wheat and vegetables);*falafel*(deep-fried balls of mashed chickpeas); and pita bread. Olives, lemon, parsley, onion, and garlic are used for flavoring. Popular fruits that are grown in the region include dates, figs, plums, and watermelons. Damascus has a number of French restaurants remaining from the time of colonial rule.

Tea is the ubiquitous drink and is often consumed at social gatherings. Soda is also very popular, as is milk and a drink made by mixing yogurt with water, salt, and garlic. Alcohol consumption is rare, as it is forbidden by the Islamic religion, but beer and wine are available, as is arak, an aniseed drink that also is popular in other Middle Eastern countries.

*Food Customs at Ceremonial Occasions.*Food is an important part of many celebrations. During Ramadan, each day's fast is broken with an evening meal called*iftar.*This meal begins in silence and is consumed rapidly.*Eid al-Fitr,*the final breaking of the Ramadan fast, entails the consumption of large quantities of food, sweets in particular. Food is also a central element at weddings, parties, and other festivities.

*Basic Economy.*The country supplies almost all of its own food needs. The proportion of the population working in agriculture has decreased significantly from 50 percent in 1970, to 30 percent in the 1980s, to 23 percent today. Despite this decline, production has increased, thanks in large part to the dam at Tabqa, which has allowed for increased irrigation. Half of the workforce is employed in industry and mining. There is less of a gap between the rich and the poor in Syria than there is in many other countries, and as more of the population gains access to education, the middle class continues to expand.

The basic unit of currency is the pound.

*Land Tenure and Property.*Before independence, urban landlords controlled the countryside, often mistreating the peasants and denying them any rights. The majority of peasants worked as sharecroppers and were economically and politically powerless. When the socialist Baath Party took control, it introduced measures to limit and redistribute land ownership and establish peasant unions. It also set up local governing organizations and cooperatives, that have allowed the peasants to attain more control of their lives and livelihood.

*Commercial Activities.*The center of commercial activity in each town or city is the souk. People from all walks of life and all ethnic and religious backgrounds come together to buy and sell a wide variety of goods. Spices, meats, vegetables, cloth, traditional handicrafts, and imported products jostle for space in the crowded booths and alleyways. Souks are not just commercial centers but gathering places as well, and haggling is a necessary part of social interactions. Shopping centers and supermarkets exist but have not supplanted this uniquely Arab institution.

*Major Industries.*The main industries are oil, agriculture, and textiles. Wheat is the largest crop, followed by cotton. Vegetables, beans, and fruits

also are grown. There is some heavy industry (metallurgyand aluminum) as well as pharmaceuticals and petrochemicals. The oil industry is controlled by the government. Other manufactures include cement, glass, soap, and tobacco.

*Trade.*Syria's primary trading partners are Germany, Italy, and France. Although Syria is not as rich in oil as other Middle Eastern nations, oil is the main export, and the exploration for deposits continues. Other exports are cotton, fruits and vegetables, and textiles. Imports include industrial and agricultural machinery, vehicles and automotive accessories, pharmaceuticals, foodstuffs, and fabric.

*Division of Labor.*Syrians are legally entitled to pursue the career of their choice; however, those choices are often limited by gender, family, social pressure, and economic hardship. There is often relatively little difference in the salaries of the working class and those of the professional class.

Social Stratification

*Classes and Castes.*Syrian society was traditionally extremely stratified. People from different classes generally do not socialize with one another, and people in the lower classes often adopt a humble attitude and an acceptance of their position. Class lines tend to coincide with racial differences, as lighter-skinned people hold higher economic and political positions and most of the people in the lower-ranked professions are darker-skinned.

The families of landholders and merchants traditionally occupied the highest position socially and politically. They usually lived in Damascus or Aleppo and managed their land from afar. Religious teachers known as*ulama*were also influential. They served as judges, teachers, and political officials as well as advisers to the government. In this role, the ulama generally supported the status quo. The towns and cities also housed artisans, small merchants, and a small working class.

The Baath government has created some shifts in that pattern. Some peasants are moving to the cities and joining the middle class; others now own land. However, there are still large numbers of indigent and landless peasants. Since the Baath takeover, the army officers who participated in the coup have succeeded the landowners as the new elite. There is also a growing middle class as a result of the spread of education.

*Symbols of Social Stratification.*The wealthy and well educated have a fairly modern lifestyle with many of the trappings of Western life. Televisions and radios are common except among the extremely poor. Appliances such as air conditioners, dishwashers, and microwaves are only for the very wealthy.

Dress is another indicator of social class. Different tribes and villages have their own distinctive patterns, designs, and colors of clothing. Men traditionally wear long gowns called kaftans, and women wear long robes that leave only their hands and feet exposed. Both men and women wear head wraps. The educated upper classes, particularly the young, tend to prefer modern Western attire. These women favor bright colors, jewelry, makeup, and high heels; men wear dressy slacks and shirts. Blue jeans and T-shirts are rare, as are shorts and miniskirts and bare shoulders or upper arms for women. Traditionally, it is a sign of wealth and status in a family for its women to dress in long robes with their faces veiled.

Political Life

*Government.*Syria adopted its current constitution in 1973. There is universal suffrage. The unicameral legislative branch is composed of the People's Council, or*Majlis al shaab,*whose 195 members are elected for four-year terms. This body proposes laws, discusses cabinet programs, and approves the national budget. The president, who serves as the head of state and is required by the constitution to be a Muslim, is elected every seven years by popular vote. The president appoints a vice president, a prime minister who serves as head of government, a cabinet, and deputy prime ministers. The president has wide-reaching powers, including serving on the supreme court. Despite the distribution of political power, in practice, the military government has the ability to overrule all decisions.

*Leadership and Political Officials.*The importance placed on the family as the central structure in society has ramifications in politics and government. Family loyalty is a primary consideration, and there is a general sentiment that family members (even distant relatives) can be trusted more than other people. The best jobs in the government generally are held by people related to the president, either of the same religious group or the same regional background or part of his extended family.

While residents generally are interested in politics both at a local level and as a part of the larger Arab world and are critical of leaders, they tend not to join political parties. Even the ruling Baath Party has relatively small numbers of members. It is more

common to belong to a labor, farm, or professional union or another organization based on family and religion that may have political goals. Within these groups, leadership positions are often hotly contested.

*Social Problems and Control.*The legal system is based on the French model, with both civil and criminal courts. There is also a State Security Court that tries political opponents of the government. The proceedings of this court violate many international standards for fair trials. There are large numbers of political prisoners in the jails. In 1992, the government announced that it would free 2,864 of these prisoners, perhaps signaling a loosening of its autocratic policies.

For cases dealing with issues such as birth, marriage, and inheritance, the system has different courts for people of different religions. The Muslim courts are called*Sharia.*There are other ciyrts for

Druze, Roman Catholics, Protestants, and Jews.

*Military Activity.*Syria has armed forces with 408,000 members. This includes an army and an air force but no navy. It spends 30 percent of the national budget on defense as a result of the state of war that has existed between Syria and Israel since the founding of Israel. Syria also has thirty thousand troops stationed in Lebanon to maintain the peace. All men are required to serve thirty months in the armed forces, with the exception of only sons, who are exempt. It is possible to buy exemption from service for a very large sum of money. Women are allowed to serve voluntarily.

Social Welfare and Change Programs

The government strictly enforces price controls on basic items as well as rent control laws, that help low-income people get by. Medical fees are covered by the state for those who cannot afford private care. The government also provides assistance to the elderly, invalids, and those suffering from work injuries. Most assistance comes from within the family structure; young people often live with their parents until and even after marriage, and children are expected to take in and care for their elderly parents.

Gender Roles and Statuses

*Division of Labor by Gender.*Traditionally, wives in towns are responsible for running the household and are restricted to the home. Rural women often work in the fields in addition to performing domestic tasks. While women are legally allowed to work outside the home, there are significant obstacles. For example, the government's Moral Intelligence Department investigates women before allowing them to hold federal jobs. Only 11 percent of women of working age are employed outside the home; among those women, 80 percent work in agriculture. They also are represented in textiles and the tobacco industry, but only 1 percent of employed women have administrative or managerial positions. There are women in the national government, and in the capital a few women work in metal or electrical workshops. It is not uncommon for women to do piecework in their homes.

*The Relative Status of Women and Men.*The Baath Party was one of the first in the Arab world to declare as one of its goals the emancipation and equal treatment of women; its constitution of 1964 states that all citizens have equal rights. While women are now entitled to receive the same education as men and to seek employment, the traditional attitude that views females as inferior beings prevails. A woman is considered the possession of a man rather than her own person. She is identified as her father's daughter until marriage; after the birth of a male child, her identity is transferred from the wife of her husband to the mother of her son.

Marriage, Family, and Kinship

*Marriage.*By Muslim tradition, marriage is arranged by the couple's families. While more leniency is now allowed, particularly in cities and among the upper classes, it is still extremely rare for a couple to marry against their family's wishes. According to the constitution, the state has assumed the duty of protecting and encouraging the institution of marriage. Nonetheless, the marriage rate has declined because of housing shortages, inflation, rising levels of education, bride money, and the prohibitive cost of weddings.

Although the state and the Muslim religion both oppose the current dowry system, it is deeply entrenched in the family structure. It places immense pressure on the husband and his family, who have to raise large sums of money, and on the bride, who often is forced to marry the suitor who can provide the biggest dowry. Syria was the first Arab country to pass laws concerning polygamy. In 1953, it passed the Law of Personal Status, under which a man was bound to demonstrate that he could financially support two wives before marrying the second one. Whereas divorce laws used to follow the Arabic tradition that a man had only to repeat three times "I divorce you" (in his wife's presence or not), court proceedings are now required.

*Domestic Unit.*The family is the primary social unit. An older male, usually the father or grandfather, has the ultimate authority and is responsible for providing for the other family members. It is customary for several generations to live together in the same house. Particularly for women, who are not allowed to leave the home, family provides the primary or only social outlet and relationships with other people.

*Inheritance.*An estate passes from the father to the oldest son in a family. Traditionally, not only property is bequeathed, but social and political position as well.

*Kin Groups.*Syrians identify very strongly with their families, both immediate and extended. While kinship ties have weakened somewhat with urbanization and modernization, the clan mentality is still a strong influence in the nation's political system.

Socialization

*Child Rearing and Education.*Children are highly valued as a blessing from God. The more children one has, the more fortunate one is considered, as children provide extra hands to work in the fields and ensure that their parents will be taken care of in old age. Children are treated with a great deal of affection. The bond between mother and son (especially the oldest son) is particularly strong.

The literacy rate is 64 percent—78 percent for men and 51 percent for women. Primary education is mandatory and free for six years. Middle school, which begins at age thirteen, marks the end of mixed-sex education. Most schools are run by the state, which combines a French structure with the rigid discipline and rote learning of the Islamic tradition. There are a few religious schools, some schools that are run by the United Nation relief program, and some that are run by the Works Agency for Palestinian Refugees.

*Higher Education.*Syria has vocational and teacher-training education as well as universities in Damascus, Aleppo, and Latakia. About 165,000 students (40 percent of them women) are enrolled in the universities. The learning situation is less than ideal, with large class sizes and outdated teaching and testing techniques. Students who can afford to obtain visas often prefer to study abroad.

Etiquette

Men and women socialize separately except on occasions when the whole family is involved. Talking is a favorite pastime, and the art of conversation is a prized skill. Men often engage in a sort of banter in which they try to one up each other with witty and eloquent insults.

In social interactions, people stand close together, speak loudly, and gesture widely with their hands and heads. Greetings hold great social significance. They are often lengthy, including questions about health. They usually are accompanied by a handshake and sometimes by a hug and a kiss on each cheek. Placing the right hand on the heart when meeting someone is a signal of affection.

Syrians are very affectionate people. Men walk linking arms or holding hands and hug and kiss a great deal, as do women. Close physical contact in public is more common between people of the same gender than it is between girlfriend and boyfriend or husband and wife.

Religion

*Religious Beliefs.*Seventy-four percent of the population is Sunni Muslim. Sixteen percent belongs to Alawite, Druze, and other Muslim sects, and 10 percent is Christian. There are small Jewish communities in Damascus, Al Qamishli, and Aleppo. As in many Arabic countries, religion is an integral part of the culture and daily life. The word "Islam" means "submission to God." The religion shares certain prophets, traditions, and beliefs with Judaism and Christianity. The foundation of Islamic belief is called the Five Pillars.

It is speculated, although not certain, that Alawite Muslims do not observe the holy month of Ramadan or make a pilgrimage to Mecca as other Muslims do and celebrate some Christian holidays. The practices of the Druze are also somewhat mysterious. A smaller group known as the Ismailis recognizes a living person, the Aga Khan, as their sacred leader.

The mystical branch of Islam called*sufi,*has a small presence in Syria, although the government sees this sect as subversive and disapproves of its practice. Sufi rituals involve chanting and dancing while moving in a circular formation.

Despite the powerful influence of Islam in people's lives, some elements of folk religion persist. Particularly in rural areas, there is a strong belief in the evil eye as well as in*jinn*(spirits). There is also a tradition of local saints to whom people pray.

*Religious Practitioners.*There are no priests or clergy in Islam. Instead, there are people with the job of leading prayers and reading from the Qur'an, the Muslim holy book. The Qur'an, rather than a religious leader, is considered the ultimate authority and holds the answer to any question or dilemma one might have. There are also*muezzins*who give the call to prayer and are scholars of the Qur'an and spend their lives studying and interpreting the text.

*Rituals and Holy Places.*The most important observation in the Islamic calendar is Ramadan. This month of fasting is followed by the joyous feast of*Eid al Fitr,*during which families visit and exchange gifts.*Eid al-Adha*commemorates the end of Muhammod's Hajj. The mosque is the Muslim house of worship. Outside the door, there are washing facilities, as cleanliness is a prerequisite to prayer, demonstrating humility before God. One also must remove one's shoes before entering the mosque. According to Islamic tradition, women are not allowed inside. The interior has no altar; it is simply an open carpeted space. Because Muslims are supposed to pray facing Mecca, there is a small niche carved into the wall that points to the direction in which that city lies.

*Death and the Afterlife.*A death is followed by three days of mourning during which friends, relatives,

and neighbors pay their respects to the family. Female relatives of the deceased wear black for several months to up to one year or more after the death. Widows generally do not remarry and often dress in mourning for the rest of their lives.

Medicine and Health Care

There are private medical practices, in addition to the free medical care provided by the state. The health care system is poor but improving. Infectious diseases are a major health threat, especially in rural areas, where water quality is poor and sewage disposal systems are not well developed. There is a high child mortality rate that is due mainly to measles and digestive and respiratory diseases.

Secular Celebrations

The major secular holidays are New Year's Day on 1 January, Revolution Day on 8 March, and the anniversary of the formation of the Arab League, 22 March. Syrians celebrate Martyrs Day in memory of the nation's heroes on 6 April; National Day (also known as Evacuation Day, celebrating independence), on 17 April; and the Day of Mourning on 29 November.

The Arts and Humanities

*Support for the Arts.*The Ministry of Culture and National Guidance promotes the national culture. Most publishing houses are owned by the state, and writers tend to be government employees. Censorship is enforced strictly, and foreign books about politics and contemporary Syrian or Middle Eastern history are banned. The National Film Centre, established in 1966, oversees the production of most films.

*Literature.*There is a long literary tradition that dates back to poets such as al-Mutanabbi in the 900s and al-Maarri in the 1000s. Writers must contend with government censorship, but fiction writing is not as tightly monitored as is nonfiction. Whereas the punishment for breaking laws concerning nonfiction is usually imprisonment, fiction writers generally are reprimanded. Perhaps for this reason, poetry and the short story are widely read and appreciated, represented by writers such as Nizar Qabbani, Shawqi Baghdadi, and 'Ali Ahmad

Sa'id. There are few women in the ranks of well-known Arab writers, but one of them is Ghada al-Samman, who was born in 1942. She writes on many of the same issues as her male contemporaries, including cultural identity and the clash between tradition and progress as well as issues specific to being a woman and writer in a male dominated society.

*Graphic Arts.*Islam forbids the artistic depiction of animals or human beings. Therefore, Syrian art until World War I consisted mainly of geometric designs in arabesque and calligraphy. These works can be seen in many palaces and mosques. After World War I, Western drawing techniques began to be taught, and fine arts was introduced as a discipline at the University of Damascus. Mostsculptureis carved in white marble and often is displayed in palaces and public buildings.

There is a lively tradition of handicraft production. Jewelry, particularly in gold and silver, is popular, as is other metalwork, such as brass and copper plates and bowls. These items traditionally were produced by Syrian Jews, and as their population has diminished, so has this art form. Mosaic woodworking is also practiced and is used in the construction of boxes, trays, tables, desks, and game boards. Damascus is a center ofglassblowingand fabric production, including the silk brocade called damask, which was named for the city. The Bedouins are known for their weaving of fabrics, including carpets and prayer rugs made on hand-built looms, and traditional clothing that is painstakingly embroidered.

Films have been produced in Syria since the 1920s. Musicals and light comedies were popular through the late 1940s. During the 1970s, film clubs were important in the resistance to the government, and for this reason they were shut down in 1980. Syria has spawned several internationally regarded filmmakers, including Omar Amirallay and Usama Muhammed, but their films, which deal with social issues, have been banned in the country, or ignored by distribution companies.

*Performance Arts.*Memorizing and reciting from the Qur'an and from secular poetry is a popular form of entertainment. There is a rich tradition of storytelling that dates back thousands of years. Even today there are coffee shops where men go to drink tea and hear nightly installments of an ongoing saga recited by a professional storyteller.

Arabic music is tied to the storytelling tradition and often recounts tales of love, honor, and family. Technically, it is repetitive and subtle.

It uses quarter notes with small jumps in the scale. Classical Arabic music makes use of the oud, an ancient stringed instrument similar to the lute; small drums held in the lap; and flutes. Contemporary music is played by an orchestra that mainly uses European instruments with a lead singer and chorus.

The State of the Physical and Social Sciences

Damascus has a museum for agriculture and one for military history. Aleppo and other important sites have museums of archaeology.

The main challenge in the area of the sciences is that most Syrians study abroad, and many do not return to Syria to work.

Bibliography

Ball, Warwick.*Syria: A Historical and Archaeological Guide,*1998.

Beaton, Margaret.*Syria,*1988.

Beattie, Andrew, and Timothy Pepper.*Syria: The Rough Guide,*1998.

Galvin, James.*Divided Loyalties: Nationalism and Mass Politics in Syria at the Close of Empire,*1998.

Hopwood, Derek.*Syria, 1945–1986,*1988.

Lye, Keith.*Take a Trip to Syria,*1988.

Mulloy, Martin.*Syria,*1988.

Quilliam, Neil.*Syria and the New World Order,*1999.

Sinai, Anne, and Allen Pollack, eds.*The Syrian Arab Republic,*1976.

South, Coleman.*Syria,*1995.

Tareq, Ismael Y., and Jacqueline S. Tareq.*Communist Movement in Syria and Lebanon,*1998.

Wedeen, Lisa.*Ambiguities of Domination: Politics, Rhetoric, and Symbols in Contemporary Syria,*1999.

Winkler, Onn.*Demographic Developments and Population Policies in Ba'athist Syria,*1998.

THE CULTURE AND CUSTOMS OF SYRIA

Religion of Syria

Syrian culture is greatly influenced by its high population of Sunni Muslims. Based on the words and actions of the Prophet Muhammad and originated in the 7th century A.D., Islam is a monotheistic faith based on the act of submission to the will of Allah. The five pillars of Islam listed include:

-Shahada: literally translated as "religious witness" which is defined as the actual act of submission

-Salat: participation in daily prayer Salat positions

-Zakat: almsgiving

-Hajj: pilgrimage to the house of Allah, located in Mecca

-Bukhari: observation of fasting during Ramadan

The primary document in Islam is the Quran, which is believed to be a literal recitation of the word of God as told to Muhammad. According to tradition, Muhammad founded the religion of Islam. He is considered the last and greastest among the prophets who emobodies the closest resemblence to perfection. Religiously, as well as politically, Muhammad established himself as a spiritual icon to Muslim followers.

Islam is divided into two main branches, Sunni and Shi'ia. Though their differences date back to early Islam, Sunni Muslims are distinct from Shi'ia due to their acceptance of caliphate (rulers following Muhammed) outside of the familial lineage. Sunnis believe in four traditions, or teachings, in accordance with the Quran, and a Muslim can choose whichever tradition they would like to fulfill. Conversely, Shi'a live by one traditon, and they believe that the cousin of Muhammad is the rightful leader of spiritual authority.

Syria has a rich religious and cultural history rooted in Islam. The Great Mosque of Damascus, built between 709 and 715 AD under caliph al-Walid I, is considered to be the oldest surviving stone mosque and an early example of monumental work in Islamic architecture. The mosque is also said to have served as a central location for Muslims during a period of Umayyad rule.

Syrian Language Characteristics

Arabic is recognized as the official language of Syria. A language with a long history and vast reach, Arabic inscriptions date back to the 4th century and it is the second most widely used writing system in the world . The history of Arabic is rooted in the Qu'ran, which Muslims believe was revealed to Mohammed in Arabic, thus making it a "high language". The widespread use of Modern Standard (MSA) acts as a great cultural unifier for the Muslim community . Followers are said to be "People of the Book" and all texts and formal speech forms across the Arab community use this classical form.

While the Muslim community uses the same written language, the spoken form of Arabic is broken into several regional dialects, which, despite different variations, are considered to be mutually intelligible . The Syrian dialect is Levantine Arabic, the informal verbal form also used in Lebanon, Palestine, and Jordan. This form of the language is used only for informal, day-to-day spoken interactions. As it is one of the most commonly used dialects, it is likely that a non-native speaker could still understand this form of Arabic, despite various different words and speech patterns.

In addition to its influence on the cultural, religious, and political language in Syria, Arabic is also an important part of the arts. The Arabic language itself is said to have developed out of the rhythmic, elevated, and rhymed language used for the public recitation of poetry . After its first textual appearance in the Qu'ran, the written form of Arabic was next seen in elaborate prose written by poets to share stories of the prophet and Arab history. They Syrian poet Abu'l-'Ala al-Ma'arri, who lived from 973-1057, is historically significant as his work questioned general conceptions regarding the afterlife . The written Arabic language has also had an enormous impact on Islamic art. Calligraphy is recognized as a high art form used for decoration in mosques and as an outlet of creative expression that complies with the Islamic ban on figural representation .

Syrian Nonverbal Communication

Both verbal and nonverbal communication in Syria are very important to maintaining social harmony and appropriate social barriers. In the Muslim faith, communication is built around Shura or "mutual consultation." Shura not only promotes effective verbal communication but nonverbal communication as well .

Muslims see nonverbal cues as very important to social harmony as nonverbal criticism such as inappropriate gestures or giving someone the silent treatment may cause misunderstanding and conflict . For example, it is seen as inappropriate to touch someone on the head, therefore patting a child on the head would be construed as very offensive in the Middle East. Specifically, Muslims believe it is best to communicate clearly and avoid nonverbal communication if it is not intended to show love, thanks or appreciation; however, it is better to verbalize these emotions .

Other cultural mannerisms are outlined by nonverbal communication as well. In most Middle Eastern countries the left hand is viewed as impure and should only be used for bodily hygiene. As a result, the left hand should never be extended to greet someone or accept a gift. Eye contact is also important to Middle Easterners; however they are often considered to have "languid eyes," as they look half closed, yet this is not interpreted to show disrespect or disinterest. In addition, when communicating people in the Middle East often stand very close to one another and are quite frank .

Gender also plays a strong role in nonverbal communication. For example, Muslim women may find it offensive if a man stands or sits to close to her, even a male physician . Young children are even taught not to touch members of the opposite sex. Yet, men are often affectionate towards each other. It is common for men to be seen walking down the street holding hands or greeting each other with a hug .

Traditional Syrian Dress

The Syrian people wear their traditional dresses on the celebrations, marriage ceremonies and the birth occasions of the new borne babies. The *traditional dress of Syria* is famous in the Arab region for its conventional crafts, embroidery and fabulous designs. Although, the modern dressing is the fusion of the traditional and western styles and the people of Syria nowadays normally wear westerly attires, yet the traditional gowns, coats and jackets are still popular among the Syrian community.

The Syrian men used to wear the traditional dress including a white shirt made of cotton. They loved to embellish the costume with blue, red and black embroidery round the neck and at the chest. Underneath the shirt men usually wore a pant (*shirwal*) made of colored or non dyed cotton fabric. They also used the traditional coats made with light fabrics as the outer wear which were wide opened at the front and embroidered on its edges. The men also used another cloak which is known as Abaya which is normally made of various light-weight silk, artificial silk or mixed silk or cotton fabrics. They cover their heads with the scarves made of fine cotton or blue or violet silky fabric with red threads.

The traditional dress for women in Syria is a garment made with triangular sleeves and it is called as *Thob*. In the past, the tailors used to apply elegant embroidery round the neck, at the chest and the sides. These dresses were further decorated with amazing patchworks in brilliant colors. The women also wore some other garments made with wool and other delicate fabrics. They also wrapped the dresses with a belt woven from red and black wool or cotton. The upper garment for the women was a coat stitched with materials in dark colors with wide sleeves and side slits. The women of Syria wrap their heads with silky scarves decorated with splendid embroidery and fringes.

The *traditional dress of Syria* can be seen commonly on the eve of the celebrations of national importance. Such events particularly take place in Damascus and Aleppo which are culturally very rich cities.

Syrian Traditions

A few of the traditions passed down through the years include Syrian cuisine, folklore dance, and festivals.

Cuisine

The typical food in Syria is centered on fruits, vegetables, grains, nuts and aromatic spices . Principally, Syrians tend to add lemons, garlic, onion and ginger into most of their recipes. All of these ingredients are used in a myriad of dishes and derive from the culture's most agriculturally rich regions of Syria.

During a typical meal, Syrians begin with hors d'oeurves and appetizers, translated as "mezze" which primarily consist of vegetables, nuts and salads.

An example of hors d'oeurve is called "kibbe." It consists of meat and pine nuts within a shell of wheat and flour, and it is one of the most difficult foods to make . Soups are also common as well.

Main dishes consist of chicken or fish and a side of rice. For most meals, pita bread is served as a means for dipping into a variety of the foods, especially "humus." After the main course, Syrians end the meal with tea or coffee accompanied with fruit and pastries .

For Syrians, presentation is everything. Making the food look appetizing and setting the table appropriately reflected her abilities as well . Everything, even the simplest dishes are garnished with fresh herbs. Because such a tremendous amount of time and effort are placed on Syrian meals, the quality of the cooking determines the competency of the individual (usually a woman) who had cooked the meal.

Festivals

Entertainment is a major aspect of Syrian life. The following explains a few of the most popular festivals held in Syrian cities.

The Traditional Festival

Taking place in May, the popular Traditional Festival, also known as the Desert Festival, is an exhilarating and entertaining event of about 40 camels racing through the ruins of Palmyra, an ancient Syrian city .

The Bosra Festival

In the month of September, the Bosra Festival, which takes place in the city of Bosra, promotes cultural exchange and diversity. During this festival, several musicians of opera, symphony, ballet and other classical genres from around the world join to celebrate their differences

The International Flower Fair

In the city of Damascus, the International Flower fair presents the most beautiful flowers of the world, including the renowned Damascus rose . Amongst the variety of competitions, visitors experience the beauty and senses of nature.

The Damascus International Fair

Another popular festival, held in Damascus, is called the Damascus International Trade Fair. Taking pace in September, this fair is "recognized as one of the most traditional business events in all of the Middle East," and over 45 countries have participated in previous fairs .

Folklore Dance: Dabka

Within Syria, modernism has altered the fundamental traditions of the past, especially in a folklore dance called Dabka. While the dance is still used in today's performances, the specific movements and characteristics of the dance have changed with time. However, the emotions that derive from the dance, including joy, excitement and anguish have lasted through the years.

Dabka is a dance "of several light coordinated steps with movements of the body that express vivacity of the males and tenderness of the females, accompanied by frequent organized movements of feet, beating the ground in harmony with a drum, a flute or any other country musical instrument."

Therefore, Dabka was primarily a rapid beating of the feet. In modern society, there are different types of Dabka that exist around Syria. Depending on the region where it is performed, the dance may be more energetic or more serene due to laborious circumstances and social nature within that specific region. The songs that originate from the dance represent the customs and the dialect of a certain region as well. Nevertheless, despite the variety of regional dances, Syrian folklore dance is a fundamental aspect of society that will be cherished for generations to come.

Family

Because of its extensive history and religious zeal, Syria is a traditional society that prides itself on several significant factors of life. The culture focuses on the importance of respect, self-discipline, education and above all, family.

Even with other significant aspects of life, including business and social duties, Syrians put family above everything else. The family background of an individual is the main reason for their reputation and social status. Furthermore, a great amount of honor and respect is placed on the family. Syrians believe that there is no loyalty as great as the loyalty found among family members, and it is not likely for a Syrian to put as much loyalty into any other aspect of his life. In fact, "There is widespread conviction that the only reliable people are one's kinsmen" . Therefore, family holds the highest value within the Syrian culture.

Marriage and the birth of children are among the greatest celebrations of Syria. However, Syrians are very strict in regards to both events. They "universally encourage endogamy or the marriage of members within the group" . This further supports their passion and attention towards family background. While the family background of a woman is still significant, tracing descent is usually more common among men. After all, since men tend to have more authority and power in this society, it is wise for a woman to marry a man with an honorable family background in order to keep the family proud. Sometimes marriages are arranged, but typically, the standard is to marry within the Arab community and to someone who has a reputable family background .

Therefore, primarily due to religious beliefs and social

expectations, Syrians put their families on a pedestal. Because Syrians depend on their families to such an extent, interrupting or upsetting family life would be foolish with devastating effects on its members. Furthermore, the attention to the family is especially recognizable in regards to the demanding expectations for the marriage of kin. Evidently, since family is one of the main stable foundations of Syrian society, given their political, economic and social unrest, they completely support their values and norms within the family context.

Syrian Business Customs

Visitors traveling to Syria must be aware and constantly conscious of the country's traditions and societal norms, and attention to such behaviors becomes increasingly important in the world of business. Foreign businesses that operate in this traditionally conservative and heavily Islamic environment cite that problems in the workplace typically arise due to differences in preferred pace, confusing government policy, and decisions based on loyalty to relationships rather than business minded . In attempting to forge new business relationships in Syria it is advised that visitors familiarize themselves with the following characteristics of the Syrian business world:

Formalities

Syrian business dress is equally formal to what is expected internationally; attire should match the conservative mindset of this setting . Women are very rarely present in the Syrian workplace, much less involved in negotiations, and are viewed as a threat; thus visiting females should particularly make an effort to dress modestly in order to assimilate more easily into the business environment.

Business cards are expected to be available for exchange . If possible, have cards readily available that also include Arabic translations. It is customary to ask many questions and get to know someone during introductions; questions regarding family, friends, and personal matters are not out of the ordinary. Syrians are also very well connected and closely tied to their extended family. Outsiders should be very conscious of what they say or comments made about other individuals as they more than likely could get back to the person or possibly offend a new acquaintance .

Work Schedule

The Syrian workweek operates Sunday through Thursday, leaving the days of Friday and Saturday as the weekend . The average workday begins at 9 am and goes until 2 pm, at which time a lunch break is taken. It is important not to place calls or attempt to conduct business matters at this time. Following this break, business resumes at 5 pm and continues to 9 pm.

Negotiations

It is standard for Syrian business interactions and negotiations to take place over food and drink, the appropriate drink being tea or coffee . Frustrations often arise from foreign businesses conscious of time as money due to the fact that Syrians do not consider time a factor of business negotiations. It is customary to become familiar with a new acquaintance and engage in "chit chat" prior to the actual negotiation .

Once negotiations have commenced, Syrian's are said to speak from the heart and tell stories, a style more personal than what is recognized as typically business-like . Negotiations are often left open and could take a matter of days, weeks or months. Syrians would rather not say anything or not come to a resolution than say something incorrect; timeliness is not considered as a Syrian business may get back to a foreign company weeks or months later, a practice that is customary but often misinterpreted abroad as very delayed or rude.

It is crucial to build a personal relationship with Syrians, as a major complaint of outside businesses is that the winning of a bid is often based upon loyalty to relationships rather than an actual business proposal . Securing a contract is one way of ensuring a solidified business relationship, however this may not be a definite solution as the influence of government policy will be discussed below.

Typologies of Syria

Cultures are dynamic and always changing, yet some of these qualities are intrinsic. These traits are often learned, cuturally distinctive and passed down through generations. Researchers have developed ways of evaluating these traits and culturally specific behaviors through the use of Hofstede's Value Dimensions, Kluckhohn and Strodtbeck's Human Nature Orientations, and Hall's High Context and Low Context Orientations.

Hofstede's Value Dimensions:

The following focuses on Hofstede's four value dimensions which include individualism/collectivism, uncertainty avoidance, power distance, masculinity/femininity, and long or short term orientation.

In determining the individualism/collectivism factor, Hofstede recommends evaluating the culture's desire to focus on the self or the group as a whole. Uncertainty avoidance defines how a culture avoids ambiguous situations. Higher avoidance shows a low tolerance for ambiguity and lower avoidance shows a high tolerance for ambiguity. The power distance of a culture is determined by how power is distributed amongst its citizens and how the power from authorities is perceived. In regards to masculinity/femininity, the culture's views towards personal achievement and acquirement of wealth versus helping others and the quality of life will determine whether the culture has high masculinity or low masculinity. Lastly, a culture is short term oriented if they live for today rather than living for tomorrow, which is characterized as long term oriented.

Collectivist – Syria upholds a unity within their nation primarily because of the Islam religion, which acknowledges sacrificing oneself for the betterment of the group. Furthermore, collectivism is represented in their motto: "Unity, liberty and socialism."

High Uncertainty Avoidance – Syrians believe in upholding traditions, making them past oriented. Because of their conservative and religious outlook, modernization is a threat to Islamic principles. Additionally, several laws were developed to govern social behavior.

High Power Distance – Syria values socialism, and therefore equality among its members. However, because of previous instability and corruption within the government, political officials control numerous aspects of society.

High Masculinity – Men dominate politics and business, leaving the women to raise the family and maintain the household.

Short Term Orientation – Since Syria is marked by instability, it is short term oriented. Although they value past traditions, they still struggle, day by day, to maintain a sense of security.

Kluckhohn's and Strodtbeck's Value Orientations:

The following are Kluckholm and Strodtbeck's value orientations which deal with five universal aspects of human behavior. The first value orientation deals with the character of human nature in that culture. The second value orientation is in regards to nature and whether humans of that culture are subservient to nature or masters of nature. The third value orientation evaluates the orientation towards time within that culture, which asks whether they are past oriented, present oriented or future oriented. The fourth value dimension discusses the culture's value in regards to current activity. This asks whether they are a being culture, a becoming culture or a doing culture. The fifth and final value dimension deals with the relationship between people and power.

Mixture of Good and Evil – Muslim is the primary religion in Syria. Because of this, Syrians view human nature as a mixture of good and evil due to the Muslim belief that people are inherently good, but the political instability which may make Syrians believe that people are also evil.

Harmony with Nature – Based on the geography of Syria, much of the terrain is desert land. This land cannot be used for agricultural purposes, and Syria has had a few problems dealing with deforestation and overgrazing in richer soiled lands. However, there has been progress towards creating more protected natural space in order to maintain the nature within Syria.

Past/Present Oriented – Syrians are past oriented because they follow many of the conservative traditions of Muslim teachings. However, they are present oriented as well because they are becoming more aware of the progressive global economy and strive to be a major contributor to its successes.

Being in Becoming – Syria is a being culture primarily due to the main religion having traditions that Muslims in Syria would like to uphold and maintain. However, it is a being in becoming culture because they are currently improving their economic and political foundations to adjust to the changing global arena.

Authoritarian – Within much of the Arab world, including Syria, many believe that certain people are born to lead while others should follow. This is in accordance with the Islam faith and social institutions.

THE SOCIETY

SYRIAN SOCIETY IS a mosaic of social groups of various sizes that lacks both a consistent stratification system linking all together and a set of shared values and loyalties binding the population into one nation.

Distinctions of language, region, religion, ethnicity, and way of life cut across the society, producing a large number of separate communities, each marked by strong internal loyalty and solidarity. Although nearly twothirds of the people are Arabic-speaking Sunni Muslims, they do not constitute a unitary social force because of the strongly felt differences among beduin, villager, and urban dweller. A perceptive observer has spoken of the "empty center" of Syrian society, a society lacking an influential group embodying a national consensus.

The ethnic and religious minorities, none of which amounts to more than 15 percent of the population, nevertheless form geographically compact and psychologically significant blocs that function as distinct social spheres and dominate specific regions of the country. Because the religious groups in each locality function as largely independent social universes, a "minority mentality," characterized by suspicion toward those of different groups, is widespread among both minority group members and those of the majority group living in minority-dominated areas where they are therefore outnumbered. Psychologically and politically, religious distinctions are by far the most significant ones. In all groups, loyalty to one's fellow members, rather than to a larger Syrian nation, is a paramount value.

The religious communities are more than groups of coworshipers; they are largely self-contained social systems that regulate much of the daily life of their members and receive their primary loyalty. The independence of the religious communities is a distinctly divisive force in society. Although Islam provides the central symbolic and cultural orientation for about 85 percent of Syrians, minority communities, most with a long history in the region, maintain cultural and religious patterns outside the Muslim consensus.

The religions, sects, and denominations differ widely in formal doctrine and belief. Nevertheless, there exists in Syria a stratum of folk belief and practice common to rural and uneducated persons of many religions. Members of various groups hold certain common beliefs in saints and spirits and observe related practices, such as exorcism and visitation of shrines, regardless of the disapproval of the orthodox religious authorities.

In addition to linguistic and religious dissimilarities, three forms of traditional social and ecological organization further divide the society. Most Syrians, including many members of religious and ethnic minorities, inhabit rural villages and earn their living as subsistence farmers. A dwindling number live the admired nomadic life of the beduin, or tribesman.

The remainder, including a substantial number of recent migrants from the countryside, live in cities and towns, many of which date from ancient times. Each of these three represents a distinct, usually hereditary, way of life, followed by particular social groups and separated from the others by such social barriers as marriage restrictions, education, and occupation.

The ascent to power of minority groups and their implementation of Baathist policies of secularism and socialism, has left most non-Muslims financially better off than the average Syrian, putting them in an anomalous position. On the one hand, many have reasserted their solidarity with Syria's opposition to Israel, the West, alleged imperialism, and capitalism. On the other hand, some observers have noted an exodus of numerous urban businessmen, professionals, and managers, particularly Christians and non-Arabs. In response, during the mid- and late-1970s, the government encouraged the return of these émigrés and attempted to develop a climate more favorable to them.

Successive Syrian regimes have attempted to consolidate a Syrian national identity by eliminating the centrifugal effects of sectarianism. Despite these efforts, Syria's postindependence history is replete with conflict between minority groups and the central government.

In part this conflict can be attributed to the French mandatory administration, from which Syria inherited a confessional system of parliamentary representation similar to that of Lebanon, in which specific seats were allocated to Christians, Kurds, Druzes, Alawis, Circassians, Turkomans, and Jews. These ethnic and religious groups were guaranteed 35 of parliament's 142 seats. Minority groups also protested what they believed to be infringement on their political rights, and in 1950 successfully blocked efforts by the Sunni Muslim president to declare Islam the official state religion. A 1953 bill finally abolished the communal system of parliamentary representation;subsequent legislation eliminated separate jurisdictional rights in matters of personal and legal status which the French had granted certain minority groups.

The struggle to balance minority rights and Sunni Islamic majority representation remains a paramount theme in Syrian domestic affairs. In 1987, the Syrian government was dominated by President Hafiz al

Assad's Alawi minority. The secular socialism of the ruling Baath (Arab Socialist Resurrection) Party deemphasized Islam as a component of Syrian and Arab nationalism. However, Baath ideology prescribed that non-Muslims respect Islam as their "national culture."

In 1986 educational and cultural institutions remained under close governmental supervision. Such institutions were designed to further government objectives by raising the general level of education and literacy, strengthening awareness of Arab cultural achievements, building public support for official policies resting on the principles of the ruling Baath Party and seeking to foster a sense of Syrian national unity. Public bodies serving these objectives multiplied during the late 1960s and by the mid1980s included the ministries of education, higher education, information, and national guidance and culture. Their activities were complemented by several directorates, authorities, and planning boards. In the consolidated budget for fiscal year (FY) 1985, nearly LS (Syrian pound) 3.43 billion, or 14.5 percent of the government's expenditure, were earmarked for education of minorities. Despite the educational system's failure to achieve the government's goals, education remained an important channel of upward mobility for minorities.

SYRIA'S STRUGGLING CIVIL SOCIETY

Authoritarian regimes have traditionally been disinclined to accept any political or social opposition and have been hostile to the development of an independent civil society that could form a counterweight to state power.

Article 8 of the Syrian constitution established the Baath party, which has prevented any independent parties from emerging since the 1963 military coup that brought it to power as "the leading party in the state and society." Yet despite this systematic repression, there has been a sustained effort by a small group of intellectuals and critics over the past decade to transform the country's political system and make it more open and accountable.

While these activists did not ignite the uprising that has shaken Syria since March 2011, their courageous defiance of Bashar al-Assad's regime has given them high standing among many Syrians. They may yet play a significant role in shaping Syria's future.

Commitment to Freedom

Bashar al-Assad's assumption of the presidency in July 2000 gave rise to a brief period of unprecedented easing of state repression known as the "Damascus Spring" whereby dozens of discussion forums and associations were created, all calling for political liberalization and democratic openness.

This sector of Syrian civil society came to light with the "Declaration of the 99," signed by numerous intellectuals including Burhan Ghalyoun, Sadeq al-Azm, Michel Kilo, Abdul Rahman Munif, Adonis and Haidar Haidar, who demanded: 1) an end to the state of emergency and martial law applied in Syria since 1963; 2) a public pardon to all political detainees and those who are pursued for their political ideas and permission for all deportees and exiled citizens to return; 3) a rule of law that will recognize freedom of assembly, of the press, and of expression; 4) freedom in public life from the laws, constraints, and various forms of surveillance, allowing citizens to express their various interests within a framework of social harmony and peaceful [economic] competition and enable all to participate in the development and prosperity of the country.

On January 1, 2001, a group of Syrian lawyers demanded a complete reform of the constitution, the lifting of emergency laws, and the concession of full civil liberties. Shortly thereafter, a group of activists published the founding charter of their civil society committee — better known as the "Declaration of the 1,000." The following day, the Jamal Atassi Forum for Democratic Dialogue was established with the participation of communists, Nasserites, socialists and Baathist critics of the regime, and on March 7, authorization was given to create independent organizations for the defense of human rights as well as cultural and social associations made up of moderate Muslims. This group included the Islamic Studies Center, headed by Muhammad Habash, a progressive scholar opposed to the Muslim Brotherhood, who served as a parliament member. By July 3, 2001, the Human Rights Association of Syria had been established with lawyer Haitham al-Malih as president.

In just a few months, two hundred discussion clubs and forums were created. Reacting to the proliferation of spaces where the future of Syria was being freely debated, the regime pushed back, fearful it might lose its monopoly on power. Invoking a need to maintain national unity in the face of external threats, beginning in September 2001, the regime arrested deputies Riad Saif and Mamoun al-Homsi, economist Arif Dalila, lawyer Anwar al-Bunni, and Atassi Forum spokesman Habib Issa, followed in short order by Kamal al-Labwani and Haitham al-Malih. All were sentenced to between three and twelve years in jail on charges of "weakening national sentiment" and "inciting sectarian strife." Other important figures were forbidden to leave the country including Radwan Ziyyade, director of the Damascus Center for Human Rights Studies, and Suhair Atassi, director of the Jamal Atassi Forum.

In an open challenge to the regime, prominent figures persisted in the demand for reform. The Damascus declaration stated that the "establishment of a democratic national regime is the basic approach to the plan for change and political reform. It must be peaceful, gradual, founded on accord, and based on dialogue and recognition of the other." This declaration also called on the government to "abolish all forms of exclusion in public life by suspending the emergency law; and abolish martial law and extraordinary courts, and all relevant laws, including Law 49 for the year 1980 [which made membership in the Muslim Brotherhood a capital offense]; release all political prisoners; [allow] the safe and honorable return of all those wanted and those who have been voluntarily or involuntarily exiled with legal guarantees; and end all forms of political persecution by settling grievances and turning a new leaf in the history of the country."

The declaration was the result of efforts made by journalist Michel Kilo to unify the main political forces, including the banned Muslim Brotherhood. Kilo had met with the group's leader, Ali Sadreddine Bayanouni, in Morocco where they agreed on a program based on nonviolence, democracy, opposition unity, and political change. A further public attack on the regime, the Beirut-Damascus declaration, which called on the Syrian regime to recognize Lebanon's independence, establish full diplomatic relations and demarcate the joint border, led to a second wave of arrests during which Kilo and Bunni were imprisoned. With this example, the regime tried to put a stop to its opponents' efforts and to ensure that their demands did not awaken Syrian society from its political lethargy.

The People's Revolt

One of the dissidents' foremost weaknesses was their inability to get their message out due to draconian restrictions on the freedom of gathering and expression. In a 2005 interview, noted activist Kamal al-Labwani provided an accurate, indeed prophetic, prognosis of the current situation when he cautioned that there is no politically mobilized street. When that happens, everything will change. Today, the opposition is purely symbolic, and this sort of opposition is incapable of uniting because it is based on personalities, on the capability of single individuals to confront the authorities... Society is watching, and when the masses begin to move, they will move behind those who represent them... So right now, we are reserving space in that arena so that when the day comes that people move to the street—either because of foreign or their internal pressures—we will be ready.

The fall of Zine al-Abidine Ben Ali in Tunisia, Husni Mubarak in Egypt, along with the upheavals in Yemen, Libya, and Bahrain, had a contagious effect across the Arab world. Most Syrian dissidents saw the uprisings as the long-awaited opportunity to introduce major changes inside the country. In an article in the Lebanese newspaper *as-Safir*, the prominent Syrian dissident Michel Kilo argued, "We are entering a new historical stage based on the primacy of citizenship, freedom, justice, equality, secularism, and the rights of men and citizens." After spending five years in prison, Anwar al-Bunni stated that "an event like this only happens once every 200 years, and it is clearly going to bring about a radical change."

On March 10, former parliamentarian Mamoun al-Homsi appealed to the Syrian people: "After fifty years of tyranny and oppression, we are beginning to see the sunlight of freedom approach." He openly accused the regime of resorting to repression, corruption, and sectarian division to remain in power. On March 15, after a first unsuccessful attempt, an anonymous Facebook group, The Syrian Revolution 2011, called for a second day of rage, which led to a mass demonstration against the regime to demand democratic openness.

Despite these appeals, few in Syria expected Assad to follow the path taken by Ben Ali and Mubarak and abdicate power. Rather, it was hoped that the new regional developments would force the regime to abandon its stubborn resistance to change and, in the face of pressure from the street, introduce reforms. As the more politicized elements in Syrian society had been decimated by successive waves of repression, there was little attempt at the outset to mobilize the masses, reasoning that they had little power to affect such change. Thus, the outbreak of popular rage surprised everyone. Suhair al-Atassi, who was in hiding at the time, recently said,

We have been subjected to suppression and murder for merely calling for freedom, democracy, general freedoms, the release of all prisoners of conscience, an end to the state of emergency, and the return of all political exiles. At the time, we said that any suppression would cause the volcano to erupt... we knew that we were working slowly but surely toward freedom, but we didn't dream of a revolution like this breaking out. It was the Syrian youth who made this dream a reality.

The revolt began in the southern city of Dar'a and then gradually and progressively spread across almost the entire country. The demonstrations, which at first mobilized a few thousand people at best, began to enjoy great prestige. In Bunni's words: In the past, only a few of us dared to call for freedom and human rights. We used to feel isolated, as the majority of people avoided us for fear of retribution from the authorities. After my release, I have realized that my demands became the demands of the entire Syrian people.

Initially, important sectors of the population demanded limited reforms, but Assad's brutal repression raised the bar. Appearing before parliament on March 30, 2011, the president made it clear that any reforms would not come about as a result of popular pressure and that the process of political liberalization would not be hurried. Some members of the intelligentsia believed that the regime would not be able to introduce reforms without collapsing:

We all know that the authorities lie and they won't permit anyone to speak out because the regime is corrupt and dictatorial, and corruption and dictatorship fundamentally contradict transparency and freedom of opinion because the first opinion that anyone would express would be opposition to the regime's corruption and tyranny and the crimes it has committed. And then they'll face arrest, interrogation, and a trial. They say, we'll enact a party law; we'll implement reform, but these are all lies because these authorities are incapable of it.

Michel Kilo added, Syria today is experiencing an existential crisis related to the distribution of wealth, social justice, freedom, and political participation, and this is not going to be resolved with repression. The police should be arresting killers, thieves, and smugglers, but not hungry people with nothing to put in their mouths.

As the uprising spread, the Syrian regime blamed the violence on armed radical elements seeking to destabilize the country. Assad told parliament that Syria was facing a conspiracy intended to provoke a sectarian war between Sunnis and Alawites. The regime tried to use this tactic to play for time in the midst of a rebellion that had taken it by surprise as well as to justify the high number of civilians killed by the security services and pro-government armed groups. Repression has intensified in the ensuing months and spread to most of the cities, but the security forces have failed to suppress the popular uprising. Faced with the success of the demonstrations, the Syrian regime was forced to back down in July and adopt a series of cosmetic reforms to try to quell the unrest, including the initiation of a national dialogue. The rebels roundly declared these measures insufficient and designed merely to buy the Assad regime more time.

As the unrest has continued, most activists have come to believe that the protest wave has transformed into a revolution that will bring about the fall of the regime. From her hiding place in July 2011, Suhair al-Atassi gave an apt description of the spirit of the demonstrations:

It's a revolution... triggered by the Syrian people seeking to stand up and say that they are citizens and not subjects, and that Syria belongs to all its citizens and not just the Assad family. This is a revolution of the youth who are demanding freedom and are being confronted with violence and murder... Today Syria is witnessing a battle for freedom by unarmed civilians urging the ouster of a regime that has utilized methods of brutal and inhumane suppression. They have brutally attacked and killed the protesters whilst the demonstrators have nothing but their words to defend them.

An Opposition Divided

As a result of fifty years of repressive measures, it is not surprising that the recent uprising has been an ensemble movement with contributions from different players. The economist and commentator Omar Dahi has identified five clearly differentiated groups taking part in the unrest: traditional opposition parties (socialists, Nasserites, and communists); dissident intellectuals; the youth movement, including the leaders of the Local Coordination Committees (LCC), which has driven the revolution and was joined by other sectors of society; a disorganized cohort of conservative Muslims; and armed Salafist groups who represent a minority.

Most of these groups (with the exception of the Salafi elements) agreed about the need to avoid violence, reject sectarianism, and prevent foreign intervention. On August 29, 2011, the LCC stated,

While we understand the motivation to take up arms or call for military intervention, we specifically reject this position as we find it unacceptable politically, nationally, and ethically. Militarizing the revolution would minimize popular support and participation in the revolution. Moreover, militarization would undermine the gravity of the humanitarian catastrophe involved in a confrontation with the regime. Militarization would put the revolution in an arena where the regime has a distinct advantage and would erode the moral superiority that has characterized the revolution since its beginning.

Initially, opposition figures urged the creation of a new social pact between the rulers and the ruled, rejecting the use of violence to force Assad from power. Bunni, for example, advocated "a peaceful solution to all the problems" while Kilo urged "a new national contract for a peaceful and negotiated end to the crisis" arguing that "a bloody conflict must be prevented given that exacerbating the sectarian tensions could lead to chaos." At the beginning of August, Kilo warned, "There are some who have chosen to take up arms against the regime, but they only represent a minority of the demonstrators. But if the authorities persist in using violence, then they will become a majority."

At first, national dialogue was also defended, but as the uprising has advanced and the repression intensified, most of the intelligentsia has come to reject this option. In March, the intellectual Burhan Ghalyoun, later named president of the National Transition Council, warned that

to get out of the crisis, the whole crisis, the use of weapons must be rejected and political logic must be accepted... The logic of negotiation and political dialogue requires credibility and the recognition of the other.

He cautioned, however, that such an attitude seemed lacking in Assad, who continued "to dream about formal reforms within the existing regime, a regime with only one ruler, one party, and one authority."

Confronted with external and internal pressure, the regime indicated its readiness for a national dialogue, authorizing a historic meeting with opposition members in Damascus on June 27. Some members of the protest movement, notably Kilo, Louai Hussein, and Hassan Abbas, chose to participate, yet most signatories to the 2005 Damascus declaration boycotted the meeting and contested the participants' right to speak on behalf of the demonstrators. While Hussein contended that the main goal of the meeting was "to organize a safe, peaceful transition from tyranny to freedom," Bunni argued that it would be exploited by the regime and used "to cover up the arrests, murders, and tortures that continue to take place on a daily basis.

Then on July 9 and 10, the regime sponsored yet another national dialogue meeting, which was boycotted by almost all opposition leaders. "While the regime is meeting—and that is what today was—there are funerals in other cities, and people continue to be killed and arrested," commented Razan Zeitouneh, a lawyer and prominent LCC member. Syrian Human Rights Association president Malih, likewise, declined the invitation, saying

Whoever attends such a dialogue with a regime that commits these crimes is a traitor to the people. After 200 martyrs, 1,500 missing persons, and 15,000 refugees, what is there to talk about? How can you have a dialogue with a person who is holding you at gunpoint?

The meeting was attended by two hundred delegates, most of them intellectuals and politicians with close ties to the regime, and was presented as a steppingstone to a transition to democracy.

Vice President Farouk al-Shara opened the meeting with the expressed hope that "it will lead to... the transformation of Syria into a pluralistic, democratic state where its citizens are equal."In a surprising development, the final statement exceeded expectations by raising the issue of releasing all political prisoners, including those arrested since the uprising began (with the exception of those involved in crimes).

It also argued that "dialogue is the only way to end the crisis in Syria" and strongly rejected any foreign interference under the pretext of defending human rights.

Furthermore, it called for deeper reforms and stronger efforts to combat corruption and requested the amendment of the constitution to make it commensurate with the rule of law, a multiparty system, and democracy.

Most Syrian activists agreed that the offer to engage in dialogue came too late and that the regime had lost all credibility. In the words of Suhair Atassi,

It has been contaminated by the blood of our people! How could we accept this [national dialogue]? It came too late! This is not to mention the lack of trust between the people and the regime. The best example of this was the arrests of the artists and intellectuals who decided to take to the streets in solidarity with the legitimate demands for greater freedoms in Syria. The Syrian regime was merely trying to buy time with this national dialogue... The Syrian opposition is united, which can be seen in its joint decision to boycott the so-called dialogue with the authorities that have been killing and suppressing the people.

In their statement, the LCC dismissed the meeting's results on the grounds that Syrians who have already been killed and tortured by the thousands will not accept any proposals or arrangements that leave Bashar Assad, the intelligence service, and the death squads in control of their lives.

As the uprising intensified and the dissidents' demands grew, the need to form a transition government, given the possible collapse of the regime, was considered.

As early as April 2011, Kilo had requested the formation of "a government of national unity," and by mid-July, Malih had gone still further, calling for a shadow government made up of "independent experts" that would unify the opposition movements and prepare for the post-Assad era.

Foreign Intervention?

The Turkish government has followed the unfolding Syrian crisis with deep concern. In the earliest phases of the uprising, Prime Minister Recep Tayyip Erdoðan and Foreign Minister Ahmet Davutoðlu advised the regime to end the repression and democratize the country. Assad ignored this "friendly advice," generating a profound unease in Ankara, which was heightened by the arrival of thousands of refugees fleeing the besieged Syrian town of Jisr Shughour.

The possibility of a full-fledged civil war troubles Ankara, which believes that the intensification of violence would significantly increase the influx of refugees into its territory. In an interview with the Qatar newspaper *ash-Sharq*, Erdoðan stressed the importance of the ties between the two countries:

For Turkey, Syria is not just another country, it's a neighbor with which we share a 910-kilometer-long border... and with which we have shared interests that cannot be ignored... We know very well that stability there is part of our national security, and we are afraid that the situation will lead to the outbreak of a civil war between Alawites and Sunnis.

The widening gap between Ankara and Damascus also means the end of Davutoðlu's "zero problems with neighbors" policy. The premise of this policy was that by way of increasing its international clout, Turkey had to maintain the best possible relationships with neighboring countries and diversify its alliances.

This required that Ankara turn its attention back to the Middle East, a region that had formed an integral part of the Ottoman Empire for centuries, thus filling a long-standing vacuum that no Arab regime had been able to fill.

The Turkish government thus warned Damascus that trade relations between the two countries, which amount to around $2.5 billion annually, could be endangered. It also hosted various opposition group meetings inside Turkey with the goal of creating a road map for a post-Assad era.

In mid-July, Istanbul hosted the National Salvation Conference, which elected Malih as its president. During the meeting, Malih rejected any dialogue with the regime: "The Syrian regime has declared war on its people, who will not go back home until the regime has fallen." The final statement from the meeting called for the formation of a shadow government, but not before the fall of the regime, and expressed its will to reach "a unified approach" between the opposition and the young demonstrators.

In a subsequent meeting, held in Istanbul on August 23, 2011, the Syrian opposition agreed to create a National Transition Council (NTC) comprised of opposition members both inside and outside the country and presided over by Burhan Ghalyoun, a Syrian academic residing in France. Despite their differences, the intensity of the repression had brought opposition members together. Basma Qadmani, their spokesperson, told the media that "the NTC represents the major forces: political parties and independent figures who symbolize the Syrian opposition." The names of Syria-based NTC members were kept secret to prevent reprisals.

In September, this group was renamed the Syrian National Council (SNC). It included members of the Damascus declaration, the Syrian Muslim Brotherhood, the Local Coordination Committees, the Syrian Revolution General Commission, Kurdish factions, tribal leaders, and independent figures. One of the first decisions of SNC was to approve a national consensus charter that defined the principles of the Syrian revolution:

1) Affirming that the Syrian revolution is a revolution for freedom and dignity;
2) Maintaining the peaceful nature of the revolution;
3) Affirming national unity and rejecting any call for sectarianism or monopolizing of the revolution;
4) Recognizing Syria is for all Syrians on an equal footing;
5) Rejecting foreign military intervention.

While the opposition members initially rejected any foreign intervention, voices favoring this eventuality began to emerge, albeit still in the minority. During the Istanbul conference, Malih urged the U.N. to put an end to the bloodshed through political and diplomatic pressure but soundly rejected any military intervention. Earlier, Kilo had also declared his desire "to see an exclusively Syrian solution... reached based on a broad, complete national understanding."

Yet given the worsening situation, the opposition has begun to consider different scenarios to bring the dictatorship to an end.

Some favor following the Libyan example where the uprising combined with foreign military intervention to bring about the collapse of the regime: Ashraf al-Miqdad, signer to the Damascus declaration living in Australia, told *Asharq al-Awsat* that the Syrian regime will never stop the repression and murders, meaning that there are only two options: foreign intervention or arming the revolutionaries... International military intervention has become the only possible solution.

The other alternative would be to divide the army, which would avoid having to arm the people.

Although these voices still represent a minority, they reflect the growing desperation of the Syrian opposition, which believes that the uprising may lose its muscle if none of the objectives are reached soon. On July 29, 2011, a group of defectors formed the Syrian Free Army (SFA). By mid October, there were an estimated 10,000 to 15,000 defectors especially active in the north and central regions. In the last months of the year, SFA began launching some operations against the Syrian army.

The LCC has tried to nip this debate in the bud, stating in a communiqué, "While we understand the motivation to take up arms or call for military intervention, we specifically reject this position as we find it unacceptable politically, nationally, and ethically." At least for now, then, it seems that a Libya-style intervention is being rejected. The communiqué stressed

The method by which the regime is overthrown is an indication of what Syria will be like in the post-regime era. If we maintain our peaceful demonstrations, which include our cities, towns, and villages, and our men, women, and children, the possibility of democracy in our country is much greater. If an armed confrontation or international military intervention becomes a reality, it will be virtually impossible to establish a legitimate foundation for a proud future Syria.

Malih concurred, "Any foreign intervention would destroy Syria, just like what has happened in Libya... the revolution in Syria will prevail, and the regime will be brought down by peaceful means." He added that "the revolutionaries will not fall into the trap" of militarizing the uprising.

An eventual militarization could have devastating effects and would likely be exploited by the regime to present itself as the guarantor of internal stability and to regain some of the territory lost to the rebels. The possibility of an outbreak of civil war could have unforeseeable effects on Syria's neighbors since it shares borders with Israel, Lebanon, Turkey, Iraq, and Jordan. As Arab League secretary general Nabil al-Arabi recently said, "Syria is not Libya... Syria plays a central role in the region, and what happens there has a direct impact on Lebanon and Iraq."

10

Tourism

Although it has some of the oldest cities in Western Asia, such as Damascus and Aleppo (a UNESCO World Heritage Site),tourism in Syria has been greatly reduced by the Syrian Civil War and its associated refugee crisis. Many former tourist attractions have been destroyed by shelling; flights by all major airlines have been suspended, and many major hotels have closed. It is estimated that considerable investment will be necessary to revive the country's tourism industry.

Overview

Before the 2011 crisis

In 2010, tourism had increased considerably compared with the previous year. According to the Tourism Ministry in January 2011, about 6 million foreign tourists visited Syria in 2009; for 2010 the figure was 8.5 million tourists, a 40-percent increase. Tourism revenue was given as 30.8 billion Syrian pounds ($8.4 billion) in 2010, 14 percent of the country's economy.Reports in 2012 from the same Syrian ministry put 2010 tourism industry revenue at $6.5 billion, accounting for 12 percent of the gross domestic product and 11 percent of the nation's employment.

After 2011

Since the beginning of the Syrian Civil War in March 2011, tourism has declined steeply. According to official reports, hotel rooms designed for foreign tourists have been occupied by refugees. In the first quarter of 2012, tourism revenue was about 12.8 billion Syrian pounds ($178 million), compared with 52 billion Syrian pounds ($1 billion) in the first quarter of 2011, and the number of foreign tourists decreased by more than 76 percent in the 2012 quarter. Employment in the tourism industry was down by "nearly two-thirds" in that period. According to UNESCO, five of Syria's six World Heritage Sites have been affected by the civil war. In 2012, Syria sent a letter to the United Nations describing the decline of its tourism industry, noting that the country's hotel-occupancy rate had fallen from 90 percent the previous year to 15 percent.

As of 2013, overall Syrian tourism revenue had declined by 94 percent, with Aleppo the worst affected, and the Tourism Minister stated, at the end of September 2013, that 289 tourist destinations had been damaged by conflict since 2011.

By 2015, the movement of tourists had declined by more than 98%. The Syrian Ministry of Tourism claimed that 45,000 tourists visited the country in the first half of 2015, but these figures were disputed by observers, according to the Syrian Economic Forum, which stated that Iranian religious tourism was all that remained. According to a 2015 article in *The Telegraph*, hotels by beaches in the Mediterranean coast in Tartus and Latakia still received internal tourists and one hotel was "full" in the summer of 2014 and 2015.

Promotion

Promotion of tourism in Syria is handled by the Syrian Ministry of Tourism. Syra's Tourism ministry maintains an active Facebook page as well as an official Syria Tourism website. In September 2016, Syria's Ministry of Tourism drew criticism from some quarters for releasing a video, "Syria Always Beatiful [*sic*]," encouraging tourists to visit its beaches. The video spotlighted regions such as Tartus, which remain somewhat peaceful, though Tartus saw an attack resulting in the deaths of over 150 in May 2016.

ATTRACTIONS

UNESCO sites

There are the six UNESCO World Heritage Sites in the country. Twelve other sites submitted to UNESCO are on the organisation's tentative list: Norias of Hama, Ugrarit (Tell Shamra), Ebla (Tell Mardikh), Mari (Tell Hariri), Dura-Europos, Apamée (Afamia), Qasr al-Hayr ach-Charqi, Maaloula, Tartus, Arwad and two sites in theEuphrates valley.

- Ancient City of Aleppo: The Ancient City of Aleppo is the historic city centre ofAleppo, Syria. The Old City of Aleppo, which is composed of the ancient city within the walls and the old cell-like quarters outside the walls approxiametly holds an area of 350 hectares (860 acres; 3.5 km), housing about 120,000 residents. Famous for its large mansions, narrow alleys, covered souqs and ancient caravanserais, the Ancient City of Aleppo became a UNESCO World Heritage Site in 1986.

- Bosra: The Ancient city of Bosra is an ancient Roman city. Famed for its Roman theatre, possibly the best preserved in the world, the city also holds many remains of the ancient city such as baths, colonnades and remains of ancient houses and temples.

- Damascus: Is the capital and one of the largest cities in Syria. It is commonly known in Syria as ash-Sham and nicknamed as the City of Jasmine. In addition to being one of the oldest continuously inhabited cities in the world, Damascus is a major cultural and religious centre of the Levant. It's famed for its ancient souks, old city, old Damascene houses and its Umayyad era Mosque, the city also has many remains from the Roman period, such as the Temple of Jupiter, and houses many of the oldest churches in the world, most notably the Chapel of Saint Paul.

- The Dead Cities of northern Syria: The dead cities are a group of 700 abandoned villages in northwest Syria between Aleppo and Idlib. Most villages which date from the 1st to 7th centuries, became abandoned between the 8th and 10th centuries. The settlements feature the well-preserved architectural remains of temples, cisterns, bathhouses and many ancient churches from early Christianity.Important dead cities include the Church of Saint Simeon Stylites, Serjilla and al Bara.

- Krak des Chevaliers and Qal'at Salah El-Din: The Krak de Chevaliers is aCrusader era fortress dating back to the 10th century, and is one of the most important preserved medieval castles in the world. The site was first inhabited in the 11th century by a settlement of Kurdish troops garrisoned there by the Mirdasids; as a result it was known as Hisn al-Akrad, meaning the "Castle of the Kurds". In 1142 it was given by Raymond II, Count of Tripoli, to the Knights Hospitaller. It remained in their possession until it fell in 1271. Together with Qal'at Salah El-Din (Citadel of Saladin), the Krak des Chevaliers is one of the best examples for Crusader era architecture.

- Palmyra: The ancient 2000 BC later Roman colonia of Palmyra is an oasis city in the Syrian desert. The ancient Palmyrenes were renowned merchants who got eormous wealth not only by trading by rare commodities from the east, but also by taking advantage of the city's position as an Oasis, bringing enormous wealth to their city. The Palmyrenes used this wealth to build great monuments, such as the Temple of Bel and the Arch of Triumph, and also to design Greco-Roman and Persian influenced Bas-reliefs of their deceased, many of which are nowadays housed in many of the biggest international museums, which show the craftsmanship of the Palmyrenes and their dedication to their religious rituals.

War tourism

The Syrian conflict is reportedly attracting adventure-seekers. According to retired Israel Defense Forces colonel Kobi Marom, who leads tours of the war zone across the Israeli border, tourists are interested in seeing the conflict and go "crazy" when they learn that they are probably being observed by Al-Qaeda militants.

TRAVEL AND TOURISM IN SYRIA

As war rages on in Syria with no end in sight, the country's travel and tourism industry has been a major causality of the conflict. Often described as the world's most brutal conflict of the century so far, the Syrian war has rendered almost all of the country highly dangerous and hazardous to all international visitors and it has also led to the biggest international refugee crisis in decades. Major tourist sites have been destroyed by shelling and the majority of source countries for inbound arrivals have imposed travel bans and called on their citizens to leave Syria immediately. The war has also caused unprecedented weakness in the Syrian economy, which has had a negative influence on outbound tourism as well.

National Airline Maintains Its Near Monopoly In Air Transportation

All major international airlines have naturally suspended flights into and out of Syria following the eruption of violent clashes near or, in some cases, inside major airports in cities such as Damascus and Aleppo. The gravity of this situation means that all international airlines have deemed it too dangerous to serve Syria and with very low demand for flights, Syrian Air remains the sole airline serving Syrian airports regularly. The airline has survived almost solely thanks to expatriate Syrians travelling between Syria and their current countries of residence.

Numerous Hotels Close Down

Syria's hotels have been another major victim of the country's ongoing conflict, with a substantial number of them having been destroyed by shelling and air strikes, notably in the city of Aleppo, which has been most severely affected by the war and has in fact been almost completely levelled by the violence. Many small travel accommodation outlets across the country are catering to displaced Syrians and offering rooms for rates as low as US$5 per night in order to provide assistance to the country's less fortunate families. Meanwhile, wealthier Syrians who can afford to flee Aleppo have fled to Damascus, where some chained luxury hotels such as the Four Seasons and Sheraton continue to operate.

Religious Tourism Remaing The Major Survivor Of Outbound Tourism In Syria

Meanwhile, almost half of total outbound departures and more than 75% of outgoing tourist receipts in Syria are generated by religious tourism, including Hajj and Umrah trips to Saudi Arabia's sacred cities of Mecca and Medina. This has allowed Syria's beleaguered travel retailers to survive during extremely difficult times. Religious tourism is known to be more resilient than other types of travel and tourism, especially during periods of economic difficulty and armed conflict.

Millions In Losses Incurred By Syria's Travel And Tourism Industry

Syria's travel and tourism balance of payments clearly demonstrated significant losses towards the end of the review period and it is expected that Syria will take years to recover from the ravages of the ongoing civil war, if and when this war comes to a definitive end. Massive investment will be required in order to bring Syria's travel and tourism industry back to life and so far reconstruction efforts have not progressed beyond the planning stage. However, before any meaningful recovery is achieved, the confidence of the Syrian people will have to be regained as well.

Delivery: Files are delivered directly into your account within a few minutes of purchase.

Overview: Discover the latest market trends and uncover sources of future market growth for the Travel industry in Syria with research from Euromonitor's team of in-country analysts.

Find hidden opportunities in the most current research data available, understand competitive threats with our detailed market analysis, and plan your corporate strategy with our expert qualitative analysis and growth projections.

If you're in the Travel industry in Syria, our research will save you time and money while empowering you to make informed, profitable decisions.

When you purchase this report, you also get the data and the content from these category reports in Syria for free:

- Car Rental
- Health and Wellness Tourism
- Tourism Flows Domestic
- Tourism Flows Inbound
- Tourism Flows Outbound
- Tourist Attractions
- Transportation
- Travel Accommodation
- Travel Retail

The Travel in Syria market research report includes:

- Analysis of key supply-side and demand trends
- Detailed segmentation
- Historic volumes and values, company and brand market shares
- Five year forecasts (of market share, market trends, market growth)
- Robust and transparent market research methodology, conducted in-country

Our market research reports answer questions such as:

- What is the market size of Travel in Syria?
- What are the major brands in Syria?

Why buy this report?

- Gain competitive intelligence about market leaders

- Track key industry trends, opportunities and threats
- Inform your marketing, brand, strategy and market development, sales and supply functions

This industry report originates from Passport, our Travel And Tourism market research database.

PLACES TO VISIT IN SYRIA

Syria is a country in the Middle East which has Damascus as its capital. The historical monuments and several other tourist spots lure travel lovers as does the courteous affection of the Syrians. Get to know some of the castles and historic travelers' spots like the Great Colonnades of Palmyra and Apamea, Temple of Bel, and Nimrod Fortress. Spiritual places of Syria are Umayyad Mosque and Sayyida Zeinab Mosque. Do not miss the Khan As'ad Pasha- described as the largest khan (inn for travelers) in Damascus city.

People who are much conscious about wellbeing and physical fitness can always visit a few health and wellness centers like Hammam Yalboughaan-Nasry, Hammam al-Sallhia, Hammam Nureddin and Hammam Bakri. Al-Nawfara Coffee shop, the Ecological and Biological Garden- also a coffee shop, Mashrabia Pub and Restaurant, Marmar Night Club, Ciao- a pleasant spot for a drink and Sissi House with an upstairs bar and a jazz pianist, are said to be the most entertainment centers in Syria.

Step into few shops and markets to buy souvenirs for your beloved ones. Sebastian, Handicrafts Lane, Souq al-Shouna, and Ezrat al-Harastani are the fine shops offering a variety of arts and crafts products. Souq- al-Hibal, Aleppo Souq, and Souqaz-Zarb sell gift articles such as family clothes, brocades, and silver, gold items. Book addicts must visit Bookshop and Librairie Avicenne, which displays newspapers, magazines, novels, and loads of story books.

Travel alert: As of today, Syria is in a state of strife. Travel to Syria is not advisable.

Places to visit in Syria

- Dumeir, the integral Roman temple
- Shahba
- Philippolis, the Roman city
- Umayyad Mosque
- Damascus National Museum

- Ba'albek fortress
- Aleppo, a major Orient commercial city
- Rasafa, the deserted city
- Dura Europos, overlooking River Euphrates
- A remote castle in Qasr al-Heir al-Sharqi
- Figure of the Virgin at Seidnaya
- Maalula, religious center of the Phoenicians
- Tartus
- Stunning crusader castle at Saldin
- Ebla, an ancient city-state in northern Syria since the Bronze Age

11

Education

With a growing population, Syria has a good basic education system. Since 2000 the Government of Syria has significantly increased the expenditure on education 1 to 6. In 2002, elementary and primary education were combined into one basic education stage and education was made compulsory and free from grades 1 to 9.

Education is free and compulsory from ages 7 to 15. Arabic is the medium of instruction in the Syrian Arab Republic. Englishand French are taught from grade 1 in the basic learning stage as the primary second language.

According to the 2007 census, 98 percent of schools in Syria are public (state run), 1.8 percent are private, and 0.2 percent are United Nations Relief and Works Agency schools for children who are refugees.

In 2007, there were 8 million students in the education system of Syria (4 million in basic education, 1.4 million in secondary and 2.3 million in tertiary). Given the current growth rate in the school age population, it is projected that by 2015, the education system in Syria will need to cater to an additional 1 million students in basic and secondary education. The school system in Syria is divided into basic and secondary education levels:

- 1st to 6th grade: Primary Education Level. From 1st to 4th grade, it's called the First Ring while 5th & 6th grade are called Second Ring

- 7th to 9th grade: Pre-Secondary Education Level

- 10th to 12th grade: Upper Secondary Education, which is the equivalent of High School.

The Arab Socialist Ba'ath Party utterly dominates the educational system in Syria in which primary school students called "Al-Ba'ath Vanguards" are injected with Baathism ideology and totalitarian beliefs.

EARLY CHILDHOOD CARE AND EDUCATION (ECCE)

The Government of Syria is also taking charge of providing pre-primary or early childhood education. Up until the early 1990s, ECCE programs were provided by mostly non-governmental institutions, of which few belonged to the government sector, while others were either private, or run by the Teacher's Syndicate, General Union of workers (GUW) or the Women's Federation.

In 1990 only 5 percent of the children between the ages of 3 and 5 were enrolled in 793 kindergartens. Ten years later 7.8 percent of that age group was enrolled. Furthermore, the data from the Syrian Ministry of Education shows an increase in the number of kindergartens from 1096 to 1475 in 2004.

BASIC EDUCATION

The gross enrollment rate in primary education under basic education level in 2000 was 104.3 and it has been steadily rising, reaching to about 126.24 percent in 2007. Still, the enrollment of females is lower than males. The gender parity index, ratio of female enrollment to male enrollment, since 2006 was 0.955.

The enrollment level in all programs at the lower secondary level has been rising significantly since early 2000, with the current gross enrollment rate of 95.3 percent.

At the secondary lower level final exams of the 9th grade are carried out nationally at the same time. The result of these exams determines if the student goes to the "general" secondary schools or the technical secondary schools. Technical secondary schools include industrial and agricultural schools for male and female students, crafts school for female students, and commercial and computer science schools for both.

SECONDARY EDUCATION

The upper secondary education is for 3 years from grade 10 to grade 12. At the beginning of the 11th grade, those who go to "general" secondary school have to choose to continue their study in either the "literary branch" or the "scientific branch". The final exams of the 12th grade (the baccalaureate) are also carried out nationally and at the same time. The result of these exams determines which university, college and specialization the student attends.

To do that, the student has to apply through a complicated system called "mufadalah".

There are wide regional disparities in post-basic education. There are lower secondary and university enrollments in rural than urban areas. Even the higher income households in rural areas do not have access to post-secondary education opportunities.

The secondary gross enrollment rate in 2007 stood at 72 percent, higher than the preceding years and one percentage point higher than the 2007 MENA regional gross enrollment rate at the secondary level.

Technical and Vocational Education and Training (TVET)

At the secondary level, the education system also includes three years of general or vocational education. Syria has a relatively large proportion of secondary school students in vocational schools; about 36 percent of total secondary school students in 2004 are in vocational schools.

According to UIS the total enrollment in technical and vocational education (both private and public) in 2007 decreased to 103 from 113,994 students in 2006. Out of the total number, 41898 are female students enrolled in TVET.

In 1990s, the government aimed to increase TVET enrollment and at one time decided to allocate 70 percent of the lower secondary graduates to vocational schools, which meant doubling the share of TVET in total enrollment from 20 percent in 1990 to 40 percent in 2000. However, this later proved unsustainable. Then in 2000 a new policy stipulated 50:50 distributions of secondary students between general and vocational secondary education, and this was later decreased to 40 percent. Students enrolled in four main specializations: commercial,industrial, agricultural and handicrafts. The TVET system in Syria is very rigid with no options of reentering the formal school system.

University Education

The earliest colleges founded in Syria were the School of Medicine (established 1903) and the Institute of Law (established 1913). The university education was founded in 1919 on a free of charge basis.

Later on, the Ministry of Higher Education was established in 1966 to supervise the scientific and educational institutions, such as, universities, academic councils, the Arabic Language Academy and educational hospitals. Most post-secondary education is state provided, but legislation passed in 2001 allows the establishment of some private · universities and colleges.

Resources for education have risen in absolute terms over the past decade, but it is difficult to match the rate of population growth. Colleges charge modest fees ($10–20 a year) if the student achieves the sufficient marks in his Baccalaureate exams.

If not, the student may opt to pay higher fees ($1500–3000) to enroll. There are some private schools and colleges but their fees are much higher.

Domestic policies emphasize engineering and medicine in Syria's universities, with less emphasis on the arts, law, and business. Most universities in Syria follow the French model of the high education, the university stages and the academic degrees are:

First stage: the License awarded after 4 years to 6 years depending on the field.

Second stage: the DEA or DESS 1–2 years postgraduate degree equivalent to the master's degree in the American-English systems.

Third stage: the doctorate 3–5 years after the DEA or an equivalent degree.

Until recently 20 private universities have been given licenses, 14 of which have actually opened the doors and 6 to be opened soon. Private universities will have an independent academic and management structure representing the owner and will be headed by the president of the university. There will also be a university board consisting of either: chancellor, faculty or division.

Virtual University

In September 2002, the president Bashar al-Assad founded the country's first virtual university through which students can obtain degrees from international institutions. The university is called "Syrian Virtual University".

Computer Literacy

This measure and others, such as making computer literacy mandatory at the high-school level and English- and French-language instruction compulsory in the elementary schools, have the goal of equipping students with computer and language skills in order to modernize the economy through the education system.

Challenges

Syria has shown great progress in providing access to basic education and to some extent, post basic education to the growing population. Still Syria has a long way to go to bring about a comprehensive change in the education system.

Access to pre primary level education is low in Syria when compared to other lower-middle income countries. The enrollment at the pre-primary level is 10 percent in Syria whereas it is 15.7 percent in the MENA region in 2007.

Government of Syriahas to make substantial investments in infrastructure to improve access to preprimary education. The government needs to prioritize expansion of schools especially in underserved areas with vulnerable populations.

According to research findings, children of disadvantaged backgrounds are the ones that benefit the most from early childhood programs by developing basic skills necessary for employment thereby moving them out of abject poverty. Currently, most of the Early Childhood Care and Education services in Syria are delivered through private kindergartens and non-governmental organizations (NGOs) based in urban areas.

Despite increasing quantity of human capital through increasing access to education at all levels, the improvement of quality of the education and training system and consequently the quality of human capital is another challenge that Government of Syria needs to address.

Weak growth in labor productivity over the past two decades has been associated with low quality and relevance of education in Syria. The results of International test scores TIMSS show that 44 percent of students who appeared in this international exam performed below the lowest international benchmark.

Therefore, there is a greater need to improve the quality of overall education system. This also involves the need to incorporate the use ofcommunication and technology to better prepare students to the demands of the globalised world. Currently, Syria's computer and internet usage is very low compared to a number of neighboring countries and is much lower than the average for lower middle income countries.

Syria also faces high repetition and dropout rates. Repetition rate at primary level has been very high, almost 12 percent in 2006 and is steadily rising since 2003.At the secondary level, repetition rate has reached almost 20 percent.

According to the latest data in 2004/05 the average repetition rate was 6 percent for grade 1-6, 13.3 percent for grades 7-9, and 7.3 percent for grades 10-12.Drop-out rates stood at 2.2 percent for grades 1-6, 8 percent for grades 7-9, and 7.3 percent for grades 10-12.Along with high repetition and dropout rates, a fairly low student –teacher ratio also signals internal inefficiency in the education system.

The ratio in Syria is low due to the relatively high recruitment of teachers in comparison to the growth of students. The number of teachers grew at an annual rate of 7 percent between 2000 and 2006, which is almost twice the growth rate for students, which resulted in STR of 19:1 in basic education and 9:1 in secondary education.

To increase the internal efficiency, the government should focus on hiring trained and competent teachers, reform the curriculum and develop testing, evaluation and measurement.

Then the increasing unemployment rate, especially among youth, implies poor education quality along with lack of infrastructure to absorb the rising population.

The youth unemployment rate in Syria stood at 19 percent in 2003. The current system is unable to provide with the skills and competencies demanded in the labor market.

Therefore, there is a need to connect education institutions, especially higher education and vocational institutes, to the labor market and to align the curricula with skills that could increase employability of the graduates. Apart from improving the curriculum the government needs to make major infrastructure adjustments to absorb the rising population of the country into the already burdened education system. In 2007, the education system in Syria catered for about 8 million students. Given the current growth rate of 4.3 percent per annum of school age population, it is projected that by 2015, the education system in Syria will need to cater for an additional 1 million students in basic and secondary education.

Impact of the Syrian Civil War

The Syrian Civil War is a major barrier to quality education for all in Syria, reversing development gains in the country. In addition to causing widespread destruction of learning spaces, the crisis has forced more than 2.1 million children and youth out of school in Syria; an additional 3.3 million in Syria need educational assistance, and 1.4 million Syrian children and youth are refugees in the five main host countries (Egypt, Iraq, Jordan, Lebanon, and Turkey).

In 2011, Syria had achieved universal primary enrolment and was near universal enrolment in lower secondary education. More concretely, 91% of primary school-aged children were in school in 2011, but by 2015 the rate had plummeted to 37%.

THE EDUCATIONAL SYSTEM OF SYRIA: AN OVERVIEW

Syria is a Middle Eastern country that borders Turkey, Iraq, Jordan, Israel, and Lebanon, and has a population of roughly 17 million people.

For much of its history, beginning with the dissolution of the Ottoman Empire, the region was occupied by France. Syria gained its independence in 1945 but the country has struggled to achieve stability since then.

While a slight majority of the population consists of Sunni Muslim Arabic-speakers, the country also has a fractious mix of other ethnolinguistic and religious communities, including Kurds, Christian Arabs, Alawites, Druze, Armenians, Assyrians, Palestinians, and many smaller groups. Since 2011, the country has been embroiled in a multifaceted and devastating civil conflict that has had a drastic impact on its system of education.

Syria has a highly centralized education system. Primary education is compulsory and is six years in length, followed by three years of noncompulsory lower-secondary education.

After lower-secondary education, students sit for the Al Kafa'a, or Brevet, examination. Depending on the results of this examination, students may attend either a three-year general academic upper-secondary program focusing on literature or science, or a three-year technical upper-secondary program.

Technical education is further divided into industrial, commercial, and vocational streams. General academic students sit for the Al Shahada Al Thanawiyya Al Amma examination, commonly known as the Baccalaureate, which is the entrance requirement for Syrian universities. Technical students sit for the Al Shahada Al Thanawiyya Al Fanniyya examination, commonly known as the Technical

Baccalaureate, and are eligible for admission to intermediate institutes. Technical students that receive high enough scores may be considered for university admission, as well, in a related field of study.

The structure of higher education in Syria is relatively simple. Intermediate institutes offer two-year programs, generally in fields such as technology, allied health professions, and teaching at the primary and lower-secondary levels.

Universities offer four-year programs in most fields, leading to the bachelor's degree, or Licence. Fields of study that require five years of study include pharmacy, dentistry, veterinary medicine, engineering, and architecture, while medical programs require six years of study. At the graduate level, master's degrees require two years of study beyond the bachelor's degree/Licence; one-year postgraduate diploma programs are also offered. Doctoral programs are a minimum of three years in duration, requiring professional research and a thesis.

The language of instruction in Syria is Arabic and, unlike in most of Syria's neighbors, official academic credentials are nearly always provided in Arabic only.

The large majority of academic institutions in Syria are state-operated; only in recent years have a few private universities been allowed to open. The curriculum is mandated by the Ministry of Higher Education and emphasizes the Arab nationalist philosophy of the governing regime.

Before the civil conflict began in 2011, Syria was—and in the government-controlled regions, still remains—effectively, a police state. No institutions of higher education were allowed to operate without the government's permission; therefore, any institution in operation would be considered recognized by the ministry. The only exceptions are in the Kurdish-held region of Syria, where two new Kurdish language-medium institutions have been established in the cities of Afrin and Qamlishle since the government lost control of the region. These institutions operate without supervision from the Ministry of Higher Education. According to news sources, these institutions intend to pursue international accreditation in the absence of resolution to the Syrian conflict.

Grading Information

The grading scale in Syria varies by the type of institution. The following tables are derived from the *NAFSA Online Guide to Educational*

Systems Around the World, compiled by the author in 2011. At the secondary level, passing the general secondary examination requires a passing score in Arabic and in all but one of the other subjects, or a passing score in Arabic and all but two of the other subjects as long as the combined score for the failed subjects is at least 25 percent. The minimum passing score is 50 percent for Arabic and 40 percent for other subjects. The minimum passing total score is 102/240 (43 percent) in the literature track and 104/260 (40 percent) in the science track.

Due to the current conflict, education in Syria has been disrupted in a variety of ways. Government-held regions of Syria account for 30–40 percent of the territory of Syria and 50–60 percent of the population. In these regions, the state-held lower- and upper-secondary examinations are still being offered. They are also being offered in the autonomous but unrecognized area held by Kurdish forces, which accounts for approximately 10 percent of Syria's population. State-held examinations are not being held in areas controlled by any of the other participants in the civil conflict; students living in these areas must travel under hazardous circumstances to government- or Kurdish-held territories in order to take the exams. Millions of Syrians have fled the country altogether. Some of them have been able to enroll in local secondary schools and sit for local examinations in the countries in which they are now living; however, a large number of students have lost the opportunity to complete their secondary education entirely.

According to the Syrian government, all Syrian universities are currently in operation; however, reports from rebel-held areas indicate that several universities in these areas are closed. Even in government-held areas, universities have come under attack, closing temporarily or holding classes at alternative locations. Currently, some university students may be able to successfully receive academic credentials, but for many students it is nearly impossible to secure transcripts or certificates from their institutions.

Higher education institutions in the United States and in other Western nations should expect to see a dramatic increase in the number of Syrian student applicants in the coming years as vast numbers of Syrian refugees have been settling, and will continue to arrive, in these countries. Flexibility and understanding is recommended as many of these students will have suffered disruptions in their studies and/or are unable to provide certain required documentation.

EDUCATION FOR SYRIAN REFUGEE CHILDREN

There are 1.5 million school-aged Syrian refugee children living in Turkey, Jordan, and Lebanon, but approximately half of them do not have access to formal education. Host countries have taken generous steps to increase enrollment, such as offering free public education and opening afternoon "second shifts" at schools to accommodate more children. But barriers such as child labor, enrollment requirements, language difficulties, and a lack of affordable transportation are keeping children out of the classroom. Children with disabilities and secondary school age children are at particular risk. Human Rights Watch is working to ensure that all of these children can realize their right to education.

Bibliography

Ahmad, Balsam. *Syria's contrasting neighborhoods : gentrification and informal settlements juxtaposed.* Fife, Scotland : University of St Andrews Centre for Syrian Studies Lynne Rienner Pub., 2012.

Baron, Xavier. *Aux origines du drame syrien, 1918-2013.* Paris : Tallandier, 2013.

Batatu, Hanna. *Syria's peasantry : the descendants of its lesser rural notables, and their politics.* Princeton, N.J. : Princeton University Press, 1999.

Belhadj, Souhail. *La Syrie de Bashar al-Asad : anatomie d'un regime autoritaire.* Paris : Belin, 2013.

Chaitani, Youssef. *Post-colonial Syria and Lebanon : the decline of Arab nationalism and the triumph of the state.* London ; New York : I.B. Tauris ; New York : Distributed in the USA by Palgrave Macmillan, 2007.

Choueiri, Youssef M. *State and society in Syria and Lebanon.* New York : St. Martin's Press, 1994.

Dam, Nikolaos van. *The struggle for power in Syria : sectarianism, regionalism and tribalism in politics, 1961-1980.* London : Croom Helm, 1981.

Firo, Kais. *Metamorphosis of the nation : the rise of Arabism and minorities in Syria and Lebanon, 1850-1940.* Brighton ; Portland, OR. : Sussex Academic Press, 2009.

Friedman, Yaron. *The Nusayri-Alawis : an introduction to the religion, history and identity of the leading minority in Syria.* Leiden ; Boston : Brill, 2010.

Gelvin, James L. *Divided loyalties : nationalism and mass politics in Syria at the close of Empire.* Berkeley, CA : University of California Press, 1998.

George, Alan. *Syria, neither bread nor freedom.* London ; New York : Zed Books ; New York : Distributed in the USA exclusively by Palgrave, 2003.

Ginat, Rami. *Syria and the doctrine of Arab neutralism.* Brighton ; Portland, OR : Sussex Academic Press, 2005.

Haddad, Bassam. *Business networks in Syria : the political economy of authoritarian resilience.* Stanford, CA : Stanford University Press, 2012.

Hashemi, Nader *The Syria Dilemma.* Cambridge, MA : MIT Press : A Boston Review Book, 2013.

Khatib, Line. *Islamic revivalism in Syria : the rise and fall of Ba'thist secularism.* Milton Park, Abingdon, England ; New York : Routledge, 2011.

Khoury, Philip S. *Syria and the French mandate : the politics of Arab nationalism, 1920-1945.* Princeton, N.J. : Princeton University Press, 1987.

Lawson, Fred H. *Demystifying Syria.* London : Saqi in association with The London Middle East Institute, 2009.

Lefeìvre, Raphael. *Ashes of Hama : the Muslim Brotherhood in Syria*. London : Hurst & Co., 2013.

Lesch, David W. *Syria: the fall of the house of Assad*. New Haven, Conn. : Yale University Press, 2013.

Lundgren Jorum, Emma. *Beyond the border : Syrian policies towards territories lost*. Uppsala : Uppsala Universitet, 2011.

Mardam Bey, Salma. *Syria's quest for independence*. Reading, UK : Ithaca Press, 1994.

Marty, Olivier. *Pour comprendre la crise syrienne* : eclairages sur un Printemps qui dure. Paris : Harmattan, 2013.

Piccinin da Prata, Pierre. *La bataille d'Alep : chroniques de la revolution syrienne*. Paris : L'Harmattan, 2012.

Pierret, Thomas. *Religion and state in Syria : the Sunni ulama from coup to revolution*. Cambridge, UK ; New York : Cambridge University Press, 2013.

Rubin, Barry M. *The truth about Syria*. New York, N.Y. : Palgrave Macmillan, 2007.

Seale, Patrick. *Asad of Syria : the struggle for the Middle East*. Berkeley, CA : University of California Press, 1989.

Sherlock, Ruth. *The fear of breathing : stories from the Syrian revolution*. London: Oberon Books, 2012.

Stacher, Joshua. *Adaptable autocrats : regime power in Egypt and Syria*. Stanford, CA : Stanford University Press, 2012.

Starr, Stephen. *Revolt in Syria : eye-witness to the uprising*. New York : Columbia University Press, 2012.

Tòauber, Eliezer. *The formation of modern Syria and Iraq*. Ilford, England ; Portland, OR. : Frank Cass, 1995.

Wedeen, Lisa. *Ambiguities of domination : politics, rhetoric and symbols in contemporary Syria*. Chicago : University of Chicago Press, 1999.

Wieland, Carsten. *Syria at bay : secularism, Islamism and "Pax Americana"*. London: Hurst & Company, 2006.

Yazbik, Samir. *A woman in the crossfire : diaries of the Syrian revolution*. London: Haus Pub., 2012.

Ziadeh, Radwan. *Power and policy in Syria : the intelligence services, foreign relations and democracy in the modern Middle East*. London ; New York : I.B. Tauris and Co. : Distributed by Palgrave Macmillan, 2011.

Ziser, Eyal. *Commanding Syria : Bashar al-Asad and the first years in power*. London ; New York : Tauris, 2007.

Index

❑❑❑

9 788819 344347 7